WORSHIP SERVICES
FOR
LIFE PLANNING

WORSHIP SERVICES
FOR
LIFE PLANNING

By

ALICE ANDERSON BAYS

ABINGDON PRESS

NEW YORK • NASHVILLE

WORSHIP SERVICES FOR LIFE PLANNING

Copyright MCMLIII by Pierce & Washabaugh

Library of Congress Catalog Card Number: 52-11311

B

SET UP, PRINTED, AND BOUND BY THE
PARTHENON PRESS, AT NASHVILLE,
TENNESSEE, UNITED STATES OF AMERICA

To

LOLA PRUDEN ACUFF

FOREWORD

This is the sixth book in a series of planned worship services written that young people may discover the will and purpose of God and find guidance in Christian living. This book has grown out of actual experience with youth in local churches, in colleges, in camps and summer conferences. The services are not offered as models to be followed without adaptation, but are intended to supplement and enrich the worship suggestions of the various denominations. They may be shortened by omitting certain parts, or used as an anthology by lifting out a poem, a story, or some other selections. The leader may offer his own prayer instead of using the prayers suggested, and other hymns and poems may be substituted. Best results will be achieved when the services are adapted to the needs of the local group.

In each worship service there is a story which sheds light on problems young people face today. Some of the stories are set in biblical times, others are about great people or important events in history, but the majority of them are modern stories set in situations quite familiar to youth today. In each case the main characters are young people facing present-day problems, making decisions, and eventually becoming mature Christian citizens. They select a vocation with the idea of rendering service, they learn to live as brothers with members of other races, and they envision a better world which they begin to build. It is hoped that through the use of this book God will speak to young people, that his will and purpose will be done in their lives as they strive to follow Jesus in a complex world.

I wish to acknowledge indebtedness and to express appreciation to all who helped in the preparation of this volume—to the young people and youth leaders of various churches for their helpful suggestions. Grateful acknowledgment is made to authors and publishers who have allowed me to use their material. Every effort has been made to trace ownership of all copyrighted material and to give proper credit.

ALICE ANDERSON BAYS

Knoxville, Tennessee

CONTENTS

SERIES ONE

SELECTING A VOCATION

1. Pioneering in Medicine (Elizabeth Blackwell) 11
2. Honoring a Great Musician (Johann Sebastian Bach) 18
3. Answering the Call to Serve (Florence Nightingale) 25
4. Being a Good Neighbor (Jane Addams) 32
5. Selecting a Vocation 38

SERIES TWO

BUILDING A BETTER WORLD

6. Opening a Continent (David Livingstone) 45
7. Seeking Peace 51
8. Bringing in the Kingdom 58
9. Changing the World (Martin Luther) 66
10. Ruling Through Love and Peace 75

SERIES THREE

LIVING AS BROTHERS

11. Appreciating Other Religions 80
12. Swinging Toward the Light (Samuel Meharry) 89
13. Giving a Cup of Water 95
14. Living as Brother to Every Race 102

SERIES FOUR

SEEKING WORTHY GOALS

15. Realizing Our Worth 107
16. Standing Firm and Bold (John Wycliffe) 113
17. Helping Each Other 121
18. Testing Our Lives by Thine 128
19. Seeking Courage and Calmness 135
20. Living on Higher Levels 143
21. Sharing in His Name 149
22. Giving—Not Seeking 156
23. Practicing His Presence 162
24. Living Abundantly 168
25. Choosing Worthy Goals 175

SERIES FIVE

SPECIAL DAYS

26. Giving Christ First Place (Christmas) 184
27. Bringing Our Gifts (Christmas) 192
28. Observing Easter 199
29. Honoring Our Mothers (Mother's Day) 206
30. Deciding for Christ (Decision Day) 212
31. Following Christ (Dedication Day) 220
32. Ministering to Others (Missions Sunday) 228
33. Serving the Least (Missions Sunday) 233

APPENDIX

Notes 238
Sources for Hymns 243
Selected Bibliography 248
Index of Stories and Subjects 253

SERVICE 1

PIONEERING IN MEDICINE

PRELUDE: "Morning Mood" by Grieg.

CALL TO WORSHIP:

> If I have faltered more or less
> In my great task of happiness;
> If I have moved among my race
> And shown no glorious morning face;
> If beams from happy human eyes
> Have moved me not; if morning skies,
> Books, and my food, and summer rain
> Knocked on my sullen heart in vain—
> Lord, thy most pointed pleasure take
> And stab my spirit broad awake.[1]
>
> —ROBERT LOUIS STEVENSON

HYMN: "Spirit of Life, in This New Dawn," or
"Breathe on Me, Breath of God."

INVOCATION:

O God our Father, we rejoice that nothing can separate us from Thy love and care. Thou art our light in darkness, our strength in adversity, our hope when all else fails. Cleanse us, we pray Thee, from our sins and give us power to put away all hurtful things. Make strong our souls; enlarge our compassion; help us to love all men, even our enemies. In Christ's name. AMEN.[2]

POEM:

> For every hill I've had to climb,
> For every stone that bruised my feet,

11

For all the blood and sweat and grime,
  For blinding storms and burning heat,
My heart sings but a grateful song—
These were the things that made me strong!

For all the heartaches and the tears,
  For all the anguish and the pain,
For gloomy days and fruitless years,
  And for the hopes that lived in vain,
I do give thanks, for now I know
These were the things that helped me grow!

'Tis not the softer things of life
  Which stimulate man's will to strive;
But bleak adversity and strife
  Do most to keep man's will alive.
O'er rose-strewn paths the weaklings creep,
But brave hearts dare to climb the steep.

—Author Unknown

Scripture:

Now faith is the substance of things hoped for, the evidence of things not seen. . . . Without faith it is impossible to please him. . . . These all died in faith, not having received the promises, but having seen them afar off, and were persuaded of them, and embraced them, and confessed that they were strangers and pilgrims on the earth. For they that say such things declare plainly that they seek a country. And truly, if they had been mindful of that country from whence they came out, they might have had opportunity to have returned. But now they desire a better country, that is, a heavenly: wherefore God is not ashamed to be called their God: for he hath prepared for them a city.[3]

Poem:

For the first man to climb the hill
And seek a prospect wider still;
For the first man to brave the sea
Unscared by its immensity;
For he who, conquering craven fear,
First found in fire a friend to cheer;
For he who first from stubborn stone

12

Wrought tool and weapon of his own;
For those the first with patient toil
To break the clod and till the soil;
For all such men, since men began,
We thank the God who made the man.
                    —AUTHOR UNKNOWN

LEADER:
We will hear the story of the first woman who entered the medical profession.

STORY:

TRAIL BLAZER IN MEDICINE

ONE fall day in 1847, a 26-year-old girl with a determined chin, her blond curls half hidden by a Quakerish bonnet, entered the Geneva College medical department in western New York. If a purple unicorn had walked in, the students could hardly have been more surprised. Up to then no woman had ever received a modern M.D. degree. That this pretty young lady would be shameless enough to try seemed incredible.

The career which Elizabeth Blackwell began that day brought her poverty, ridicule and social ostracism. But it also made her the daring medical pioneer who saved many lives and opened the doors of medical schools to women in many parts of the world. Her influence still endures.

Elizabeth Blackwell felt that God was directing her life. She hated being with sick people, and the mere thought of a dissection turned her pale. But when the notion of becoming a doctor kept recurring, she began a determined assault on the medical schools. After 12 shocked refusals, she was at last admitted at Geneva College.

Here Elizabeth's serious purpose and good humor soon gained her the respect of her classmates. But Geneva matrons, when they passed her on the streets, held back their skirts pointedly. Surely no female with a shred of decency would expose herself to the dreadful things that are taught in a medical school. Despite such hostility, Elizabeth stuck it out and was graduated in 1849 at the head of her class.

Her ambition was to become a surgeon. Since no American hospital would admit her, she went hopefully to Paris, only to suffer a severe disappointment: the French doctors would not recognize her degree. "Enroll at La Maternité as a student midwife," she was advised.

Life at La Maternité proved to be desperately hard. The little doctor often spent 18 hours a day in backbreaking drudgery. All Paris lay just over the wall, but only once in six months was she permitted to leave the grounds.

It was in this gloomy setting that Dr. Blackwell met romance. A handsome young intern, Dr. Hippolyte Blot, fell in love with her. But God, she believed, had unmistakably directed her to open medical careers for women. "Because of the stern life I have chosen, all thoughts of love and marriage must be put aside," she wrote in her diary. She never forgot the young intern; 45 years later she wrote wistfully of his unfailing devotion.

Her European studies over, Elizabeth returned to New York to start practice, only to find that no respectable boardinghouse would take her in. "If I let a female doctor's shingle be shown on my premises," one landlady said, " a mob might come and wreck the place." Elizabeth eventually had to buy a house with borrowed funds.

While waiting for patients who didn't come, she noticed the laced-in waists of the young girls, their heavy clothing and sunproof veils, their lack of exercise and the birdlike meals they ate in order to appear dainty. Might not such habits account for their high tuberculosis rate?

This observation marked a turning point in Elizabeth's career. A series of lectures she gave on the subject so impressed a group of Quaker matrons that they established a small dispensary for her in one of New York's poorest wards. Elizabeth gladly went to work in this disease-ridden district.

Soon she had patients enough—these desperate people were too poor to afford prejudice. But busy though she was, Elizabeth felt terribly alone. In general, the medical profession refused to have anything to do with her. Men accosted her when she went on night calls. "It's hard, with no support but a high purpose, to live against every species of social opposition," she wrote. "I *should* like a little fun now and then."

Now her adventurous mind began to plan a new project—the first hospital in the world staffed entirely by women doctors to serve tenement patients who had trouble being admitted to the overcrowded municipal hospitals. Such an institution would offer young women medical students the practical training that other hospitals refused them.

For nearly six years the determined little doctor worked in poverty and professional isolation. Then, slowly, her situation began to change.

Horace Greely sent a reporter to see her. The famous Dr. Willard Parker spoke approvingly of her work. And with the help of $10,000 raised largely by Henry Ward Beecher, Elizabeth proudly opened the doors of the New York Infirmary for Women and Children in May 1857. They have remained open to this day.

Now she started a health crusade which kept her busy the rest of her life. Remembering the usual hospital squalor, one of her first innovations was to put white spreads on the beds and ruffled curtains at the windows. "Ugly, dirty surroundings dishearten people," she said. "It is harder for them to get well." Visiting doctors saw no connection between Elizabeth's almost fanatical cleanliness and the absence of childbed fever, but they were impressed by the low death rate in maternity cases.

Elizabeth was convinced that sunlight, good food, uncontaminated milk, fresh air and pure water would prevent many illnesses and help cure others which doctors were treating with harsh remedies. She appointed Dr. Rachel Cole of her staff a full-time "sanitary visitor." Dr. Cole, the first Negro woman to receive an American medical degree, taught immigrant mothers the proper diet for small children and the benefits of soap, fresh air and sunlight. Her efforts paved the way for modern visiting nurses.

By 1867 Elizabeth had established a medical college for women in connection with the infirmary. An early drawing shows young ladies with ruffled aprons and cascading bustles cutting up cadavers. But despite the quaint costumes, her medical college was superior to most of the men's schools of that era, where the teaching consisted chiefly of "canned" lectures. Young M.D.'s frequently began practice without having examined a living patient.

Dr. Blackwell's students served in the hospital wards, interviewed dispensary patients, attended the sick in crowded tenements. No pupil could receive a diploma without passing a stiff examination in bedside diagnosis.

The fame of the school spread. One day an emissary from the Czar called on Elizabeth and asked to be taken through the college: 25 ladies, having heard of Dr. Blackwell, were seeking admission to the medical schools of St. Petersburg. Then word came that a girl had entered a medical college in Algiers. Soon afterward, there was a query from the Swedish Government—15 young women wanted to study medicine in Stockholm. Dr. Blackwell's vow to open the profession to women was being realized.

15

But in England, women who wished to become doctors still faced a bitter fight. Elizabeth went to their aid, leaving the hospital and college in competent hands. A few months after Elizabeth's arrival in England, the struggle flared into violence. Seven young women who had dared to enroll in the medical department of the University of Edinburgh—called in the press "the shameless seven"—were mobbed by enraged men students and pelted with mud. There was an investigation. But it was the girl students, not the mob leaders, whom the faculty finally dismissed.

"Start a medical college of your own!" was Elizabeth's advice. She helped raise the money and plan the courses for the London School of Medicine for Women—an institution that is still educating women medical students from many parts of the world.

Despite advancing years and illness, Elizabeth's fervor was unabated. To broadcast her ideas on preventing disease, she founded the National Health Society, with the motto, "Prevention is better than cure." When she delivered a series of health lectures to London working people, her words were distorted by certain factory owners who didn't want employees to become dissatisfied with their living conditions, and the press gave her a slanderous mauling. This, of course, didn't stop her. She lived to see hygiene taught to English children in every tax-supported school.

.　.　.　.　.　.　.　.　.　.　.　.　.　.

Obliged at last to give up lecturing, Elizabeth carried on campaigns from her study. She wrote of the sufferings of matchmakers, threatened by death from phosphorus poisoning; of ragpickers, exposed to many forms of contagion; of clothing makers, shut up for long hours in airless lofts. She was in the vanguard of the fight for sickness and old-age insurance, for better housing, for coöperatives to reduce the cost of nourishing food. . . .

Elizabeth grew venerable in appearance, but her mind remained many years ahead of the times. Young women doctors all over the world brought her their problems by correspondence. When she died in May 1910, at the age of 89, she had realized her lifelong dream. As one of her admirers said: "She lived to see the river of her individual life expand into the ocean of a world movement." [4]

PRAYER:

O Thou Master Workman, who has imparted to every man some talent and hast called all men to serve Thee, help us to find our places.

Show us the work Thou wouldst have us do; give us breadth of vision and charity of heart toward those who seek to serve Thee in other ways. Guard us lest we draw a circle about our own group, to shut out those who do Thy work but do not follow with us.

Eternal God, the Giver of every good and perfect gift, who has given us life and love and labor and above all, the gift of Thy blessed Son, make us more fit for Thy service. In Him we see Thee; in His words we hear Thee; through His deeds we know Thee; by His death we are won to Thee; by His glorious resurrection we find power in Thee for triumph over pain and sin and death. To Thee we give all the praise of a grateful heart and pledge our witness. . . . Through Christ our Lord. AMEN.[5]

HYMN: "O Master, Let Me Walk with Thee," or
        "Go, Labor On!"

BENEDICTION:

To Father, Son, and Holy Ghost, the God whom we adore, be glory, as it was, is now, and shall be evermore. AMEN.

SERVICE 2

HONORING A GREAT MUSICIAN

PRELUDE: "Sonatina" from "God's Time Is Best" by Bach.

CALL TO WORSHIP:

> How many of us ever stop to think
> Of music as a wondrous magic link
> With God; taking sometimes the place of prayer,
> When words have failed us 'neath the weight
>   of care?
> Music, that knows no country, race, or creed;
> But gives to each according to his need.
>   —AUTHOR UNKNOWN

LEADER:

Andrew Fletcher once said, "I knew a very wise man who believed that . . . if a man were permitted to make all the ballads, he need not care who should make the laws of a nation."

POEM:

> God sent his Singers upon earth
> With songs of sadness and of mirth,
> That they might touch the hearts of men,
> And bring them back to heaven again.[1]
>   —HENRY W. LONGFELLOW

HYMN: "Joyful, Joyful, We Adore Thee," or
        "Let All the World in Every Corner Sing."

POEM:

> Music is a soaring bird;
> Ecstatic in its flight;
> Music is the crooning heard
> In tall pines' arms at night;

18

HONORING A GREAT MUSICIAN

> Music is the laughing sea
> Embracing moon-white shores;
> Music is the flashing key
> Unlocking heaven's doors.
> Music is the silver seine
> Flung gaily in life's shoals;
> Music is God's cool, gray rain
> On parched and thirsty souls.
>
> —AUTHOR UNKNOWN

SCRIPTURE:

He hath put a new song in my mouth, even praise unto our God. . . .
I will sing with the spirit, and I will sing with the understanding also.
. . . Praise ye the Lord. Praise God in his sanctuary: praise him in the
firmament of his power. Praise him for his mighty acts: praise him according to his excellent greatness. Praise him with the sound of the
trumpet: praise him with the psaltery and harp. Praise him with the
timbrel and dance: praise him with stringed instruments and organs.
Praise him upon the loud cymbals: praise him upon the high sounding
cymbals. Let every thing that hath breath praise the Lord. Praise ye
the Lord.[2]

INVOCATON:

> O God, cause our spirits
> To feel the fellowship of thy Spirit,
> Our minds to apprehend thy thoughts,
> Our hearts to love thy love,
> Our wills to unite with thy will,
> Until thy life in our lives shall achieve
>   thy purposes,
> Through the eternal Christ. Amen.[3]
>
> —CHAUNCEY R. PIETY

LEADER:

Bach spent the greater part of his life in the service of the church,
composing its music and training its choirs. When we listen to Bach's
music, we have the opportunity of sitting at a great spiritual feast, a
feast of music. Albert Schweitzer, one of the great interpreters of Bach,
said that any room becomes a church in which Bach's sacred works are
performed and listened to with devotion.

19

STORY:

CONSECRATED GENIUS—JOHANN SEBASTIAN BACH

LITTLE Sebastian Bach felt his way noiselessly down the stone stairway and into the room in which the book of wonderful music was locked in the cupboard with the latticed door. Eagerly he slipped his small hands through the lattice and drew out the book, then took it to the window where the moonlight flowed in like a bright river. For six long months the ten-year-old boy had worked every moonlight night making a copy of the forbidden music.

The book belonged to his married brother, Christoph, who gave the orphaned Sebastian a home in his own house and taught him to play the clavichord, an ancestor of the piano. Christoph considered this music too difficult for the little boy to play and had locked the expensive book in the cupboard, forgetting how small Sebastian's hands were.

That night Sebastian completed his copy. He was eager to play it, but he must wait.

It seemed a long time, but at last there came an afternoon when the family was away. Sebastian took his own copy of the great music into the parlor and spent hours of ecstasy playing it on his brother's clavichord. But he forgot to watch the clock and, the first thing he knew, his big brother was standing beside him, scowling.

Christoph was only twenty-four and never dreamed that his little brother possessed one of the greatest musical talents of all time. To punish him for handling the forbidden volume, he took the copy away from him, returning it years later.

How Sebastian grieved for the music! One night, sleep-walking, he wandered downstairs into the parlor and began to play the music he had copied. By the time his playing had awakened the household—and himself, too, he realized that copying the music had etched it on his memory. He did not need the copy. It was only then that Christoph began to realize that Sebastian's talent was unusual even for a member of the Bach family.

It would have been strange if Johann Sebastian Bach had not been a musician, for of the sixty adult male members of the Bach family of whom we have a record, fifty-three were professional musicians.

Johann Sebastian Bach was born in 1685, the sixth and last child of the town musician of Eisenach, Germany. The environment in which he spent his early childhood had a profound influence on his whole life for it was here in Wartburg Castle that the prisoner, Martin Luther, had translated the New Testament into German. It was here that he had written many of his fine chorales. One of them, "A Mighty Fortress Is Our God," Bach later used as the principle theme of one of his own cantatas.

Sebastian's father taught him to play the violin, but the little boy wanted more than anything else in the world to become an organist. His father, an organist himself, promised him organ lessons as soon as his hands had grown enough.

Unfortunately, both Sebastian's parents died when he was only nine years old. In Ohrdruf, where he lived with Christoph, he was sent to school and given as many advantages as Christoph could afford. Sebastian earned money when he could, sometimes by playing his violin and singing on the street.

He was able to save some of this money and, when he was fifteen, he went to Luneberg to study. For a time in Luneberg he received a small salary as choirboy, but his voice soon changed and he lost that income. He did not mind so much, however, because he had more time to spend at the organ.

Sebastian went frequently to other cities to hear concerts by well-known artists, especially organists, but his purse was so slim that he had to walk. Once, he had walked to Hamburg to hear the famous organist, Reinken, and walking back to Luneberg without any money he became so hungry that he felt faint.

Sebastian stopped to rest on the shady side of a building, but it was a restaurant, and the odor of food tantalized him. The door opened and someone threw two fish heads at his feet. He was so very hungry he picked them up. Imagine his joy at finding two gold pieces in their mouths! He bought only a little food, for there was enough money for another trip to Hamburg.

When Sebastian Bach was eighteen he accepted a position as organist and choir director in Arnstadt. He was there for one stormy year. When the church officials voted him four weeks' leave of absence to go to Lubeck to hear the organist, Buxtehude, he could not tear himself away from such great music and remained four months.

Buxtehude, who was about to retire, offered young Bach his own excellent position if he would marry Buxtehude's daughter. But Sebastian was in love with a distant cousin, Maria Barbara Bach. There were complaints about his prolonged absence in Lubeck, so when he was offered a better position in Mülhausen he accepted gladly.

He had hardly arrived in Mülhausen when an uncle died, leaving him a small legacy. The first thing he did after receiving the money was to marry Maria Barbara.

Bach was becoming so well known that after a year in Mülhausen an offer came from Prince Wilhelm Ernst to be court violinist and chapel organist in Weimar. His contract also called for one new composition each week. He accepted joyfully and spent nine happy years in Weimar. While there he wrote many of his greatest organ works and a large number of cantatas.

With maturity, Bach's early religious training bore fruit. He declared that "the object of all music should be the glory of God," and every one of his manuscripts bore, in his handwriting, the dedication, "For the glory of God," or the supplication, "Help me, Jesus."

Bach had become famous, and people came to Weimar to hear him just as he had gone to other cities to hear great musicians. His music attracted the attention of Leopold, Duke of Cöthen, who offered him a much more lucrative position than the one in Weimar.

The prince, however, refused to permit his favorite musician to leave his employ. When Bach insisted on leaving, the prince had him imprisoned. Bach went calmly about his composing, and several of his immortal organ works were composed in prison. After a month, the prince relented and released Bach, who promptly moved to Cöthen.

In Cöthen, the Bach family lived in the palace in a charming apartment overlooking the palace gardens. The children were free to play among the flowers and trees. From a business standpoint the move was excellent, but it deeply disturbed Bach that here he could not dedicate his music to God. His compositions must be secular.

The duke liked to travel and frequently took Bach with him on his journeys. Three of Bach's seven children had died and upon returning from one of his trips he was stunned to learn that Maria Barbara, also, had died.

Some time later, he fell in love with a young singer, Anna Magdalena Wulcken, and married her. It was for her that he wrote some of his loveliest songs. Because she wanted to learn to play the harpsichord, he wrote music for her to play.

Finally, the duke, who had been a bachelor up to this time, married a lady who did not care for music. Consequently, the concerts at the court became fewer and less important in the court life.

Another thing that troubled Bach was that his children were not receiving the religious instruction he felt they should have. He decided to leave Cöthen and find a position where he could secure such instruction for his children and where he could dedicate his own music to God. He obtained the position of music director of St. Thomas School for Boys in Leipzig.

Bach spent twenty-seven years at St. Thomas School teaching music, training the choirs for the four leading churches in Leipzig, and composing his greatest music. One of these, "The Passion of Our Lord According to S. Matthew," is considered the greatest oratorio ever written.

Bach made important innovations. He curved his fingers and used all five instead of only three held flat on the keyboard. Music was written only in certain keys because in other keys it sounded out of tune. Bach devised a new system of tuning and wrote compositions in every major and minor key, to prove that his ideas were feasible. All pianos today are tuned according to his ideas.

Several of Bach's twenty children became famous musicians. He went to Berlin to visit his son, Karl Philip Emanuel, a musician at the court of Frederick the Great. When the king learned that Bach had just arrived, he canceled the evening concert which was about to begin, announced, "Gentlemen, old Bach is here!" and demanded that Bach sit down immediately and play. Bach had been interested in a newly invented instrument which he had not yet seen, the pianoforte. The king had bought fifteen and insisted that Bach try all of them. While he was playing, the king walked back and forth behind the musician's chair muttering, "Only one Bach! Only one Bach!"

In his last years Bach was afflicted with blindness caused by eyestrain which began when he copied the book of music by moonlight many years before. Shortly before his death his vision returned and he was able to see his family again.

Bach died in 1750, at sixty-five, but his music, whose deeply spiritual quality reflects the faith of its composer, is a heritage for every musician and music lover.[4]

Poem:

> In the still air the music lies unheard;
>   In the rough marble beauty hides unseen:
> To make the music and the beauty, needs
>   The master's touch, the sculptor's chisel keen.
>
> Great Master, touch us with Thy skilful hand;
>   Let not the music that is in us die!

Great Sculptor, hew and polish us; nor let,
  Hidden and lost, Thy form within us lie!

Spare not the stroke! do with us as Thou wilt!
  Let there be naught unfinished, broken, marred;
Complete Thy purpose, that we may become
  Thy perfect image, Thou our God and Lord! [5]

—HORATIUS BONAR

PRAYER:

Our Father, we are grateful for the consecrated musicians who dedicated their talents to thy cause. We are thankful that they not only helped the people of their day to a better understanding of thee, but that they have brought us nearer to thee. Their music reveals thy majesty, thy love and concern for us, and reminds us of our dependence upon thee. It encourages us to love thee more, and furnishes us an avenue through which we may express that devotion. Grant that the enrichment that has come to the lives of many people through sacred music may encourage us to put our selfish interests in the background, and dedicate whatever talents we may have to thy cause. Help us to use the works of the great musicians to express our thoughts to thee, and may we through our lives glorify thee in everything we do. In Jesus' name. AMEN.

HYMN: "All Things Are Thine, No Gift Have We," or
  "Let Us with a Gladsome Mind."

BENEDICTION:

May the love of God, which passeth all understanding, keep you from henceforth for evermore. AMEN.

SERVICE 3

ANSWERING THE CALL TO SERVE

PRELUDE: "Evening Song" by Schumann.

CALL TO WORSHIP:
> Christ claims our help in many a strange disguise;
> Now, fever-ridden, on a bed he lies;
> Homeless he wanders now beneath the stars;
> Now counts the numbers of his prison bars;
> Now bends beside us, crowned with hoary hairs.
> No need have we to climb the heavenly stairs,
> And press our kisses on his feet and hands;
> In every man that suffers, he, the Man of
> Sorrows, stands!
>
> —AUTHOR UNKNOWN

HYMN: "O Master, Let Me Walk with Thee," or
"Now in the Days of Youth."

SCRIPTURE:
Jesus called them unto him, and said, Ye know that the princes of the Gentiles exercise dominion over them, and they that are great exercise authority upon them. But it shall not be so among you: but whosoever will be great among you, let him be your minister; and whosoever will be chief among you, let him be your servant: even as the Son of man came not to be ministered unto, but to minister, and to give his life a ransom for many. . . . No man can serve two masters: for either he will hate the one, and love the other; or else he will hold to the one, and despise the other. Ye cannot serve God and mammon.[1]

PRAYER:
O Lord, let us learn of thee to be meek and lowly. Pour into us the whole spirit of humility. Fill, we beseech thee, every part of our souls

25

with it, and make it the constant, ruling habit of our minds, that all our other tempers may arise from it; that we may have no thoughts, no desires, no designs, but such as are the true fruit of a lowly spirit. AMEN.[2]

POEM:

> Lord, let me not die until I've done for thee
> My earthly work, whatever it may be.
> Call me not hence with mission unfulfilled;
> Let me not leave my space of ground untilled;
> Impress this truth upon me that not one
> Can do my portion that I leave undone.

—AUTHOR UNKNOWN

LEADER:

We will hear the story of the woman who dignified the profession of nursing and made it attractive to women.

STORY:

LADY WITH THE LAMP

> A Lady with a Lamp shall stand
> In the great history of the land,
> A noble type of good,
> Heroic womanhood.

SO WROTE Henry Wadsworth Longfellow of the slender, darkclad figure with the white cap and apron who walked down the long rows of cots on which the wounded soldiers lay. If it was night she carried a small, shaded lamp that threw a tiny beam of golden light across the beds. This lamp she would set on the floor as she looked after the needs of her patients. The suffering soldiers blessed her name and eagerly awaited her visits. They called her the "Lady with the Lamp."

Often, especially after a major battle had filled the hospitals with wounded, she worked twenty hours without stopping to rest. She was never too tired, it seemed, to speak a kind and encouraging word, or to write the letter home for someone unable to do so himself. As a consequence, the name of Florence Nightingale stands today as a symbol for devoted and conscientious work in nursing. One soldier, writing to his family at home, said: "We call her the Angel of the Crimea."

Florence Nightingale was born in Florence, Italy, in 1820, and was named for her birthplace by her parents, who were English. Most of her childhood was spent in England, however, for the Nightingale family returned there to live.

Like many another little girl Florence loved to play with her dolls. She liked to make believe they were ill, then put them to bed and tenderly care for them. Sometimes they met with accidents, imaginary ones of course, and had their arms and legs tied up with splints until the fractures healed. Even as a child she was making ready, quite unconsciously, and training herself for her lifework. She had pets, too, to play with—a dog who followed her everywhere outdoors and a pony she loved to ride around the countryside. Her mother taught her to hemstitch and embroider, and by the time she was twelve she could do fine needlework. From her father she learned about English literature and Latin and Greek.

A very dear friend was the vicar of the local church. Once when they were walking through the fields near her home they came upon a shepherd who was having trouble with his flock of sheep. The vicar inquired as to the difficulty and the man explained that his dog, who ordinarily helped in caring for the sheep, had been injured in a mishap and would probably have to be killed. Florence at once wanted to see the dog. At the shepherd's cottage she gave first aid to the injured animal, returning every day until the dog recovered.

Very soon she came to be a help to sick people, too, for whenever her mother heard of anyone who was ill or in need, she would send Florence with baskets of food or flowers. Nor was the little girl with the lovely brown hair content merely to deliver the gifts her mother sent—she always tried to do something to relieve pain and suffering if she could, or by a cheerful and pleasant word lift the spirits of the afflicted one. As she grew older she made it a practice to visit the sick in the neighborhood, ministering to their needs, and reading to them from her Bible or prayer book. At the chapel in the little village of Lea Hurst, near where the family lived, she taught a Bible class for young girls.

When about eighteen or twenty she met Mrs. Elizabeth Fry, the Quaker woman who had founded an order of nursing sisters, and whose work in prison reform was well known. Mrs. Fry was then an elderly lady, with a long career spent in working for the unfortunate and underprivileged. She made a deep impression on Florence Nightingale, and it may well be that it was at this time the young Englishwoman decided to make nursing her lifework. For soon afterwards she spent some time in London hospitals, later visiting others in Ireland and Scotland. What she saw there did not please her, for the English hospitals of that time were not at all like the clean, well-kept institutions of today.

Even the buildings were unsanitary and poor, and inefficiently operated. The nurses were careless and ignorant, with very little if any training. Then she went to France and Germany where she found conditions much better. She heard about Pastor Fliedner and his work in organizing the Protestant Deaconesses at Kaiserswerth on the Rhine, and in 1850 visited the institution. She studied the work and methods of the Sisters, and made this entry in a diary she kept: "I am thirty, at the age at which Christ began His mission. Now no more childish things, no more vain things. Lord, let me think only of Thy will."

After two periods of training at Kaiserswerth Miss Nightingale returned to England to become the superintendent of the Harley Street Home in London. This was primarily a hospital for governnesses and gentlewomen of the teaching profession. She found running this hospital no easy task for, in addition to the work, she had to go out and secure the money by gift and subscription on which to operate it.

In 1854 the Crimean War broke out, with France and England on one side fighting Russia on the other. The battleground was the Crimea, where President Franklin D. Roosevelt met Churchill and Stalin in the conference at Yalta during World War II. The British were totally unprepared for the campaign and their armies found themselves without enough surgeons and nurses to care for the sick and wounded, at one time without even bandages and other necessities. Sidney Herbert, the head of the War Department in England, asked Miss Nightingale to organize and superintend a force of nurses to serve in the Crimea.

She had been planning to do exactly that, even before she was asked, and a few days later left England with a group of thirty-eight nurses. At Scutari, near Constantinople, the British had turned a large barracks building into a hospital. Here were some five miles of beds and cots, the wounded were even lying on the floor. Cholera, typhus, and dysentery were rampant because of unsanitary conditions, for the Barracks Hospital was not equipped with any hospital appliances.

Miss Nightingale was faced with an appalling situation—the bed sheets, where there were any, were made of canvas, rats overran the place, there were no laundry facilities, and the wounded were even expected to do their own cooking! To make matters still worse, only twenty-four hours after her arrival, the wounded from the Battle of Inkerman began pouring in. Every available space was filled, and hundreds of wounded men had to be laid on the muddy ground outside, no room for them even on the floor.

Out of this chaos of mismanagement Florence Nightingale, as Superintendent of Nurses, had to bring order. First of all she fitted out a kitchen and put into effect measures of sanitation. Many days she worked for twenty hours without a rest—in spite of the fact that she was of a frail physique she possessed remarkable powers of endurance. One of her assistants described a night visit around the wards of the hospital in a letter home: "It seemed an endless walk. As we slowly passed along, the silence was profound; very seldom did a moan or cry from these deeply suffering ones fall on our ears. Miss Nightingale carried her lantern, which she would set down before she bent over any of the patients."

Even when supplies were available, they were often unobtainable because of "red tape." She became an expert cutter of red tape, being a born diplomat. When necessary, however, she could use more direct methods. Once, when certain supplies were urgently needed, she was told they were in a near-by warehouse but could not be released until inspected by a committee. The committee appeared to have vanished nor could its members be located.

"Open the door," said the Lady of the Lamp. "I take the entire responsibility upon myself. Open the door!"

She got the supplies. It is said that when she came to the Scutari hospital the death rate was sixty per cent. A few months later it had been reduced to one per cent, which pretty well tells the story of the effectiveness of her work.

Visiting the Crimean hospitals near the battle lines, she contracted a fever and almost succumbed. But she recovered and continued her work until the close of the campaign. Back in England she found a grateful people had subscribed a Nightingale Testimonial Fund of 50,000 pounds (about $250,000). Everyone gave with enthusiasm—the well-to-do large sums, those of smaller means lesser amounts, the children pennies, the soldiers and sailors a day's pay each. The money was used to establish a training school for nurses.

In 1859 Miss Nightingale suffered a severe illness that left her practically an invalid the rest of her life. But though pretty well confined within four walls, her mind remained as active and energetic as her body had been in the Crimea. She wrote two books—*Hospital Notes* and *Notes on Nursing*—and everything connected with hospital or army reform interested her deeply. Everything connected with India, too, though she lived in England. She was an avid reader, and she loved statistics. Though in frail health for many years, the Lady with the Lamp lived to the age of ninety, passing into the Great Beyond on August 13, 1910.[3]

POEM:

> O God of life, by whom our lives are given,
> Quicken our sight to see Thy gracious hand
> In all the good for which great souls have striven,
> And help us humbly by Thy power to stand.
>
> O God of toil, who callest us to labor
> Within the common life of mills and marts
> Help us to see each human soul as neighbor;
> Grant us the gift of understanding hearts.
>
> O God of peace, in whom all men are brothers,
> Speak to this sundered world, by hatreds rent;
> Teach us to praise Thee by our love of others,
> And give us peace, whose strength by war is spent.
>
> O God of might, high over class and nation,
> Who dwellest in each humble, contrite soul,
> To Thee we look in hope and adoration;
> Lead on in triumph to Thy gleaming goal.[4]
>
> —GEORGIA HARKNESS

PRAYER:

Our Father, we are grateful for the life of Florence Nightingale, for her courage, determination, and dedication to the profession of nursing. We thank thee that through her life she dignified the vocation of nursing and made it more attractive to others. Help us to realize that all work ranks the same with thee, that all honorable work is important if it furnishes an opportunity to serve thee. We ask for guidance in the type of work we shall do. Lead us into the vocation in which we can render the most acceptable service, and grant us patience and strength to endure the long period of preparation for our work. Make us willing to serve in the needy places, forgetting the praise and acclaim of men, seeking only to forward thy cause and help to bring in thy rule of righteousness. For Jesus' sake. AMEN.

HYMN: "We Thank Thee, Lord, Thy Paths of Service Lead," or "Master, No Offering Costly and Sweet."

BENEDICTION:

Let thy blessing rest upon us as we seek to serve thee by doing thy will. AMEN.

SERVICE 4

BEING A GOOD NEIGHBOR

PRELUDE: "Andante Cantabile" by Tschaikowsky.

CALL TO WORSHIP:

> The world is weary of its pain,
> Of selfish greed and fruitless gain,
> Of tarnished honor, falsely strong,
> And all its ancient deeds of wrong.
>
> Almighty Father, who dost give
> The gift of life to all who live,
> Look down on all earth's sin and strife,
> And lift us to a nobler life.[1]
>
> —JOHN H. B. MASTERMAN

INVOCATION:

We implore thy tender mercies in the forgiveness of all our sins whereby we have offended either in thought, word, or deed. We desire to be truly sorry for all our misdoings and utterly to renounce whatsoever is contrary to thy will. We desire to devote our whole man, body, soul, and spirit, to thee. And as thou dost inspire us with these desires, so accompany them always with thy grace, that we may every day with our whole hearts give ourselves up to thy service. AMEN.[2]

SCRIPTURE:

And, behold, a certain lawyer stood up, and tempted him, saying, Master, what shall I do to inherit eternal life? He said unto him, What is written in the law? how readest thou? And he answering said, Thou shalt love the Lord thy God with all thy heart, and with all thy soul, and with all thy strength, and with all thy mind; and thy neighbor as thyself. And he said unto him, Thou has answered right: this do, and thou shalt live. But he, willing to justify himself, said unto Jesus, And who is my neighbor? And Jesus answering said, A certain man went down from Jerusalem to Jericho, and fell among thieves, which stripped him of his raiment, and wounded him, and departed, leaving him half dead. And by chance there came down a certain priest that way: and when he saw him, he passed by on the other side. And likewise a Levite, when he was at the place, came and looked on him, and passed by on the other side. But a certain Samaritan, as he journeyed, came where he was; and when he saw him, he had compassion on him, and went to him, and bound up his wounds, pouring in oil and wine, and set him on his own beast, and brought him to an inn, and took care of him. And on the morrow when he departed, he took out two pence, and gave them to the host, and said unto him, Take care of him: and whatsoever thou spendest more, when I come again, I will repay thee. Which now of these three, thinkest thou, was neighbor unto him that fell among the thieves? And he said, He that showed mercy on him. Then said Jesus unto him, Go, and do thou likewise.[3]

HYMN: "The Light of God Is Falling," or
   "Where Cross the Crowded Ways of Life."

LEADER:

If you stated your creed, what would be it? Someone has given this as his creed.

POEM:

Let me be a little kinder,
   Let me be a little blinder
To the faults of those about me;
   Let me praise a little more;
Let me be, when I am weary,
   Just a little bit more cheery;
Let me serve a little better
   Those that I am striving for.

Let me be a little braver
   When temptation bids me waver;
Let me strive a little harder

33

To be all that I should be;
Let me be a little meeker
With the brother that is weaker;
Let me think more of my neighbor
And a little less of me.

—AUTHOR UNKNOWN

LEADER:

We will hear the story of the woman who pioneered in our country in social service.

STORY:

THE HEART OF HULL HOUSE

LITTLE Jane Addams, holding tight to her father's hand on a visit to the poorer quarters of Freeport, looked up at him out of her gray-blue eyes and said:

"When I'm a grown-up lady, I'm going to live in a great big house but I don't want it to be near other nice ones. I want to live right next door to poor people, and the children can play in my yard."

Some twenty years later two young women rented an old mansion on Halstead Street on Chicago's West Side. Their plans were simple. They intended, they said, to be good neighbors to the potpourri of races—Italian, Russian, Polish, Irish, Scandinavian, German, Swiss, French, and twenty-eight other nationalities who lived about them. The year was 1889. One of the young women had been the child who had visited the slums of Freeport with her father two decades ago.

Jane Addams had a rich background for this daring experiment. In the first place she had been reared in a large family where she learned the game of give-and-take. Her Quaker father had taught her to put first things first. If the thoughts of youth are long, long thoughts, then his daughter's ideas must have possessed extra depth and purity. The keynote of her whole life was service.

But the world did not know that back in 1889. It was merely a not-too-strong girl in her late twenties with an A.B. from Rockford College. Jane Addams had been abroad twice. On her second visit she had seen Toynbee Hall in the slums of London. The sight of the working practicality of that institution stirred her to action.

Nor was she alone; it also moved Ellen Starr Gates, her traveling companion and college friend. Slowly through the weeks and months that followed, the two Americans conceived the idea of a similar project in their own land. "T'ole Hull House" where they, with an older woman, Miss Mary Keyser, first spent the night on September 14, 1889, was the seed of a movement that would one day make Jane Addams the acknowledged leader of social work in America.

The girls had worked for weeks to bring back the original beauty of the fine old house built in 1856 in the then fashionable part of town. Left behind in the stream of on-moving Chicago, it was being used as a storage place for a furniture factory when Jane Addams and her friend rented it. Fired with enthusiasm, they got down on their knees and polished the exquisite old floors; they painstakingly scraped hideous brown paint from rare Italian marble mantels; they brought treasures from their homes—a beautiful Della Robbia to hang over the fireplace, vases, and pictures from abroad, a grand piano purchased from their slender funds.

Hull House fast became a focal point for the thousands who entered its doors. Within two years after it opened, the register showed an annual list of more than a hundred thousand people. In birth, life, or death, Jane Addams was constantly in demand. In spirit and in fact she became one of the people she served. She showed that her ideals were harnessed to reality when she accepted the post of garbage inspector of the Nineteenth Ward. Only a study of the neglected, odorous, stinking alleys and byways of the slums of that day could begin to portray the immensity and distastefulness of the job she accepted and carried through to completion. Yet she could return from the duties of her revolting task, bathe, don fresh clothing, and become the leading spirit that the Italians called *la Casa di Dio*—the House of God.

Jane Addams' vision, her powers of organization, her eagerness were endless. But she was no mountaintop idealist. Her concern for people was genuine. Residents of Hull House remember the night she awoke to see a burglar in her room. Realizing his situation, he bolted for the nearest window. She, fearing he would leap out and break his neck, sat up in bed and wailed:

"Don't take the window—take the stairs!"

Such was her ability to command that the young man turned and fled for the nearest stairs and safety.

Jane Addams loved her neighbors, and the activities of Hull House showed it. But her regard did not stop with personal aid. Early in her career she threw down the gauntlet in the battle for child labor laws and better working conditions. In the political campaign of 1912, she supported Theodore Roosevelt and the new Progressive party because she believed that he would do most for social betterment. She presided over the International Congress of Women at the Hague in 1914 in a vain attempt to halt the onrushing flood of war. In 1915, although she knew the gesture was an empty one, she allowed her name to be used in Henry Ford's Peace Ship movement and was afterwards branded by patriotic organizations. Yet she lived to receive the Nobel Peace Prize in 1931, or rather to divide it with Dr. Nicholas Murray Butler.

Seventy-five years is too short for the Jane Addamses of this world. She found it so, too. When she was confronted in 1935 with an operation which proved to be her last, she begged for time to finish the book she was reading because, she said, she *must* know how it came out. In love with life, she gave with both hands.

The secret of her fame is an old one. *He that is greatest among you . . . shall be your servant.*[4]

POEM:

If you sit down at set of sun
And count the acts that you have done,
  And counting find
One self-denying deed, one word
That eased the heart of him who heard;
  One glance most kind,
That fell like sunshine where it went—
Then you may count that day well spent.

But if, through all the livelong day,
You've cheered no heart, by yea or nay—
  If, through it all
You've nothing done that you can trace
That brought the sunshine to one face—
  No act most small
That helped some soul and nothing cost—
Then count that day as worse than lost.[5]

—GEORGE ELIOT

PRAYER:

O thou whose mercy is over all, we beseech thee for our brethren in every place, and most especially for those who are in any way distressed.

Visit the sick with thy comfort and healing power. Come to the bereaved with thy peace, and increase in them the faith that love is stronger than death. Hasten with thy protection to those who are sorely tempted; make them strong to resist and conquer. Draw near to all who are lonely, all who are anxious, all who are cast down and discouraged, and to those who suffer in the suffering of those they love, that they may be strengthened with all power for all endurance and patience.

Look in thy might upon those who have no helper. Defend the poor, and save the children of the needy. Make haste for the relief of those who know the pains of hunger and those who have nowhere to lay their head. Bring near the deliverance of those who are persecuted and those who are discriminated against, exploited, and oppressed. Show thy compassion to every victim of injustice, and to those who inflict loss and pain upon others show the demands of thy righteousness and the inexorable working of thy holy laws.

Reveal unto us, we beseech thee, those things in ourselves which are adding to the sum of human misery. Help us to repent of these our sins, and give us grace to consecrate ourselves to thy service, that we may be used of thee to help one another and to set forward thy blessed kingdom; through Jesus Christ our Lord. AMEN.[6]

HYMN: "More Love to Thee, O Christ," or
      "Saviour, Thy Dying Love."

BENEDICTION:

Grant us a larger portion of thy Spirit as we strive to live as neighbors with all races and classes of people. AMEN.

SERVICE 5

SELECTING A VOCATION

PRELUDE: "Largo" from *Xerxes* by Handel.

CALL TO WORSHIP:

> Is your place a small place?
> Tend it with care;—
> He set you there.

> Is your place a large place?
> Guard it with care!—
> He set you there.

> Whate'er your place, it is
> Not yours alone, but His
> Who set you there.[1]

—JOHN OXENHAM

HYMN: "O Master Workman of the Race," or
"Go, Labor On!"

SCRIPTURE:

God hath spoken once; twice have I heard this; that power belongeth unto God. Also unto thee, O Lord, belongeth mercy: for thou renderest to every man according to his work. . . . Man goeth forth unto his work and to his labor until the evening. . . . Study to show thyself approved unto God, a workman that needeth not to be ashamed, rightly dividing the word of truth. . . . So teach us to number our days, that we may apply our hearts unto wisdom.[2]

SELECTING A VOCATION

INVOCATION:

> God of all being,
> Grant us power for seeing
> The intrinsic sublime
> In space and time;
> For beholding beauty
> In toil and duty;
> For knowing pure joy
> In ordinary employ
> For perceiving thee
> In ubiquity. AMEN.[3]

—CHAUNCEY R. PIETY

LEADER:

What is our motive in the selection of our vocation? What is uppermost in our minds, the material gains coming to us, or the service we can render? Let us ask ourselves whether we are willing for God to guide us in the selection of our vocation.

POEM:

> Teach me, my God and King,
>   In all things thee to see,
> And what I do in anything,
>   To do it as for thee.
>
> . . . .
>
> All may of thee partake;
>   Nothing so small can be
> But draws, when acted for thy sake,
>   Greatness and worth from thee.
>
> If done to obey thy laws,
>   E'en servile labors shine;
> Hallowed is toil, if this the cause,
>   The meanest work, divine.
>
> Thee, then, my God and King,
>   In all things may I see;
> And what I do, in anything,
>   May it be done for thee!

—GEORGE HERBERT
ALT. BY JOHN WESLEY

STORY:

ANSWER TO HER PRAYER

THE metallic clank of the knocker on the parsonage door brought Jane Harrison wearily from the kitchen. She had just finished removing untouched food from her aunt's breakfast tray. A month of twenty-four hours a day, caring for her Aunt Bess, a returned missionary, had been exhausting for all in the parsonage—Jane, her family. Through the door curtains she saw the outline of Dr. Doug Kramer's medicine case.

She hadn't expected Doug to call so early in the day. Jane knew of course that he was concerned about her aunt's failure to show improvement. "It's her mental attitude," he kept insisting. "If there were some way to get the woman to feel that she did not need to go back to the kind of life that ruined her health, then perhaps she could relax and regain some of her strength."

Jane and Doug had been together in high school, and Doug's years away, in college, in the Navy, in medical school, and as an interne had never changed their friendship. And now Doug was waiting for her answer to *the question*. He had a right to expect her answer to be a foregone conclusion. Actually, she had not given it.

"Doug—" she said. "I must talk to you. In this room over here, where Aunt Bess can't hear. A letter came from the Mission Board this morning, addressed to me. It was a reply to the one Aunt Bess begged me to write. Aunt Bess lives for the day when she can return to the natives she left."

Doug sat up quickly. "That's out of the question."

"—after the report you, as her physician, sent, the Board is positive, too, that Aunt Bess can never go back to Africa."

As always when Doug was near, the answer seemed so easy. Their town was one of the few which had more practitioners than it actually needed. But Doug Kramer could afford to take life easy. His wealthy father had a wide practice. Who wouldn't dream of being the wife of a young physician, under such circumstances?

Doug had finished reading the letter from the Mission Board. "She'll have to know about this in time, naturally."

Bracing herself against the impulse to give her answer then and there, Jane said, "I don't think we should wait longer than is necessary. Do you? . . ."

"If I decide that she is strong enough, I'll have you do it this morning."

Ten minutes later Dr. Doug Kramer . . . asked Jane to come up. "I don't think we will tell her this morning, but your aunt insists on talking to you." Jane stepped inside the door.

"Did you get that letter from the Board yet?" her aunt asked. "Did you tell them, when you wrote, how good I have been feeling lately?"

Doug stepped up then. "You are showing some improvement. But you must relax—rest."

Aunt Bess was silent a minute, then smiled. "That's right. God has never failed to answer prayer, in his own time."

Jane sensed what her aunt's prayer was. She longed to return, but if she was never to go back, then someone else must go. In the letter the Mission Board had given no indication that anyone was available to go. They had said hopefully, "The Lord will raise up someone to take your aunt's place."

Doug had counted pills into an envelope. "Isn't it about time you let them find someone else?" he asked.

Aunt Bess did not seem to hear.

Jane walked beside Doug as they went downstairs. Sometimes she detected in Doug what seemed to be a more serious attitude toward life. He was attending church frequently.

"I don't see how we can ever tell your aunt what the letter actually means," Doug said. Turning his back to the door, he lowered his voice, "Jane, I'm strong enough to take your answer—any time."

In a flash Jane realized that her eyes had said too much. She looked away quickly, so that Doug could not see her face. She longed for the kind of future Doug could give her. Most of all, she wanted Doug himself. But in a few minutes he would be gone, and she would have to face Aunt Bess. She would keep talking about the "harvest," the "lack of laborers."

"I will give you my answer, Doug," she promised. "Soon."

That afternoon Jane dialed Doug's office number. "I believe the suspense is harder on Aunt Bess than the truth."

"Perhaps you are right," Doug said. "Go ahead. Read the letter to her."

Ten minutes later Jane concluded her reading. A glance at the pale cheeks on the pillow told Jane that Doug was right—absolutely. Then Doug knocked on the bedroom door and came in.

The face on the bed forced a smile. "They don't know how good I've been lately. You'll have to write to them again."

Suddenly learning that you could never return to people you loved, and longed to help, would be a blow, Jane told herself. In a way Jane felt that she, too, had lived with those African natives. There had been the regular letters from Aunt Bess while on the field, the snapshots, and then the furlough years. Silently, Jane reread the concluding paragraph. "Perhaps it is his will that others shall go now. . . ."

Aunt Bess said, "I can still pray."

Doug bent over his patient. "Try to relax. You need all the rest you can get." Nodding to Jane, he started for the door.

"Your aunt shows some improvement. Perhaps I ought to be encouraged. In time she should be able to lead a restricted life."

"Perhaps you think this is queer of me. But I can understand how Aunt Bess feels about not going back. She loves her native friends. Unless she goes back, or someone. . . ."

"In a while she will be strong enough to write letters. And letter writing is one way of living with others vicariously. We've both done all that we can for the patient. Now let's talk about ourselves. You will marry me, won't you? Or have I been taking too much for granted?"

"I know I've been stalling a long time. I'm not being fair to you either, Doug. But my answer—I can't."

"You didn't mean that. I know you didn't mean that."

Jane spoke. "I do mean it. That day Aunt Bess went to bed with her first attack, I knew she would never go back and that only one thing would ever satisfy her, or me. She would really be living with her people again, vicariously, if I went in her place. I kept dodging it, but I won't dodge the truth any longer."

"You are serious?"

Jane nodded.

"Naturally you realize what you will be giving up?"

"There is no other way. I'm sorry. I should have decided long before this. It is harder for both of us now. If you'll let me, I'll go up right now to tell Aunt Bess. I think she needs just that."

When she reached the first landing of the stairway, Doug stopped her. "Jane, you're the type. Perhaps I understood you better all along than you understood yourself. I always knew you were the type."

Jane opened the door of her aunt's room and went in. Leaning over the bed, she said, "I have made my decision. I want to go."

SELECTING A VOCATION

"Are—you—sure?"

"Yes. I am sure now."

"But Doug—," she said. "You love Doug."

"I think he understands."

A light knock on the door told Jane that Doug was waiting in the hallway. She hoped he had not heard what her aunt had said. "Come in."

Doug came over to the bed next to Jane. "This will be a surprise to both of you, perhaps. Caring for your aunt, talking to her, has made me realize some things about my own life. I'm not really needed in this town. We could go together, Jane. Couldn't we?"

Then Jane felt the warmth of Doug's fingers as they closed on her hand. No, it wasn't a dream. Doug's hand was solid and real. His lips had actually said those words. His brown eyes, directed toward her, were still waiting for the answer. Closing her own hand on his, she gave it.

Aunt Bess spoke. "Where was my faith? He always answers prayer—in his time." [4]

POEM:

Upon thy bended knees, thank God for work,—
Work—once man's penance, now his high reward!
For work to do, and strength to do the work,
    We thank Thee, Lord!

Since outcast Adam toiled to make a home,
The primal curse a blessing has become,
Man in his toil finds recompense for loss,
A workless world had known nor Christ nor Cross.

Some toil for love, and some for simple greed,
Some reap a harvest past their utmost need,
More, in their less find truer happiness,
And all, in work, relief from bitterness.

Upon thy bended knees, thank God for work!
In workless days all ills and evil lurk.
For work to do, and strength to do the work,
    We thank Thee, Lord! [5]

—JOHN OXENHAM

PRAYER:

As we look across the vast field of our work, O Master, we feel the challenge of thy call and turn to thee for strength. So much to do for thee, and so little wherewith to do it!

O Christ, thou who art touched with a feeling of our infirmities and hast been tempted even as we, look with thy great sympathy on thy servants. Thou knowest the drain of our daily work and the limitations of our bodies. Thou knowest that we carry but a little candle of knowledge to guide the feet of the erring amid the mazes of modern life. Thou knowest that our longing for holiness of heart is frustrated by the drag of our earthliness and the weight of ancient sins.

Fit us for our work, lest we fail thee. We lean on thee, thou great giver of life, and pray for physical vigor and quiet strength. We call to thee, thou fountain of life, to flood our minds with thy radiance and to make all things clear and simple. We submit our inmost desires to thy will, and beseech thee to make thy law sweet to our willing hearts.

Give, Lord, what thou askest, and then ask what thou wilt. We make our prayer, O God, by faith in Christ, our Lord. AMEN.[6]

HYMN: "O Son of Man, Thou Madest Known," or
"O Jesus, Prince of Life and Truth."

BENEDICTION:

Now may God bless us and keep us, and may his Spirit guide us into the vocation in which we can best serve him. AMEN.

SERVICE 6

OPENING A CONTINENT

PRELUDE: Hymn tune "Crusader's Hymn."

CALL TO WORSHIP:

> "I seek Truth," said Science;
>   Faith cried, "I seek God!"
> Faith on wings went questing,
>   Science needs must plod.
>
> Though by ways far-parted,
>   To one goal they came:
> Found, when search was ended,
>   God and Truth the same.[1]
>
> —EFFIE SMITH ELY

HYMN: "There's a Wideness in God's Mercy," or
"Love Divine, All Loves Excelling."

INVOCATION:

O God, what shall we render unto thee for all these thy manifold mercies? O that we were able to serve thee all the days of our lives! O that even for one day we were enabled to do thee service worthy of thyself! For verily thou art worthy of all service, all honor, and praise without end. AMEN.[2]

SCRIPTURE:

When he saw the multitudes, he was moved with compassion on them, because they fainted, and were scattered abroad, as sheep having no shepherd. Then saith he unto his disciples, The harvest truly is plenteous, but the laborers are few; pray ye therefore the Lord of the harvest, that he will send forth laborers into his harvest. . . . Then the eleven disciples went away into Galilee, into a mountain where Jesus had appointed them. And when they saw him, they worshipped him; but some doubted. And Jesus came and spake unto them, saying, All power is given unto me in heaven and in earth. Go ye therefore, and teach all nations, baptizing them in the name of the Father, and of the Son, and of the Holy Ghost: teaching them to observe all things whatsoever I have commanded you: and, lo, I am with you alway, even unto the end of the world.[3]

LEADER:

In the following poem the author gives us a glimpse into the life of one of the world's greatest missionaries, David Livingstone.

POEM:

> Patient he worked in the dingy mill,
>   Amid the lint and gloom,
> Who was destined a richer fabric to weave
>   Upon a vaster loom.
>
> Little they dreamed who saw him toil
>   Where droning spindles whirled,
> He would help to fashion the mighty web
>   Of a diviner world;
>
> That over a somber continent,
>   With shuttles of love and light
> He would send a fadeless golden thread
>   Through the warp of Afric night.[4]
>
> —EFFIE SMITH ELY

STORY:

DAVID LIVINGSTONE

DAVID LIVINGSTONE was born in 1813. He died in 1873. The story of these sixty years is one of struggle with hardships and triumphs over difficulties. His life was a demonstration of bravery and patience, as he overcame obstacles before which ordinary men would have admitted defeat. Although born in poverty, he carved for himself a career that was honored at his death by his burial in Westminster Abbey.

The driving forces in his amazing career as an explorer, missionary, scientist and traveler were a thirst for scientific knowledge, a desire to alleviate suffering, a spirit of adventure, a longing to be a pioneer, ambition to open new fields for commerce, and a yearning to find new soil in which to plant the seed of the gospel of Christ. He was equally at home as a botanist, ethnologist, zoologist, doctor, preacher, sociologist, and traveler. For sheer grit, resoucefulness, love of truth and devotion to the welfare of humanity, he surpasses all ordinary travelers and missionaries.

Livingstone's ancestors were farmers on the Island of Ulva, off the west coast of Scotland. His parents were industrious, though very poor. At the age of ten David entered a cotton mill as a "piecer" boy, and helped to support the family. The parents loved their children and took great pains with their education. From the father they acquired the rudiments of learning and a great thirst for knowledge.

As a piecer boy, David worked from six in the morning until eight at night. He fastened a book which he was studying to the loom in such a way that he could glance at it and snatch a sentence or two, as he passed to and fro at work. From eight to ten in the evening he attended a night school, which the owners of the mill provided. On many occasions at midnight his mother had to take a book from him and send him to bed. This disregard of fatigue was one of the outstanding traits of his personality.

On holidays David found great pleasure in wandering over the countryside, seeking new information. Thus early in life he developed an attitude of alert, accurate observation and a passion for scientific information. Books on travel and adventure and the lives of great men fascinated him. When nineteen years old, he took up the duties of a cotton spinner. He began to attend classes at the University of Glasgow, and in six years had sufficient knowledge and understanding of medicine to be given a surgeon's diploma. He was also fitted to expound the gospel, as a lay preacher.

Like many others of his day who felt the burden of poverty, he worked his way without any outside help. For him knowledge and professional skill were not ends in themselves. They were not merely means of making a living. He looked upon them as resources that enlarged his ability to render service to those whose lives were painful and barren.

In choosing a vocation, Livingstone was influenced by his fondness for travel, his genuine piety, and the spirit of adventure. He decided to become a Christian missionary. At that time Robert Moffat was in England on furlough. Reports of Moffat's achievements in South Africa deeply impressed young Livingstone, who sought an interview with him. David was twenty-five years old when he received a summons to go to London for an examination by the officials of the London Missionary Society. Doubtless Moffat had recommended that he be given consideration. David was thrilled when the report on his examination was favorable. He attended a training school at Chipping Ongar, and after two years was licensed as a preacher and sailed for Africa. He landed at Cape Town toward the close of 1840.

Livingstone began his life as a missionary at Kuruman. There he found Moffat and remained for several months where he had an opportunity to study the manners and customs of the Bechuana people, the native language, and the surrounding country. Bakatla, chief of the tribe, was favorable to his purpose, and permitted him to make excursions into the country and to settle for six months at a place called Lepelole. With this isolated place as headquarters, he went a ten-day journey still farther toward the north, to the lower part of the river Zonga. This trip proved his pluck and stamina. He gave the natives who went with him such relentless marching that they were played out. Thus he won their respect. Driven from Lepelole during a war with a neighboring tribe, Livingstone found a new location in the valley of Mabotsa.

On his journeys he saw many traces of the slave trade. His flaming indignation at the cruelty of the slave traders, and his statesmanlike efforts to put an end to this traffic, form one of the most commendable phases of his career.

He married the daughter of Robert Moffat. The training of this noble young woman, in her father's mission station, was scant preparation for intimate companionship with a man whose restless spirit led him into an unending series of dangerous adventures. Her services to the native women and children were a constant source of gratitude and friendliness. Sometimes as many as a hundred children came to her school, and her sewing classes for girls were very popular.

In 1851, Mrs. Livingstone and her three children went with the explorer on his third attempt to cross a desert and reach Sebituane, a strategic point in his journey across the continent. Their native guide missed the way, and it seemed that the children would perish before they reached the other side of the desert. All but blind and hardly able to walk, they staggered on, knowing that to stop was to die. At last the sight of birds told them that their sufferings were nearly at an end. The endurance and devotion of Mrs. Livingstone fill one with amazement. On her fell the major task of rearing the five children. Mrs. Livingstone had to return to England, and after sixteen years of service Livingstone returned also. His wife accompanied him on the next return to Africa, but died of tropical fever on this trip. She was buried under the shadow of a giant baobob tree, mourned by black friends as well as white.

In the national memorial to Livingstone, in Blantyre, Scotland, his birthplace, are eight bronze tableaux, beautifully sculptured, depicting his vision, love of truth, faith, perseverance, courage, renunciation, and utter devotion. One scene pictures him in an African hut, kneeling by a bed. The figure is in the position in which he was found by natives when death came in 1873, at Ilala, in Besa Country. He had been ill for months. Unable to ride a donkey, he now was carried forward. His will outlasted his physical resources. His black companions removed his heart and buried it reverently in African soil. On April 18, 1874, his body found a final and suitable resting place in Britain's most sacred mausoleum—Westminster Abbey. It had been carried for six months by faithful servants from the interior to the sea coast.[5]

LEADER:

The following poem from *Punch* was written for the occasion of the burial of Dr. Livingstone in Westminster Abbey in 1873:

> He knew not that the trumpet he had blown
>   Out of the darkness of that dismal land
> Had reached and roused an army of its own
>   To strike the chains from the slave's fettered hand.

> Open the Abbey doors and bear him in
>   To sleep with kings and statesmen, chief and sage,
> The missionary come of weaver-kin
>   But great by work that brooks no lower wage.

He needs no epitaph to guard a name
　Which men shall prize while worthy work is known;
He lived and died for good—be that his fame:
　Let marble crumble, this is Living-stone.

—AUTHOR UNKNOWN

LEADER:

A great English poet contributed the following lines concerning the death of Livingstone:

POEM:

Great Heart is dead, they say—
What is death to such a one as Great Heart?
One sigh, perchance, for work unfinished here—
Then a swift passing to a mightier sphere,
New joys, perfected powers, the vision clear,
And all the amplitude of heaven to work
The work he held so dear.
A soul so fiery sweet can never die
But lives and loves to all eternity.[6]

—JOHN OXENHAM

PRAYER:

Our Father, we thank thee for the inspiration coming to us from the lives of the great missionaries who put self in the background and are concerned only with carrying the gospel to the people in the far corners of the earth. We are grateful for their accomplishments, their example, and their devotion to thy cause. Help us, like them, to be willing to do the work that no one else wants to do, to work in the hard places, and to be satisfied with serving thee, regardless of whether praise or blame comes to us. Help us who do the commonplace tasks at home, to stand steadfastly for the right, to overcome evil with good, to face each temptation bravely and remain true witnesses for thee. Grant that we may take up our cross daily and face our tasks with courage. In Christ's name. AMEN.

HYMN: "We've a Story to Tell to the Nations," or
　　　"Spirit of Life, in This New Dawn."

BENEDICTION:

Hasten the time when every knee shall bow and every tongue confess thee to be Lord and Master of us all. AMEN.

SERVICE 7

SEEKING PEACE

PRELUDE: "Andante Serioso" by Ketelbey.

CALL TO WORSHIP:
> Down the dark future, through long generations,
>> The echoing sounds grow fainter and then cease;
> And like a bell, with solemn, sweet vibrations,
>> I hear once more the voice of Christ say, "Peace!"
>
> Peace! and no longer from its brazen portals
>> The blast of war's great organ shakes the skies!
> But beautiful as songs of the immortals,
>> The holy melodies of Love arise.[1]
>> —HENRY W. LONGFELLOW

HYMN: "O Master, Let Me Walk with Thee," or
"O Son of Man, Thou Madest Known."

SCRIPTURE:

I will hear what God the Lord will speak: for he will speak peace unto his people. . . . The Lord will give strength unto his people; the Lord will bless his people with peace. . . . Moreover I will make a covenant of peace with them; it shall be an everlasting covenant with them. . . . Yea, I will be their God, and they shall be my people. . . . Blessed are the peace makers: for they shall be called the children of God.[2]

STORY:

THE GREATEST OF THEM ALL

REACHING for the telephone, I heard a voice explain, "This is Bill Cooper. Busy tomorrow?"

51

Mr. Cooper was president of Cooper's Incorporated, a member of the church board of trustees, a generous giver to every community project.

"No," I answered.

"How about you and Anne driving down with me tomorow, to see the 'Ticonta' sail?"

Eager for anything that might break the chain of frustrated thoughts surrounding me, I blurted, "Sure. Glad to." After a moment I queried, "The 'Ticonta'?"

"You will forgive my pride, I hope," he said, "but that shipment for the hospital in India is going out on the 'Ticonta.'"

"Forgive me," I sputtered, "for forgetting." In a world desperately searching, gifts of $15,000 worth of medical equipment for the mission field meant hope. "I'll be delighted to go. I know Anne will, too."

In vain, I had been trying all day to whip thoughts into shape for a talk to our young people on Sunday evening. These young men and women, many of them college seniors, would soon be going out into the world to become leaders. Confused about world conditions, they would be gathering to hear something that would give them courage. But, like the murky weather outside, a mood of despondency was crowding in on me; for I did not have a message of inspiration to give.

As I stepped outside, I passed the stained-glass picture of the Good Shepherd. In darkness, I reached the side entrance, opened a door and picked my way through a room filled with blackboards and small chairs. Jane Donovan was at the console in the main auditorium, rehearsing for the Sunday services. The music stopped instantly, and the player's fingers fell from the keys, to lie motionless before her.

"Sorry," I apologized quickly. "I'll be leaving in a second."

"I don't mind an audience," she said, smiling. "Maybe that is what I need."

I stood there a while, and then she exclaimed suddenly, "Is it worth the trouble?"

"Being organist carries with it a lot of work that doesn't show," I pointed out, encouragingly. "Still, people do appreciate your efforts, Jane."

"It's more than that. Sometimes I wonder, is there anything to it at all?" In that explosive instant she had gestured toward the cross, the Bible, and other symbols of our faith, standing inside the chancel.

Then, flushing with a sense of guilt as she realized what she had said, she lapsed into silence.

"All of us have moments of doubt. Bringing them out into the light may help to dissolve them."

When she did not speak, I felt compelled to. "A-bombs, now H-bombs, hatred, ignorance, ugliness everywhere, people grabbing for all they can get, you keep trying to tell yourself there is a better way, and yet—?"

"Jane," I said, with concern, "there is something else, isn't there? It's about Dick?"

Frequently I stopped in at the *Daily Herald* office during late afternoon, when the press back shop was rolling, for a chat with Dick Patterson over his typewriter. On one of those afternoons he had asked me bluntly, "Where does idealism fit into the dog-eat-dog world we have today?"

Trying to appear relaxed, I sat back in the chair and waited for Jane to speak, if she would.

"I keep putting Dick off," she explained. "I can't do that forever, I know."

"You love him?"

"If I didn't love him," she pointed out, with new color in her cheeks, "I wouldn't have a problem."

Dick was just about number one on my list, I told her. Realizing I was being of small comfort, I added, "He's in a tough game. A newspaper reporter contacts the police, sees crime firsthand almost, the seamy side of life all the way through."

Jane's blue eyes showed plainly how disappointing my words had sounded. I began to feel how little I must have been able to help any troubled soul in my months on the campus.

Suddenly an idea popped into my mind. "Mr. Cooper is driving down to the dock tomorrow to see off his shipment of medical equipment. He has invited Anne and me to ride along. Suppose I talk to Mr. Cooper, suggest that he take you and Dick along, too?"

Hope shone from her eyes for an instant, then it was gone.

"Mr. Cooper has objected to the publicity up to now," I explained. "But if I make him see the point about having Dick along, I feel sure that he will consent. Why should evil be given page one in a newspaper, and good deeds not even mentioned?"

"If Dick consents to go," she agreed, "I will, too."

Hurrying back to the study, I dialed Mr. Cooper. It took a few minutes of explanation and pleading, but he accepted my plan. He shoved the responsibility for results on me, "If you think it will do the public and Dick Patterson any good, okay."

A little later I located Dick in the *Herald* office, working over his typewriter. I decided to go directly to the point. "Do you suppose that you could get away from this place for a day? Tomorrow?"

I outlined the trip and its purpose. "You could get a story—have a day's vacation besides." After that, I emphasized Mr. Cooper's generous gift to the cause.

Dick put on a cynical scowl. "Publicity. Someone is always demanding page one for his upstanding contribution to the public welfare."

"But the publicity angle is my own idea," I said quickly. "In fact, Bill Cooper did not want the gift mentioned. But, it seems to me, when newspapers make such a point of dealing out words to the bad side, they could do a little for the better side now and then."

The four of us—Dick and Jane, Anne and I—made the trip with Mr. Cooper. Murky weather in the low places delayed us an hour or more. The majestic vessel was beginning to slide outward, into the fog which hung over the river, when we finally pushed our way through the crowd on the dock. Mr. Cooper's face showed keen disappointment in not getting there sooner.

As the "Ticonta" became less and less distinct in the haze over the river, a sense of responsibility for the trip haunted me. Hadn't I suggested that Dick come along, so that he might see something beyond the day-to-day realism that hung over a newspaper office?

Apparently through taking pictures, Dick stood beside me. "There's something priceless on that vessel," I said. "Equipment desperately needed to alleviate suffering among the downtrodden of this earth."

Dick's hand slid a pad from his coat pocket, and began scribbling notes. "I'll make an edit out of this, too. Timely theme, local angle. Thanks for the idea. The Old Man ought to be tickled with me when I get back."

I glanced at Jane, and realized anew what a failure my effort to help her turned out to be.

A gaunt, middle-aged man, who had been absorbed in watching the disappearing vessel, moved a little to one side and saw Mr. Cooper. The stranger's face showed plainly that he was anxious to know what Mr. Cooper's interest was in the "Ticonta's" sailing.

With justifiable pride, Mr. Cooper told of his gift to a hospital in India. The other man listened carefully. The gaunt, middle-aged man's fingers groped for Bill Cooper's hand. I thought his own hand trembled a little as he shook Mr. Cooper's.

"Few people can realize what such a gift means," the stranger said. "Surely an answer to someone's prayer."

"Oh, not much of a sacrifice," Mr. Cooper pointed out. "I canceled a trip to Florida for the winter. That's all."

No longer could I ignore the half smile on Dick's bored face. Suppose Mr. Cooper should notice it, too? The mortification would be more than I could stand. I was ready to admit my error in urging Dick Patterson to come along, and the pained expression in Jane's face told me that she felt it, too.

Relieved, then, I saw that Bill Cooper was too wrapped up in conversation to pay any attention to Dick's cynicism. "You talk like someone who might understand the mission field," he was saying to his new acquaintance.

Staring back at the "Ticonta," the stranger did not seem to hear Mr. Cooper's remark. What was there about the great ship to engross his thoughts?

"Pardon me for being curious," Bill Cooper said, "but may I ask, friend, what brought you here?"

"My daughter. She is on the 'Ticonta.'"

Bill Cooper was a little confused by the situation he had created for himself. Uncertain what he should say, he asked, "You have a family?"

The stranger's silence made a hush fall on our whole group. "Elaine was my family," he replied minutes later.

"And she has gone? May I ask where?"

"For South Africa—as a missionary."

Understanding our curiosity, as well as our reluctance to ask more questions, it was the stranger who spoke. "Seven years is a long time. I hope I can stand here on the dock some day to see her come home."

Tired gray eyes told me that the great decision of his life had not come easily. I saw Dick straining to catch every syllable the man uttered.

Elaine's father turned toward the river again. "If you saw the 'Ticonta' sailing out in midocean, and if you didn't know better, you'd say she was alone, lost, going nowhere. Yet, all the while, she would have a captain, there'd be a chart, and she would be sailing toward a port somewhere."

Humbly, to myself, I said, "This is faith."

Bill Cooper's hand went out quickly to grasp the stranger's, and shake it. "Compared to yours, my gift is no gift at all," he blurted. Spotting Dick, he came closer. "I don't want mine mentioned in the *Herald*."

I felt Dick Patterson's fingers on my coat sleeve, drawing me to one side. When we were out of hearing range, he said, "Maybe Bill Cooper's gift was real, too. I won't say now that it wasn't. Only it didn't get through to my skin at first."

"Jane," I called her over to us. "Dick has something to tell you."

Leaving them together, I walked toward the river. "We, of today, are a suspicious generation," I told myself, "calling things phony often, when they aren't. Our skins may have grown callous, but self-sacrifice still touches the heart."

Exploring every peace plan, I had failed to respond to the full meaning of one—the greatest of them all: "I am the Way." The "Ticonta" was sailing in confidence, because she had a course to follow.

Suddenly I realized that I had my message—a vision to hold before my audience on Peace Sunday evening.[3]

POEM:

"Only through Me!" . . . The clear, high call comes pealing,
Above the thunders of the battle-plain;—
"Only through Me can Life's red wounds find healing;
Only through Me shall Earth have peace again.

"Only through Me! . . . Love's Might, all might transcending,
Alone can draw the poison-fangs of Hate.
Yours the beginning!—Mine a nobler ending,—
Peace upon Earth, and Man regenerate!!

.   .   .   .

"Only through Me shall Victory be sounded;
Only through Me can Right wield righteous sword;
Only through Me shall Peace be surely founded;
Only through Me. . . . *Then bid Me to the Board!*"

Can we not rise to such great height of glory?
Shall this vast sorrow spend itself in vain?
Shall future ages tell the woeful story,—
"Christ by His own was crucified again"? [4]

—JOHN OXENHAM

SEEKING PEACE

PRAYER:

O Lord, forgive us for our prejudice, our lack of understanding of other races. Enlighten our minds and give us a clearer vision of what it means to live as brothers with people of all races. Help us to practice in our lives those things which we believe in our hearts. Give us the discernment to see our brothers' needs and a willingness to share the privileges and opportunities that come to us. Help us to follow Christian principles in our lives and eventually to create better relations between ourselves and our neighbors, and thus bring peace to a troubled world. In the name of the Prince of Peace, we pray. AMEN.

HYMN: "Dear Lord and Father of Mankind," or
"Prince of Peace, Control My Will."

BENEDICTION:

As we have therefore opportunity, let us do good unto all men, especially unto them who are of the household of faith. AMEN.

SERVICE 8

BRINGING IN THE KINGDOM

PRELUDE: Hymn tune "Germany."

CALL TO WORSHIP:

Who shall ascend into the hill of the Lord? or who shall stand in his holy place? He that hath clean hands, and a pure heart; who hath not lifted up his soul unto vanity, nor sworn deceitfully. He shall receive the blessing from the Lord, and righteousness from the God of his salvation.[1]

HYMN: "These Things Shall Be," or
      "O Young and Fearless Prophet."

SCRIPTURE:

After this manner therefore pray ye: Our Father which art in heaven, Hallowed be thy name. Thy kingdom come. Thy will be done in earth, as it is in heaven. . . . Whereunto shall we liken the kingdom of heaven? It is like a grain of mustard seed, which a man took, and cast into his garden; and it grew, and waxed a great tree; and the fowls of the air lodged in the branches of it. . . . It is like leaven, which a woman took and hid in three measures of meal, till the whole was leavened. The kingdom of heaven is like unto a merchantman, seeking goodly pearls: who, when he had found one pearl of great price, went and sold all that he had, and bought it. . . . Not every one that saith unto me, Lord, Lord, shall enter into the kingdom of heaven; but he that doeth the will of my Father which is in heaven. . . . The kingdom of God cometh not with observation: neither shall they say, Lo here! or, lo there! for, behold, the kingdom of God is within you.[2]

INVOCATION:

O God, from whom all goodness, truth, and beauty come, we

pray for a better spirit in ourselves and throughout the whole church, because we have been weak in thy service and blind in the vision of thy kingdom; praying that those who represent us may have imagination and courage, wisdom and ability and charity among themselves. In Christ's name. AMEN.

POEM:

> God's call sounds through the centuries:
>   Awake, O Youth, and know
> Your total capabilities,
> The waiting possibilities,
>   What you should do, where you should go.
>
> God's call rings through the universe:
>   Advance, O Youth, today
> Where things are bad and growing worse,
> Where thinking straight is called a curse,
>   Where tyrants hold the sway.
>
> God calls you to make history:
>   Advance, O Youth, and dare
> Gethsemane and Calvary
> To light and lead humanity
>   Where life gives life to share.
>
> God calls to world community:
>   Heed him, O Youth, extend
> His love, good will, and unity,
> And kingdom's opportunity
>   To every foe and friend.[3]

—CHAUNCEY R. PIETY

STORY:

THY KINGDOM COME

"YOU used to want to help on things. . . ."

At the rear of the store, in the office of Whitaker Hardware Company, Gladys Moore found herself standing on one side of a half-century-old mahogany desk. Dwight Whitaker, Jr., was on the other. The girl raised her eyes to the level of a firm, determined chin. Something else was standing between them, too. She had come

59

to realize that lately. The desk, the business, the name which it represented, was a symbol of that.

"This is different. The people of Hadley are getting fed up. Drives for this. Drives for that—I tell you we must begin to look out for ourselves."

Dwight's word always sounded convincing; but what he didn't realize was that he had changed. Three years ago he became a partner in his father's hardware business. Since that time his interests had narrowed steadily, until Gladys found herself wondering whether he even remembered that there was a world outside the massive brick walls of the Whitaker store.

"I'm sorry," he said. "Tell the young people of your group I'm really sorry that I can't go along with them on this project."

Looking down, Gladys saw her left hand and the ring on its third finger. Dwight could have been such a help . . . his influence . . . the name. The name? As Mrs. Dwight Whitaker, Jr., would she, too, be just another "puppet on Whitaker strings"?

"There are things we need for ourselves," Dwight pointed out. "There's our drive to raise money for a set of carillon chimes."

Gladys nodded, but without looking up. Those people still needed food, clothing. Most of all, if they were to be kept from drifting into paganism which had helped cause two wars, they needed encouragement, to feel that people in America were concerned.

Dwight laughed. "Don't you realize that our neighbors across the street have a finer church building than we do?"

"St. Paul's isn't so bad, for looks," Gladys defended. There was something else. How would she say it? "You remember that place in the service, where the congregation chants the Lord's Prayer?"

Of course, he remembered. As choir director, he had tried for months to help the congregation, and the choir, to get that just right.

She continued, "As I played the accompaniment for the words, 'Thy kingdom come. Thy will be done,' I caught myself wanting to pause there, play that part over and over. 'Thy kingdom come. Thy kingdom come.' Do the people at St. Paul's really want the kingdom to come? Maybe they're looking for some miracle to change this mixed-up world into a grand paradise."

Dwight was looking at her in astonishment. Realizing how her words must have sounded, Gladys added quickly, "Oh, I have no right to talk like this. My father is a minister. I guess a minister's daughter sort of gets his slant on things."

"Your father is a credit to our congregation. We are proud of Dr. Moore, of that inspection trip he made to Europe."

"Three years ago you would have appointed yourself a committee of one to put this drive over, even if there had been a half dozen before," she reminded him.

"I've settled down," he explained. "If that is what you mean. I was going to keep this as a surprise. We have just completed arrangements to have St. Paul's Sunday morning service broadcast."

"That's fine," she said. Once she could have talked frankly to Dwight, made him see that all these things, pleasant as they were for St. Paul's, were only secondary. Now he had "settled down." He had two interests left—the hardware business, the choir at St. Paul's. She must say nothing to hurt him.

After a week of choir rehearsals, Gladys began to think that perhaps she had underestimated the importance of it all. "We must get this right," Dwight kept saying. "St. Paul's has a reputation to maintain." He paced across the floor in front of the choir loft. "Let's stop for tonight. I guess we're all tired."

Dwight dropped in a front pew. Gladys said, "You're trying too hard. You're too tense. That makes everybody tense."

"But this thing has to be right. We'll be on the air—thousands listening in."

"Maybe we're getting out of harmony," she said.

"What did you mean by that?" he asked ruefully.

"I mean," she said, "we want everything to be as good as we can make it. But a mistake now and then is a small thing—is to be expected in a choir like ours."

"I don't know what to think. People expect something of us. We're an old congregation. We have a tradition to uphold."

"Dwight, I have to tell you this. You don't know what you want. You're all mixed up inside."

"Yes, I am."

"With one hand you're trying to play in a minor key. Tradition, you call it. You're still young enough to want to play in a major key with the other hand—to reach out to the future. You used to be ready to try new things, even in music. Failures, mistakes, didn't mean so much to you then."

"People need things to depend on," he replied.

"Security is all right in its place," Gladys explained. "Only you're holding on to it so hard that you're missing the fun of living, of reaching out."

"I hardly know what to think sometimes," Dwight confessed. "I came back determined to do a lot of things. They didn't pan out. The store. I wanted to modernize."

"St. Paul's needs modernizing, too."

Dwight jumped to his feet. "Well, we do agree on that then," he exclaimed.

"You're talking about the physical part of St. Paul's." She stopped, then laughed. "Here I go again. You'd think I was pastor here, instead of Dad."

"No. Go on," Dwight encouraged.

"The real church—well, it's something you can't put your fingers on. It's what we do, what we want to do, what we hope for."

Dwight asked, "What do we hope for?"

"A better world," Gladys said.

"A better world?" Dwight shook his head. "I've about given up on that, too."

"It does look bad," Gladys admitted. "But there is hope."

"Hope?" Dwight pondered the word. "I can't see it."

"You might call it the seeds of hope. Christianity, faith in Christ for a shattered world."

"Oh, I see," Dwight laughed. "I thought there was a catch to it. You're getting ready to ask me to do something on that drive again."

"In fact I was," she told him frankly. "Only I was trying to make you see that if the kingdom is ever to come, we must do something." The girl stopped. Maybe the whole subject was getting to be an obsession with her. That afternoon, when she had slipped in for an extra hour's practice, she played through the musical setting of the Lord's Prayer. She caught herself playing "Thy kingdom come," then repeated, "Thy kingdom come."

She waited for Dwight to say something. He did. "Another drive. More for Europe. So far as I'm concerned, that's out. Dad thinks this give-away idea has gone far enough."

"And you? What do you think?"

"I'm afraid I agree."

Gladys felt something of a throb in her temples. She saw Dwight hold the door for her. But her feet refused to move. The fingers of her right hand closed over the ring. Suddenly they slid it from her finger. "Here," she said, and forced it back into his hand. She had made up her mind. Never could she consent to be a puppet on the Whitaker string.

The night was a miserable one. A hundred times she asked herself why she had been so impulsive and given Dwight's ring back. A week of rehearsals followed—a week of nights in which she kept asking herself, did Dwight care?

Then the broadcast itself. She must get herself under control somehow. A slip, the slightest slip, would ruin everything for Dwight.

Everyone was doing his best. Gladys tried to relax and listen to the sermon. Then came her father's momentous words: "We pray for the kingdom to come. Do we mean it? Then we must help to answer that prayer."

"Thy kingdom come." What she had tried to say was a faint echo of what her father was saying so eloquently now.

The sermon ended. Everyone would join in the Lord's Prayer. "Our Father which art in heaven. . . . Hallowed be thy name. . . . Thy kingdom come. . . ."

Voices were singing on. Suddenly, gasping, Gladys realized what she had done. She had repeated the accompaniment for the words "Thy kingdom come," just as she had done that afternoon.

Dwight's face was pale. The chant was almost completed before she got her fingers back again into time with the words. A perfect broadcast had been ruined by her fumbling! The service ended. Startled by someone standing beside her, she looked up. "All I can say," she stammered, "is that I'm sorry."

Dwight was smiling. "A mistake, now and then, is to be expected."

"I ruined the broadcast for you—for everyone."

"On the contrary. You have helped to make this a memorable occasion."

Memorable? Everybody would remember a blunder like hers this morning.

Dwight must have read her thoughts. "I don't mean it that way," he said. "I mean that never again can I repeat the words 'Thy kingdom come' without thinking about what they mean."

Gladys raised her eyes. Dwight's fingers held the ring. With a warm smile, she held out her hand toward him. Her finger was extended.[4]

POEM:

Would you win all the world for Christ?
    One way there is and only one;
You must live Christ from day to day,
    And see His will be done.

But who lives Christ must tread His way,
    Leave self and all the world behind,
Press ever up and on, and serve
    His kind with single mind.

No easy way,—rough—strewn with stones,
    And wearisome, the path He trod.
    But His way is the only way
    That leads man back to God.

And lonesome oft, and often dark
    With shame, and outcastry, and scorn,
And, at the end, perchance a cross,
    And many a crown of thorn.

But His lone cross and crown of thorn
    Endure when crowns and empires fall.
The might of His undying love
    In dying conquered all.

Only by treading in His steps
    The all-compelling ways of Love,
Shall earth be won, and man made one
    With that Great Love above.[5]

—JOHN OXENHAM

PRAYER:

O Christ, thou hast bidden us pray for the coming of thy Father's
kingdom, in which his righteous will shall be done on earth. We have
treasured thy words, but we have forgotten their meaning, and thy
great hope has grown dim in thy Church. We bless thee for the
inspired souls of all ages who saw afar the shining city of God, and
by faith felt the profit of the present to follow their vision. We rejoice
that today the hope of these lonely hearts is becoming the clear faith

64

of millions. Help us, O Lord, in the courage of faith to seize what has now come so near, that the glad day of God may dawn at last. As we have mastered Nature that we might gain wealth, help us now to master the social relations of mankind that we may gain justice and a world of brothers. For what shall it profit our nation if it gain numbers and riches, and lose the sense of the living God and the joy of human brotherhood?

Make us determined to live by truth and not by lies, to found our common life on the eternal foundations of righteousness and love, and no longer to prop the tottering house of wrong by legalized cruelty and force. Help us to make the welfare of all the supreme law of our land, that so our commonwealth may be built strong and secure on the love of all its citizens. Cast down the throne of Mammon who ever grinds the life of men, and set up thy throne, O Christ, for thou didst die that men might live. Show thy erring children at last the way from the City of Destruction to the City of Love, and fulfil the longings of the prophets of humanity. Our Master, once more we make thy faith our prayer: "Thy kingdom come! Thy will be done on earth!" [6]

HYMN: "O Master Workman of the Race," or
"O Brother Man, Fold to Thy Heart."

BENEDICTION:
May we set our affections on eternal things, seeking first the kingdom of God and his righteousness, in Jesus' name. AMEN.

SERVICE 9

CHANGING THE WORLD

PRELUDE: "Prayer" from *Rienzi* by Wagner.

CALL TO WORSHIP:

> The days of pack and clan
> Shall yield to love of man,
> When war-flags are furled;
> We shall be done with hate,
> And strife of state with state,
> And man with man create
> A brave new world.

—AUTHOR UNKNOWN

HYMN: "God of Grace and God of Glory," or
"The Voice of God Is Calling."

INVOCATION:

O God, who dost prefer before all temples the upright in heart and pure, and who dost instruct us in all truth: we know that if we walk with thee, what in us is dark thou wilt illumine; what is low, raise and support; what is shallow, deepen; so that every chapter of our lives will witness to thy power, and justify the ways of God to men. In Christ's name. AMEN.

SCRIPTURE:

But in the last days it shall come to pass, that the mountain of the house of the Lord shall be established in the top of the mountains, and it shall be exalted above the hills; and people shall flow unto it. And many nations shall come, and say, Come, and let us go up to the mountain of the Lord, and to the house of the God of Jacob; and he will teach us of his ways, and we will walk in his paths:

66

for the law shall go forth of Zion, and the word of the Lord from Jerusalem.

And he shall judge among many people, and rebuke strong nations afar off; and they shall beat their swords into plowshares, and their spears into pruning hook: nation shall not lift up a sword against nation, neither shall they learn war any more. But they shall sit every man under his vine and under his fig tree; and none shall make them afraid: for the mouth of the Lord of hosts hath spoken it.

For, behold, I create new heavens and a new earth: and the former shall not be remembered, nor come into mind.[1]

LEADER:

We will hear an incident in the life of one of the great reformers.

STORY:

ONE MORE SONG

NIGHT was lowering over the mining village of Mansfeldt in Prussian Saxony. A bluff wind swept up and down the crooked narrow streets, across the burghers' houses with their pointed roofs, timberwork, and overhanging stories, across the small Gothic church, the distant castle of the territorial lord, and the hovels of the miners. From many windows firelight and candles sent faint yellow rays into the gloom. Snow crested the town wall with a circle of white. A golden half-moon hung in an inky sky, and twinkling stars were just beginning to peep out.

A boy in worn garments walked swiftly over the frozen ground, as if to warm his unwrapped legs. His thin body shivered, but he trudged purposely on, a basket hung over one arm. Fair hair framed his lean face under a ragged hood. He rubbed his unmittened hands briskly together.

Three of the boys in the village had planned to sing with him tonight. Martin attended the church school of hymns. Ever since he could remember there had been delight for him in singing, especially the joyful songs. He often found himself singing words of his own to new tunes which came from inside him. All week he had practiced the "Carol of Jesus" with the three, singing in four parts the wonderful words. It was extremely cold tonight, so that the parents of the others had forbidden them to come. Martin had come alone.

The wind could not stop him tonight. The frosty air could not keep him at home. There was no time in all the year when the hearts of the villagers opened as well to song, and he must take advantage of that. Already there were six hunks of bread in his basket, five wild apples, three big onions, and a slice of goose. There was never an abundance in the cupboard at home. There had been more lately since his father had the smelting furnaces, but Martin and his mother continued to chop wood, tying it in great bundles, carrying it on their backs to the houses of the burghers to exchange for food. His flesh pained from cold. His back ached from lifting the heavy bundles. But there was something he *must* do before he went home to crawl under the scant bedding with his mother and father.

Martin needed a pardon piece to buy a pardon from the peddler monk who stayed at the inn. A sense of sin was smothering him. He knew he could not rest well until he had forgiveness. The day before his father had struck him so hard the blood had come. In anger Martin had run away. He had hastened to the municipal pasture ground and stayed hidden there all day in the swinekeeper's hovel until the keeper came home. He felt very unhappy inside because of what he had done. He decided not to leave Mansfeldt after all. And when he had returned to their one-room home his mother was weeping bitterly. He had looked at her red eyes and known then that he had committed a dreadful sin.

That morning he had gone to the peddler monk in the vestry of the church. The monk, who sat behind a long table, was short and broad with a full face, straight mouth and nose. He was a pompous man with a blustery voice. A lock of white hair hung down straight over his forehead between two bald spots and sloping eyebrows. He was clean-shaven and wore the dark garb of the Dominicans. A red wooden cross hung around his neck on a gold chain. He had told Martin how deadly his sin was, and how necessary it was to get the money to buy a papal indulgence.

Another monk was there who also wore Dominican garments. He was tall and grave with a beaked nose and kind eyes. While the peddler had been telling Martin all about purgatory and how terrible his sin was, the tall one kept shaking his head. The peddler monk paid no attention, but went on collecting coins from hands thrust at him, rapidly giving out pardon papers. Martin had wanted to ask the thin monk about it, but the man was soon surrounded by those who asked questions all about a city named Florence and about Rome.

CHANGING THE WORLD

Martin paused timidly in front of a two-story house where there was no light, wondering if the people were too poor to waste candles. He felt very scared to sing before such a big house in the night all alone. But surely people who could live in such a house were not poor and would give good alms. He knocked and began, lifting one foot at a time from the ice. A frowzy-looking woman with deep-set eyes and a dark shawl over her head came out muttering, and handed him a piece of stale wheaten bread.

"My bit for the poor," she said grudgingly. She waved him on and slammed the door.

Martin thought of the warmth of his father's smelting furnaces. His steps lagged. But he must sing one more song at the inn before he went home. He walked on past the houses of the burghers. Inside their homes were warmth and laughter. His mother and father loved him. He was sure of that, even if they spoke harshly and sometimes treated him severely. But they never laughed. Maybe it was because they were so poor. They had always been poor, ever since he could remember.

A gust of wind whipped his garments above his knees. He hurt all over now. He knew he should go home. But wonderful things can happen on the Eve of the Nativity. He might earn a pardon piece for his song. Hope burned in his heart. He moved on.

Yes, he would sing one more song. Ragamuffins infested taverns on Nativity Eve, but perhaps there would be fine gentlemen, too. One might like his song enough to give him a florin. How he wished he could help build the basilica of St. Peter, too. He had heard the fat monk telling the people about that need, and how God would redeem the poor souls in purgatory, if the basilica was built.

The fruiterer's shop was still open. There was the butcher's next to it, and beyond the grocer's. He passed them longingly, thinking of all the good things they contained, especially the hares in the butcher's window. He felt hungry, but he wanted to take his basket home to divide with his mother and father.

At last the lighted windows of the tavern showed in the shadows at the end of the dimly-lit street. As Martin drew near the irregular stone building he paused. There came the sound of laughter, men's voices raised in talk.

Old Nichen, the innkeeper, was a gruff man. Once two years before he had poured icy water on the boys as they sang. Again Martin shivered. He wanted no icy water tonight. He was very frightened at singing all alone, and of what Nichen might do. Tremblingly he opened his mouth and began to sing. In a moment the door opened. A heavy step on the threshold brought terror to Martin's heart. His legs felt like jelly. A huge figure cast its shadow across the snow in front of him.

"Be off with you!" a loud, strident voice bellowed.

It was Nichen, and his heavily jowled face was dark. He stood with one hand on his hip, the index finger of the other hand pointing in the direction from which Martin had come.

"It is Nativity Eve," Martin pleaded in a small voice. "I would sing of the Saviour."

"Sing!" Nichen sneered. "We have no need of your noise here. Be off!"

"One moment, Nichen," a deep, quick voice interrupted. "Your guests would hear the boy. Have you forgotten, Nichen, what eve this is? Come, boy. Come inside. Nichen's guests would hear your song."

Martin looked up at the tall, kindly monk he had seen at the church that morning.

"Come, child," the man repeated softly. "It's suppertime. Dine with me. Then we'll hear your song."

Wonderingly, shyly, Martin took the hand the monk offered, and let him lead toward the ruddy blaze. A shiny kettle was steaming on the hearth. There were smells of meat and bread and spice.

Martin looked around the big room from the red berries against glossy green on the shelf above the fire to the hangers-on and the square-faced peddler monk sitting at a spread table facing him. The peddler monk's eyes were hard. His brow was creased. The pardon box was on the table beside him.

Then Nichen was setting the table near the fire with a hare and fruit and bread. The friendly monk smiled down from above.

"The wonder of the Nativity," his host said, "is that it makes all men brothers. We are all children of one father, one family. Little brother, it gives me pleasure to have you here with me this night."

After the food had been blessed, Martin began to eat hungrily. The food warmed him. Firelight threw long shadows over the unplastered walls and ceiling.

Martin was so happy and busy for a little while that he forgot to be unhappy because he had no pardon piece. Then he looked over at the peddler monk, who was staring at him, and remembered why he had come. His heart began to beat again in slow, painful strokes.

But you couldn't ask a friend for alms. There were no rich gentlemen here tonight. This monk had given him a good supper, the finest he had ever had in all his twelve years. He would come again on the morrow and sing for coins.

Martin got up slowly. He knew no words great enough to thank this kind monk. And he wanted to thank him. There came a swift urge to sing. His song would express the thanks he could never convey! Clasping his small red hands together he broke forth in full song.

To his amazement his mouth was not singing the "Carol of Jesus." Words were coming out of his heart into his mouth and out into the warm, hushed air. Even the hangers-on grew very quiet. Martin knew not whence the words came into his heart. He only knew that he must sing. And he sang in a sweet, clear voice and his soul was in his song:

"All praise to Thee, Eternal God,
Who wore the garb of flesh and blood,
And chose a manger for Thy throne
While worlds on worlds were thine alone.
Hal-le-lujah!

A little child, Thou art our guest,
That weary ones in Thee may rest.
Forlorn and lowly is Thy birth
That we may rise to heaven from earth.
Hal-le-lujah!"

Young Martin Luther sang on with glad radiance, lingering over the words, not wanting them to stop pushing up out of the inside of him, not wanting the song ever to end. He sang the praises of a Saviour who redeemed from darkness of night unto light.

"All this for us, Thy love hath done
By this to Thee our love is won
For this our joyful songs we raise
And shout our thanks in ceaseless praise.
Hal-le-lujah!"

When he had finished he stood in the hallowed silence. Nobody spoke. Even old Nichen stood quietly as if under a spell. He wasn't frowning now. Nobody was frowning except the peddler monk.

71

A minute later Martin reached for his basket. He pulled up his hood. "I'll be on my way," he said.

Quietly, lest he wake the others from their trance, he slipped toward the door.

"Wait," the friendly monk called in a quick whisper.

He came after Martin, reached for his hand, and slipped something hard into it. At the door Martin opened his hand a crack to look. Two gold coins lay in his palm, two beautiful gold coins! He transferred one swiftly to one hand, turned, and carried his pardon piece happily toward the peddler. And when he had his pardon paper, holding it tightly, the basket swinging over his arm, he retraced his steps, clenching the hand that held the other coin as if he were afraid that what it contained might be snatched away. He went out into the night.

In a moment he was back. With slow steps he shuffled once more to the table of the peddler, looked lovingly at the shiny piece in his fingers, and then dropped it into the carved box.

"For the basilica of St. Peter," he whispered, crossing himself, "and the lost souls in purgatory."

When the heavy oak door finally closed upon his small figure Girolamo Savonarola of Florence sat very still, looking at the strange shadows on the ceiling.

Again came assurance that God must be sovereign, that Rome with Pope Alexander VI did not pay true allegiance to God as King. Alexander's hope was to subjugate all Italy to him, and extract vast treasure from the meek and trusting, such as this pitifully small boy. Boys, like young Martin, who seldom enjoyed a good meal, denied themselves to make Alexander and his family rich. Savonarola could see a body burning in the square outside the Palazzo Vecchio. It was his own.

But he knew he must go on with his work of preaching penitence and God's sovereignty. At all costs truth must be proclaimed.

He turned to his companion. He wiped a tear from his eye. "A boy like that may one day change the world," he said.

His companion sneered. "Who wants it changed?" he threw out, taking the leg of a hare in his hand and pulling it apart with yellow teeth.

"A lot of folk," Savonarola said, lifting his eyes once more to the shadows playing above his head.

72

Suddenly he threw himself to the inn floor there before them all where he knelt, eyes closed, lips moving fervently.

"What are you doing?" his companion demanded with a frown. Savonarola opened his eyes. He stood up.

"You wouldn't understand," he said slowly, "but 'the meek shall inherit the earth!' " [2]

POEM:

> God grant us wisdom in these coming days,
> And eyes unsealed, that we clear visions see
> Of that new world that He would have us build,
> To Life's ennoblement and His high ministry.
>
> . . . .
>
> To pledge our souls to nobler, loftier life,
> To win the world to His fair sanctities,
> To bind the nations in a Pact of Peace,
> And free the Soul of Life for finer loyalties.
>
> Not since Christ died upon His lonely cross
> Has Time such prospect held of Life's new birth;
> Not since the world of chaos first was born
> Has man so clearly visaged hope of a new earth.
>
> Not of our own might can we hope to rise
> Above the ruts and soilures of the past,
> But, with His help who did the first earth build,
> With hearts courageous we may fairer build this last. [3]
>
> —JOHN OXENHAM

PRAYER:

O thou great Companion of our souls, do thou go with us today and comfort us by the sense of thy presence in the hours of spiritual isolation. Give us a single eye for duty. Guide us by the voice within. May we take heed of all the judgments of men and gather patiently whatever truth they hold, but teach us still to test them by the words and the spirit of the one who alone is our Master. May we not be so wholly of one mind with the life that now is that the world can fully approve us, but may we speak the higher truth and live the purer righteousness which thou hast revealed to us. If men speak well of us, may we not be puffed up; if they slight us, may we not be cast down;

remembering the words of our Master who bade us rejoice when men speak evil against us and tremble if all speak well, that so we may have evidence that we are still soldiers of God. Amen.[4]

HYMN: "Rejoice, Ye Pure in Heart," or
"Rise Up, O Men of God."

BENEDICTION:

Unto God's gracious mercy and protection we commit ourselves. May the Lord bless us, preserve us from evil, and bring us to everlasting life. AMEN.

SERVICE 10

RULING THROUGH LOVE AND PEACE

PRELUDE: "L'Heure Mystique" by Bedell.

CALL TO WORSHIP:

> Come! Peace of God, and dwell again on earth,
> Come, with the calm that hailed thy Prince's birth,
> Come, with the healing of thy gentle touch,
> Come, Peace of God, that this world needs so much.
>
> Break every weapon forged in fires of hate,
> Turn back the foes that would assail thy gate;
> Where fields of strife lie desolate and bare
> Take thy sweet flowers of peace and plant them there.
> —MAY ROWLAND

HYMN: "O Thou Who Camest from Above," or
"Rejoice, Ye Pure in Heart."

INVOCATION:

O God, the source of all good gifts, deliver us, as we draw nigh to thee, from coldness of heart and wanderings of mind, that with steadfast thoughts and kindled affections we may worship thee in spirit and in truth, through Jesus Christ our Lord. AMEN.

SCRIPTURE:

Many nations shall come, and say, Come, let us go up to the mountain of the Lord, and to the house of the God of Jacob; and he will teach us of his ways, and we will walk in his paths. . . . Let us then pursue what makes for peace and for mutual upbuilding. . . . They shall beat their swords into plowshares, and their spears into pruning hooks: nation shall not lift up a sword against nation, neither shall they learn war any more. . . . Recompense to no man evil for evil. Provide

75

things honest in the sight of all men. If it be possible, as much as lieth in you, live peaceably with all men.[1]

POEM:

> O God, whose will is life and peace|
>   For all the sons of men,
> Let not our human hates release
>   The sword's dread power again.
> Forgive our narrowness of mind;
>   Destroy false pride, we plead:
> Deliver us and all mankind
>   From selfishness and greed.
>
> O God, whose ways shall lead to peace,
>   Enlighten us, we pray;
> Dispel our darkness and increase
>   The light along our way.
> Illumine those who lead the lands
>   That they may make at length
> The laws of right to guide the hands
>   That wield the nations' strength.
>
> O God, who callest us to peace,
>   We join with everyone
> Who does his part that wars may cease
>   And justice may be done.
> Enable us to take the way
>   The Prince of Peace hath trod;
> Create the will to build each day
>   The family of God.[2]

—ROLLAND W. SCHLOERB

LEADER:

There is a legend stating that the shepherds who followed the star of Bethlehem still roam the world today. The following story reveals some of the things about which they were concerned.

STORY:

AND YET THEY SEEK HIM

THE OTHER Shepherd wondered! As he sat on a little knoll watching his flock contentedly grazing, he was pondering what the Master had said: "The world had forgotten—forgotten—forgotten!" He and the Boy

Shepherd had made an earlier start than usual to the fields hoping to greet the Master as he passed that way. And they found him there already, troubled and grieved, for he knew of the unrest in the world—of the rumors of wars, of the bitterness and revenge men hold in their hearts today. The Boy Shepherd, too, could not understand, for had not Jesus walked among men as the Prince of Peace—had he not left as a heritage the message of the Love of the Father? Had he not commanded his disciples to take that message to all mankind? And of course ere *this* year had dawned—there could not be those who know not of Jesus nor those who do not heed His voice!

Many hours had passed since the Master left them there, and now as was his custom the Older Shepherd was coming to sit with them and watch the lambs. Carrying his favorite wee lamb in his arms, the Boy Shepherd ran to the little bridge that he might tell of their hour with the Master.

"And He kept saying—'The world has forgotten—forgotten!' Thinkest thou that in two thousand years there are yet men who hate each other—men who would kill their fellows for gain?

"If His followers have been faithful, and have taken His message to the far places, the world today must be a wonderful world! Rememberest thou the words He spake—'A new commandment give I unto you—that ye love one another as I have loved you'; and He said, 'Peace I leave with you; my peace I give unto you.' If love permeates the world, then wars have ceased—yes, surely in two thousand years love must rule the world." And so recalling the words of the Master they joined the Other Shepherd.

"Our boy is questioning whether or not love and peace rule the world!"

"Yes, when the Master left us we were troubled. Would that thou had been here! The ways of the world seem to grieve the Master. We cannot believe but that all nations live in peace one with the other, and that his disciples have preached and taught God's love till the world is Christian!"

"When the Master passeth this way again let us all three be here to talk with Him about it more!"

So they lingered, the Older Shepherd giving of his wisdom and humor, the Boy Shepherd occasionally walking among the sheep, watching the lambs at play. But the Other Shepherd held in his heart the words of the Master and pondered them.

Many times they met on this their favored hill and always they lived over again those wonderful strange days in Judea, when the star had led them to the manger and the Christ Child. . . .

And then once again they were together, and the Master was with them, and said to them:

"Ye shall journey over the world and when ye have found where the Father's love reigneth and peace abideth, ye shall return and rest from your journey and give a report."

In his eagerness the Boy Shepherd answered, "We will not be long, Master, for through two thousand years the governments of the world shall have found the way to live peaceably one with the other. It is to *them* I shall go. And I am sure *I* shall be the one to find it!" But the Master made him no answer.

The Other Shepherd turned to them and said: "Governments there have been since the beginning of the world, and always strife among them. But I have always felt sure the mothers of the world would one day rise up and say, 'There shall be peace in the lands. No more shall our sons go to war and slay each other.' So I know ere this the women will have rid the world of wars, and *I* shall find the peace we seek because of *mother love.*"

Then the Wise Older Shepherd spoke: "Remember ye not that the disciples organized the church in the world to teach and preach Jesus —the Father's love—brotherhood—and peace? On our quest *I* shall find that the *church* has established peace throughout the world."

And so the Master sent them forth. The Boy Shepherd, so confident, visited government halls and conferences and rulers' thrones, to find everywhere rumors of war and preparation for conflict. And his youthful enthusiasm began to wane; his confidence was shaken. He is yet seeking peace.

The Other Shepherd had not been long in the lands till he found the mothers of the world were interested in many things other than peace in the hearts of men. There were jealousies among them. Their days were crowded with so many inconsequential activities that they had forgotten the heritage that was theirs. He, too, is still searching— searching.

The Older Shepherd, in his calm deliberateness, went to the churches, sure that his mission would soon be accomplished. Today he wanders—searching—seeking—hoping yet that the church will bring to the world through the Gospel story the Peace of God. For he found much of the world still pagan—and even strife within the church at times.

And so today, as in the long ago—the shepherds watch for a guiding star to show them where peace abides, and where God's love reigneth.[3]

POEM:

> There is a stranger in the council hall
>> Where nations meet to plan the peace again.
> He sits unnoticed by the farther wall,
>> His eyes upon the leaders among men.
> His ears attend their clearly laid designs
>> For living in tomorrow's homes and marts,
> As though beneath their spoken words and lines
>> He hears the inner voices of their hearts.
>
> But when the delegates of all the world
>> Have cried their million wants, and lists are long,
> And after blueprints, charts, and plans are hurled
>> In varied protest at the core of wrong,
> He is our hope; He is the peace we seek.
>> O Listen, world, and let the Stranger speak! [4]
>
>> —ESTHER BALDWIN YORK

PRAYER:

Our Father, help us to look within our own hearts and acknowledge our part of the world's sin—the unjust practices which we often condone, the greed which we fail to condemn, the hatred and prejudices which still exist between races and classes of people. Give us courage as we strive to live in peace and good will with all people. Bless the work of the United Nations, grant unto its leaders sufficient understanding and a willingness to deal wisely with the perplexing problems of the world, that all nations may be drawn closer together. Guide us in our efforts to build stronger bonds of peace, good will, and brotherhood between our country and other nations. Give us a sense of thy presence, greater faith in thee, and obedience to thy will. In the name of the Prince of Peace. AMEN.

HYMN: "Prince of Peace, Control My Will," or
"Peace, Perfect Peace."

BENEDICTION:

Now unto him that is able to do exceeding abundantly above all that we ask or think, according to the power that worketh in us, unto him be glory throughout all ages. AMEN.

SERIES THREE

LIVING AS BROTHERS

SERVICE 11

APPRECIATING OTHER RELIGIONS

PRELUDE: "Jesu, Joy of Man's Desiring" by Bach.

CALL TO WORSHIP:
>   Thou Light of Ages, Source of living truth,
>   Shine into every groping, seeking mind;
>   Let plodding age and pioneering youth
>   Each day some clearer, brighter pathway find.
>
>   Thou Light of Ages, shining forth in Christ,
>   Whose brightness darkest ages could not dim,
>   Grant us the spirit which for Him sufficed—
>   Rekindle here the torch of love for Him.[1]
>   —ROLLAND W. SCHLOERB

HYMN: "Fairest Lord Jesus," or
      "O Jesus, Prince of Life and Truth."

SCRIPTURE:
In the beginning was the Word, and the Word was with God, and the Word was God. The same was in the beginning with God. All things were made by him; and without him was not anything made that was made. In him was life; and the life was the light of men. And the light shineth in darkness; and the darkness comprehended it not.

There was a man sent from God, whose name was John. The same came for a witness, to bear witness of the Light, that all men through him might believe. He was not that Light, but was sent to bear witness of that Light. That was the true light, which lighteth every man that cometh into the world. . . .

I am the light of the world: he that followeth me shall not walk in darkness, but shall have the light of life.[2]

POEM:

> O Thou, to whose all-searching sight
> The darkness shineth as the light,
> Search, prove my heart; it yearns for thee;
> O burst these bonds, and set it free!
>
> Wash out its stains, refine its dross,
> Nail my affections to the Cross;
> Hallow each thought; let all within
> Be clean, as thou, my Lord, art clean!
>
> If in this darksome wild I stray,
> Be thou my Light, be thou my Way;
> No foes, no violence I fear,
> No fraud, while thou, my God, art near.
>
> . . . .
>
> Saviour, where'er thy steps I see,
> Dauntless, untired, I follow thee;
> O let thy hand support me still,
> And lead me to thy holy hill!

> —NICOLAUS L. ZINZENDORF
> Tr. JOHN WESLEY

STORY:

LIGHT FROM THE PAST

"SEE HERE, you young rascal! You nearly knocked me over!" Joseph Allenby glared at the rosy-cheeked youth who was trying to balance an armful of packages.

"Sorry, Mister," replied the boy cheerily. "I couldn't see where I was going, with all these bundles. Merry Christmas!"

Joseph Allenby continued to elbow his way through the holiday throngs, his lips twisted slightly into a bitter smile. He heard the laughter around him, but in his heart there was no laughter—only a bristling impatience to escape the milling crowds and return to the shelter of his home.

Finally he reached the outskirts of town and saw his house before him, looming out of the darkness. It was beginning to snow. A shower of white, misty flakes that dropped on the ground shivered for an instant and then settled into the frozen earth. Just as Joseph was about to turn the key in his lock, he heard a shrill young voice calling to him from the neighboring lawn. It was Tommy, six-year-old son of his neighbors, the Wilkins.

"Mr. Allenby, I've been waiting for you." A small figure came tumbling toward him, exhaling little clouds in the frosty air.

"What is it, Tommy?" Joseph nodded vaguely at the child, scarcely looking at him.

"Mommy and Daddy want you to come over to our house tomorrow, you know—to celebrate Christmas with us. You should see our tree! It's beautiful—all covered with colored lights. Will you come?"

Joseph Allenby shrugged his shoulders and said sharply, "You can tell your parents I thank them; but I have no time for such foolishness." With that, he turned his back on the bewildered child and entered the house.

Inside it was cold and bleak. Joseph thrust a log on the dwindling fire and watched the flames shoot up. 'A beautiful tree with colored lights, indeed," he muttered. "That's all Christmas means today—a time for parties, for fancy decorations, for extravagance. People have forsaken God; they no longer have ideals; they think only of frivolity."

Joseph Allenby stood before the hearth—a tall, lean man of about forty-five years, with sagging shoulders and a shock of prematurely white hair. A flicker of lights moved restlessly over his body, illuminating a worn, lined face and steely, blue eyes, narrowed into slits. As he stared into the heart of the fire, the figure of Mathilde rose up before him. Sweet, gentle, childlike Mathilde—gone these fifteen years. Ever since her departure, Joseph had isolated himself from the rest of the world, reliving his grief from day to day.

Suddenly the doorbell, clanging through the silence, brought him back to the present.

"Now who do you suppose . . ." He opened the door cautiously. Outside stood a young woman, holding a flimsy coat around her small frame. She was smiling pleasantly.

"Mr. Allenby? My name is Feldman, Esther Feldman." She went on cordially, with a faint trace of a foreign accent. "My husband and I just moved into the house at the corner. We want so much to be friends with the people in the neighborhood."

Joseph stood stony-faced, resenting this intrusion, eager only to return to his dreams and his fireplace.

The woman continued with some embarrassment, her voice trembling a little. "You know, this time of the year, while you observe Christmas, we celebrate the Jewish holiday, Hanukkah . . ."

"I am well aware of it," replied Joseph impatiently.

"Well, we're having a big Hanukkah dinner this evening, and we thought it would be nice if you and some of the other neighbors could join us. There will be plenty of good food and I'm preparing a special holiday dish—pancakes." Her voice trailed off uncertainly, "You see, this is our first . . ."

"Pancakes, eh?" Joseph shouted the word as if it were an insult. "Plenty of good food! Is this the way you remember those ancient heroes, the mighty Maccabees? What of their sacrifices? What of their courage and their faith in God? What of their struggle for religious freedom? Today, these are forgotten—all we think about is stuffing ourselves!" He paused, his face white with fury. "No, thank you, I respect your ancestors too much to remember them with such tomfoolery."

He fairly slammed the door in her face.

Shortly afterwards, Joseph was struck with remorse. There had been no need to burst out with such violence at a perfect stranger. Poor woman—she was not to blame. She was only a victim of the times— times when people denied the glorious past and thought only of revelry and gluttony.

Restless and uneasy, Joseph sought relief where he had found it many times before—in the Bible. He picked up the tattered volume, thumbed idly through the pages, whispering to himself, "If only I could go back to the past, even for a moment, before Christmas trees and Hanukkah festivals, before department-store Santa Clauses and empty celebrations—back to biblical times when people were close to God and spiritual values counted for something." All at once a great weariness came over him. He leaned back and closed his eyes.

"Snap out of it, Joseph—no time for dozing now—we're going on a long journey."

Joseph bolted out of his chair and looked around. Outlined in the doorway was a powerful-looking gentleman, impeccably dressed in a dark suit, wearing white gloves and brandishing a walking stick.

"Who are you—where did you come from? How do you know my name?" Joseph sputtered.

"Hold on there," laughed the man. "Is that the way to greet a guest? I must say you're not very courteous. As for my identity, you may call me Lumen. The other questions are highly irrelevant. And now, to get down to business. Were you serious about wanting to return to the past?"

Joseph's astonishment turned to irritation. "Of course; but what's that to you?"

"You don't have many manners, do you?" The stranger chuckled. "Well, never mind. I'll take you anyway. Ready?"

Before Joseph had a chance to reply, he experienced a curious sensation—as if he were spinning in space. Fireplace, armchair, living room —all seemed to melt away and he whirled about in a circle of inky blackness. Then the atmosphere cleared and he found himself in an ancient, walled city, on a cobblestone thoroughfare. The stranger who called himself Lumen was close beside him.

"Does this place look familiar to you?" asked Lumen genially. "We're in Jerusalem. Oh, don't let the clothes worry you," he added quickly, noticing Joseph's astonishment at the strange apparel of the passers-by. "We're back in 165 B.C."

Joseph rubbed his eyes. To be sure, the men and women looked as if they had stepped out of the Old Testament, but Joseph was still suspicious. He would soon find out. He signaled an elderly, bearded gentleman who was hurrying by.

"No use, Joseph," chuckled Lumen, "he can't hear you. In fact, he can't even see you. We're invisible."

Joseph swallowed hard and tried to regain his composure. Finally, he asked, "Where are the people rushing?"

"They're on their way to the Temple, of course. It's the great day of rededication. Just a few short weeks ago the place was a shambles. But everyone got busy and now wait until you see it. It's as beautiful as it was the day three years ago when the Syrians took possession of it and forbade the Jews to worship God there."

Joseph's eyes flashed. "Do you mean to tell me we're about to see the rededication of *the* Temple—the one that was defiled by the Syrians?"

"None other," laughed Lumen. "But what are we waiting for—we'd better get going if we want to arrive in time for the ceremony. Let's hurry."

Joseph's legs moved mechanically. This was certainly a miracle. Only this afternoon he had been in the twentieth century on the day when

Jews throughout the world were celebrating Hanukkah. Now, he was about to witness the very event they were commemorating.

He recalled the details of this great battle for religious freedom, one of the earliest on record: how Antiochus, the Syrian tyrant, had invaded the holy Temple and desecrated it; how he had tried to force the Jews to worship Greek idols and how they had remained stubbornly loyal to God; how the Jews, under the leadership of the mighty warrior, Judah Maccabee, had struggled for three years against overwhelmingly superior Syrian forces; how they had finally triumphed over oppression and restored the Temple.

Just as the two men reached the courtyard they heard shouting and the blaring of trumpets, and saw a host of warriors in shining armor march into the Temple. The tallest and grandest among them halted at the entrance and addressed the crowd in a strange tongue.

Joseph turned to Lumen, shaking with excitement. "Why, that must be—it can only be . . ."

Lumen laughed. "Yes, it *is* Judah Maccabee, better known to friends and enemies alike as The Hammer."

Joseph followed his companion into the Temple, his heart pounding with anticipation. Inside, he stood motionless as he watched one of the greatest dramas of all time unfold before his eyes—the rededication of the Temple. He saw a priest advance to the altar and apply oil to the sacred lamp, or Menorah, symbol of everlasting light, which had not burned for three long years.

"And that is why Hanukkah is called the Festival of Lights," chanted Joseph half aloud.

In the middle of the ceremony, a woman swayed slightly and cried out —a long, piercing wail of lamentation. Joseph seized his friend's arm.

"That woman—who is she?" he asked breathlessly.

"It's Hannah—her seven sons were slain by Antiochus when they refused to bow down to false gods."

"But she looks like—why, she might be the mother of that woman who came to visit me today . . ."

"Mrs. Feldman?" suggested Lumen softly. "Yes, she does, doesn't she? Well, in a way, Esther Feldman is very much like Hannah."

"Like Hannah?" said Joseph scornfully. "That's nonsense. The young woman who came to see me knows nothing of suffering or of religious ideals. She thinks only of feasting and parties."

Lumen shook his head. "You're wrong, my friend. Esther Feldman knows a great deal about suffering *and* about ideals. She and her husband were tortured by the Nazis for their religious faith. For years they kept their courage high in a concentration camp. Esther Feldman arrived in the United States only a few weeks ago. The Hanukkah celebration she asked you to attend was to be her first in many years in a country where she need fear no persecution. You see, Joseph, in your world there are hundreds of thousands of human beings who have shown great courage and heroism for their principles, just as in ancient times."

Joseph was silent for a moment. "I have lived too much in the past. Lumen, take me back to my world."

"Not yet, Joseph. We have still another journey to make. Are you ready?"

Instantly, the Temple, the altar, the Menorah, the crowds of people all vanished and Joseph was hurled into clouds of space. When the mist cleared, he found himself in a large meadow, with Lumen at his elbow. It was a cold, clear night and the sky was ablaze with stars that drenched the whole countryside in a silver glow.

"I have never seen a night so bright," whispered Joseph to his companion," or so hushed. It terrified me a little. Where are we, Lumen?"

Even Lumen was solemn; the laughter had gone from his lips; the twinkle had vanished from his eyes.

"We are only a short distance from the Temple in Jerusalem, Joseph; more than 150 years have passed since the Jews celebrated the first Festival of Lights."

Joseph started to speak but his words froze within him. There was something mystical and awesome about this night—something that set it apart from all other nights. He walked on in silence.

Finally the two men came to an old, weatherbeaten barn and Joseph's wonder grew. From within came the sound of music, a music so strange and ethereal that it might be the harmony of the stars.

Slowly they entered and Joseph stood transfixed. Before him, illuminated by the starlight which streamed in from a crack in the roof, was a manger filled with straw and on the straw lay a new-born Babe in swaddling clothes. Beside him, on the hay, lay a woman; and bending over her, gently caressing her hand, was a man. Everywhere there were animals—oxen and cows, donkeys and lambs, goats, dogs and hens, and not a creature among them stirred or uttered a sound.

Joseph could restrain himself no longer. With a muffled sob, he knelt beside the Infant. "It is the Christ Child; it is the Prince of Peace." Then he rose and his voice rang out in the silence, "Glory to God in the highest, and on earth peace, good will toward men." As he spoke, the music swelled until it seemed as if all heaven were alive with sound. Gently Lumen took his friend's arm and led him out into the frosty evening.

The two men walked for a time without a word. Then Joseph began to weep softly.

"What is it, Joseph?' asked Lumen. "Are you thinking of the Christ Child and what became of him?"

"No, Lumen," replied the man, "I am thinking of another child and what is to become of me."

"The child wouldn't be Tommy Wilkins, by any chance, would it?" Lumen's eyes sparkled roguishly.

But Joseph was lost in thought. "We used to have Christmas trees," he recalled, "trees that glittered with silver tinsel and shining balls and gifts in gay wrappings and colored ribbons."

"But I thought you said all that was foolishness, that people had lost their ideals and forsaken God."

"It is I who have forsaken God," said Joseph sadly. "It is I who slammed the door on Mrs. Feldman and turned away little Tommy Wilkins. For fifteen years I have shut myself up in a large, gloomy house and locked out all warmth and love and light . . . light," Joseph repeated the word tenderly and looked curiously at his companion. "Lumen . . . Lumen . . . why, that *means* light."

"Yes, Lumen is Latin for 'light.' "

For the first time Joseph truly appreciated his new friend. "Thank you, Lumen. Thank you for bringing light back into my life."

As he spoke, a giddiness swept over him and he felt a sinking sensation. When he recovered, he was back in his living room, shivering with cold before a dying fire. Peering into the darkness, he called softly, "Lumen, are you there?" There was no reply.

Slowly he arose, slipped into his coat and walked out into the night. The snow was falling thick and fast now and already a white, gleaming blanket covered the town. As he passed his neighbor's house, Joseph paused for a moment before the large window to watch Mr. and Mrs. Wilkins as they placed gifts under the Christmas tree.

Yes, it *was* a beautiful tree, just as Tommy had said—tall and proud and blinking with colored lights that told of warmth and hospitality inside. Tomorrow, he thought, tomorrow he would go to Tommy and apologize. Little as he deserved it, he knew the Wilkins would be charitable and forgive him.

He continued along the street, the snow crunching underfoot, until he came to a tiny house on the corner. Through the window, the lights of a Menorah flickered and beckoned to him. Drawing closer, he could see a young woman, her face radiant and smiling, arranging flowers in a vase on the table.

Suddenly Joseph wanted to leap into the air, he felt so exhilarated. This was his world! Not the dead world of the past, but this blessed country, this pleasant street, these good people who lived side by side, sharing everything in true friendliness. While they enjoyed their precious freedoms, they respected the rights of their neighbors to live in dignity and to worship God as they pleased. This was a world where brotherhood and liberty and justice were not merely ideals; they were pulsating realities and he was proud to be part of such a world.

"Peace on earth, good will toward men." Joseph placed his forefinger on the doorbell marked "Feldman" and pressed it.[3]

PRAYER:

Our Father, we are grateful for the gift of thy Son to the world, for the record of his life and teachings. We thank thee that the good news of the gospel has been brought to us, and may we show our gratitude by striving to live by the law of love and service to others. Help us to get rid of any prejudice, and to have a friendly attitude toward people of all religions and races. May we strive to appreciate the historical backgrounds of all of the people we meet. Make us kind one to another, merciful, forgiving, and compassionate. Reveal to us ways by which we can be neighborly, and open doors of opportunity by which we can carry the Christian message to those who are still in darkness. May the joy of the Christmas season enter into the hearts of thy children everywhere. In Christ's name. AMEN.

HYMN: "Light of the World, We Hail Thee," or
    "As with Gladness Men of Old."

BENEDICTION:

Now the Lord of peace himself give you peace always and be with you all. AMEN.

SERVICE 12

SWINGING TOWARD THE LIGHT

PRELUDE: "Deep River" by Coleridge-Taylor.

CALL TO WORSHIP:

> O brother man, fold to thy heart thy brother;
> Where pity dwells, the peace of God is there;
> To worship rightly is to love each other,
> Each smile a hymn, each kindly deed a prayer.
>
> Follow with reverent steps the great example
> Of him whose holy work was doing good;
> So shall the wide earth seem our Father's temple,
> Each loving life a psalm of gratitude.
> —JOHN G. WHITTIER

HYMN: "Where Cross the Crowded Ways of Life," or
"At Length There Dawns the Glorious Day."

SCRIPTURE:

From the rising of the sun even unto the going down of the same, my name shall be great among the Gentiles; . . . for my name shall be great among the heathen, saith the Lord of hosts. . . . The Lord hath made known his salvation: his righteousness hath he openly showed in the sight of the heathen. . . . The Gentiles shall come to thy light, and kings to the brightness of thy rising. . . . We have also a more sure word of prophecy; whereunto ye do well that ye take heed, as unto a light that shineth in a dark place, until the day dawn, and the day-star arise in your hearts. . . . For God, who commanded the light to shine out of darkness, hath shined in our hearts, to give the light of the knowledge of the glory of God in the face of Jesus Christ. . . . Arise, shine; for thy light is come, and the glory of the Lord is risen upon thee.[1]

89

POEM:

"I do believe the world is swinging toward the light,"
So spoke a soul on fire with holy flame.
Amid the dark such faith pierced through the night,
The dreamers wrought, and living fruitage came.
To give of self, and not to count the cost,
To learn, to teach, to labor, and to pray,
To serve like Christ the least, the last, the lost,
These were the beacon fires that lit the way.

Our light grows dim; the air is thick with doom,
And everywhere men's souls are crushed with fears.
Yet high above the carnage and the gloom
The call resounds across the teeming years,
"Lift high Christ's cross! Serve God and trust His might!"
I do believe the world is swinging toward the light! [2]

—GEORGIA HARKNESS

LEADER:

We will hear the story of an act of kindness which led later to the
establishment of a college that has been a training center for the Negroes of the South.

STORY:

MUSTARD-SEED PEOPLE

ABOUT the year 1860, a sixteen-year-old youth by the name of Samuel
Meharry set out from Ohio, his wagon piled high with supplies, to
seek his fortune in the West. One afternoon in Indiana his wagon
became bogged down in a deep mudhole on a wilderness road. Meharry tried everything he knew to get the wagon out, but to no
avail. Nightfall was coming on. In the twilight he discerned a distant
light. Meharry made his way toward a cabin from which the light
shone. Now, I failed to mention that this was a white youth. But he
could not help it. He was born that way. It made no difference, however, as we shall see.

Meharry knocked on the cabin door. A friendly farmer opened it.
"Howdy, son!" he said. "Won't you come in?" Now the farmer was
black. He could not help it either. He, too, was born that way. But
his color had prevented him from obtaining an education in those
days.

"My wagon is stalled in a mudhole out on the road," said Meharry. I thought maybe you might help me get it out."

"Sure I'll help you. But it's too dark now. We'll 'tend to that in he mornin.' Had yoh supper yet, son?"

"No, sir, I was too busy with the wagon," replied the lad.

"Well, we's just poh folks, and ain't got much to eat, but you're most welcome to what we have. Sit down, son, and eat."

The boy ate a warm supper. Then his friend said, "We ain't got no eds, son, but you can sleep on the bes' pallet in the house. You'll be afe here. Nuthin's gointer harm you. You're in a God-fearin' home. Res' now, and in the mornin' we'll see 'bout the wagon." The family had prayers and all retired.

After an early breakfast, the farmer and Meharry worked at the mudhole. One scraped away the mud and the other threw in gravel. The two of us workin' together will soon have this wagon out on dry ground," said the farmer. Shortly afterward he said, "Now son, whip up yoh mules. I'll put my shoulder to the wheel and push. She oughter ome out!" Out came the wagon!

"Thank you, good neighbor," said Meharry as he prepared to drive off. "If I ever make any money out West, I'll remember you and lo something good for your people. Good-by!"

"Good-by, son, and may God bless and prosper you," responded he farmer. The farmer's name is unknown. The location of the farm has been lost. Maybe these details are not important. Suffice it for the kingdom of God that two strangers met—members of two different races, where one held the other in chattel slavery—met, and saw "that of God" in each other and were unafraid. Suffice it that an unknown farmer helped a young traveler and gave him a warm welcome into his heart. This was the beginning of the miracle.

Sixteen years passed. Meharry had made his fortune. One day when he walked the streets of Nashville, Tennessee, he saw poverty and disease taking a heavy toll of the former slave refugees there. Meharry's compassionate heart was touched. Then he remembered his good neighbor back in the Indiana woods, and the promise he had made. He decided then and there, "I will start a medical school for Negroes here in Nashville. Their young men and women will learn the science of medicine and the art of healing. Here we will train nurses and doctors and dentists and pharmacists. They will minister to the sick and afflicted, and save human life, by the grace of God. I will persuade my brothers to join me and bring in other trained men to teach here. Then we must have a good hospital. God helping me, I'll find the men to run it," said Meharry. And he did. Four other Meharry brothers came and worked and taught with Samuel. The Hubbard brothers joined them and established the famous school and hospital. The Methodist church contributed to the project and money flowed in from many sources. The little seed of brotherhood planted in an act of kindness around a mudhole was growing into an astonishing tree.

If you should visit Nashville today, you will not find Samuel Meharry or any of his brothers, but instead a monument built by them and scores of others who believed in the divine possibilities of all men. You will see one of the finest medical colleges and health centers in the country. The buildings, grounds, equipment, and endowment combined are worth several million dollars. But this is not the real monument to Samuel Meharry. The true memorial and the true miracle of the mudhole is alive today in the thousands of graduate doctors, dentists, and nurses, and their services of mercy. During the past seventy years these winged messengers of health have not only ministered to the needs of their own people, but have served men and women of all races, in and out of the United States, and in the armed forces of the nation around the world.

Truly the tiny mustard seed of faith in one's brother man, planted by that Indiana roadside, has become a veritable tree of refuge for all pain-racked humanity. Here they come by the thousands for release from suffering, and rest under its beneficent branches. And here too, Negroes and white men, and brown men also, have studied and worked together in mutual confidence and respect for one another—worked and fought as strong comrades united against man's common enemy: disease and death. For seventy long years they have been winning two battles. One against diseases of the body, the other over diseases of the mind. Since race prejudice is a disease of the mind, it has been dealt a body blow by the Meharry miracle. "Blessed are the pure in heart; for they shall see God," said Jesus. Meharry and the farmer saw God in each other at the mudhole, and the miracle of healing followed.[3]

LEADER:

Meharry Medical College, Nashville, Tennessee, with an average enrollment of 475, is a member of the Association of American Medical Colleges. It was organized in 1876 as the medical department of Central

SWINGING TOWARD THE LIGHT

Tennessee College, but it has had a separate existence since 1915, when a new charter was granted by the state of Tennessee. Meharry has three schools: medicine, dentistry, and nursing. Its graduates represent more than half of the Negro physicians and dentists in this country.

POEM:

> Men! whose boast it is that ye
> Come of fathers brave and free,
> If there breathe on earth a slave,
> Are ye truly free and brave?
> If ye do not feel the chain,
> When it works a brother's pain,
> Are ye not base slaves indeed,
> Slaves unworthy to be freed?
>
> Is true freedom but to break
> Fetters for our own dear sake,
> And, with leathern hearts, forget
> That we owe mankind a debt?
> No! true freedom is to share
> All the chains our brothers wear,
> And, with heart and hand, to be
> Earnest to make others free!
>
> They are slaves who fear to speak
> For the fallen and the weak;
> They are slaves who will not choose
> Hatred, scoffing, and abuse,
> Rather then in silence shrink,
> From the truth they needs must think;
> They are slaves who dare not be
> In the right with two or three.
>
> —JAMES RUSSELL LOWELL [4]

PRAYER:

Once more a new day lies before us, our Father. As we go out among men to do our work, touching the hands and lives of our fellows, make us, we pray thee, friends of all the world. Save us from blighting the fresh flower of any heart by the flare of sudden anger or secret hate. May we not bruise the rightful self-respect of any

93

by contempt or malice. Help us to cheer the suffering by our sympathy, to freshen the drooping by our hopefulness, and to strengthen in all the wholesome sense of worth and the joy of life. Save us from the deadly poison of class-pride. Grant that we may look all men in the face with the eyes of a brother. If any one needs us, make us ready to yield our help ungrudgingly, unless higher duties claim us, and may we rejoice that we have it in us to be helpful to our fellow men. AMEN.[5]

HYMN: "The Light of God Is Falling," or
     "O Jesus, Master, When Today."

BENEDICTION:

Now unto the King Eternal, immortal, invisible, the only wise God be honor and glory forever and ever. AMEN.

SERVICE 13

GIVING A CUP OF WATER

PRELUDE: "Liebestraum" by Franz Liszt.

CALL TO WORSHIP:

> The common hopes that make us men
> > Were his in Galilee;
> The tasks he gives are those he gave
> > Beside the restless sea.
>
> Our brotherhood still rests in him,
> > The Brother of us all,
> And o'er the centuries still we hear
> > The Master's winsome call.[1]

—OZORA S. DAVIS

HYMN: "O Master, Let Me Walk with Thee," or
"In Christ There Is No East or West."

INVOCATION:

O Lord, make us aware of the needs of others—the poor, the downtrodden, and the oppressed. Make us sensitive to their desires and longings, and willing to do something to relieve their suffering and to bring to them equal opportunities. We thank thee that thou hast shown us the way and hast led in service to the poor and the unfortunate. Help us to do our part whatever the cost. In Christ's name. AMEN.

LEADER:

What was Jesus' attitude toward the poor, the outcasts, and those that are usually considered unimportant? Did he ever miss an opportunity of ministering to needy persons? In the following word of Jesus we see that they had a definite place in his ministry.

SCRIPTURE:

The Spirit of the Lord is upon me, because he hath anointed me to preach the gospel to the poor; he hath sent me to heal the brokenhearted, to preach deliverance to the captives, and recovering of sight to the blind, to set at liberty them that are bruised, to preach the acceptable year of the Lord.[2]

LEADER:

Have we tried to imagine what life is like to the poor, the hungry, the despised minorities, and displaced persons? What have we done to help them? Are we willing to help when it costs us something? What was Jesus' attitude toward people who needed help? Does he ask us to do anything which he has not already done?

How many times have we neglected to give a cup of water, to speak kindly, to encourage people who seemed disreputable or unimportant to us? Let us notice the words of Jesus at this point.

SCRIPTURE:

Whosoever shall give to drink unto one of these little ones a cup of cold water only in the name of a disciple, verily I say unto you, he shall in no wise lose his reward.[3]

POEM:

>The cup of water given for thee
> Still holds the freshness of thy grace;
>Yet long these multitudes to see
> The sweet compassion of thy face.
>
>O Master, from the mountain side,
> Make haste to heal these hearts of pain;
>Among these restless throngs abide,
> O tread the city's streets again,
>
>Till sons of men shall learn of thy love
> And follow where thy feet have trod;
>Till glorious from thy heaven above
> Shall come the city of our God! [4]

—FRANK MASON NORTH

GIVING A CUP OF WATER

HYMN: "O Jesus, Master, When Today," or
"O Brother Man, Fold to Thy Heart Thy Brother."

LEADER:

We will hear the experience of a group of missionaries in Africa with sharing a cup of cold water. Let us meditate on what we would do in a similar circumstance.

STORY:

A CUP OF WATER

A CUP of water is a simple thing, but that afternoon all the complexities of a world-wide conflict focused on a single cup of water.

We had traveled all day, three riding in the cab of a truck, four in the open back. Two were missionaries, three Africans and two visitors from America. One of the Africans was a preacher, a gifted linguist, one of the most loved men in his tribe. Another was our cook, and the third the general handy man—both devoted Christians.

The road was rough, the country wild. Elephant tracks were common. Antelope, lions, water buffalo, crocodiles and hippos were numerous in that region. Villages were few. We had planned few stops, for on the outward trip we had held many services and our schedule was already full. But we forgot the magnetic appeal of the word that a missionary doctor would return down that road that day. Mothers and babies, families with ill members, sick who were able to get to the road, waited in the hot sun. A swampy section, the region is a vast malaria hole and the persistent fever, when it does not kill, weakens resistance to other diseases. Year old babies were brought with enough diseases for a lifetime. . . .

So the day wore on. Heat fatigue and thirst took their toll of our strength. Late in the day we boarded a primitive ferry. The three Africans and I were in the back of the truck. The wind and dust had left us parched. Then a missionary offered me a cup of water.

Suddenly the world's strife seemed to me to focus in that cup. . . . The Africans watched the missionary, and me, and the cup. I had treasured my fellowship with them. We had shared discomforts, talked about many things, laughed at many things, prayed together at the Angelus Hour. They knew that cup was not intended for them. What would you do? I hope you are wiser than I was. What I did is not important to this story, but the problems focused in that scene are some of the most important ones confronting mankind.

How much is the white man going to share his cup of water with other races? His cup overflows with treasures: health, education, comfort, opportunity. Theirs often is empty, often broken. The missionary movement is the most generous, creative manner of sharing our blessings this world knows, yet it is a very human movement with very human frailties. Many Africans think that some missionaries have racial prejudice against them. Perhaps they are right. Certainly that is not true of all missionaries, nor of most. What a strange paradox, that people will give their lives in service of those against whom they have such prejudices! Yet it is no more strange than our naïve assumption that we Americans can send from our midst missionaries untainted by our racial prejudice.

As those Africans that day silently watched two white men with a cup of water, so the colored races of mankind today watch the white man with our overflowing treasures. A cup of water is a simple thing. Love is a simple thing. Sometimes simple things hold worlds of meaning. What do you do to share your cup of water, to show your love? [5]

POEM:

I slept. I dreamed. I seemed to climb a hard, ascending track,
And just behind me labored one whose face was black.
I pitied him, but hour by hour he gained upon my path.
He stood beside me, stood upright, and then I turned in wrath.
"Go back," I cried, "What right have you to stand beside me here?"
I paused, struck dumb with fear, for lo! the black man was not there—
But Christ stood in his place!
And oh! the pain, the pain, the pain that looked from that dear face.
—AUTHOR UNKNOWN

LEADER:

We will hear the experience of missionaries in the Philippines.

STORY:

A CUP OF COLD WATER IN THE JUNGLE

WE were climbing a mountain in the Philippines in Northern Luzon and had gone through jungle trails for four hours, finally hiking up the mountain to the habitat of a wild tribe of Negritos. They are a diminutive people, resembling our American Negro, but short enough to stand under the armpits of a man of average height. They live in trees, eat nuts and roots, and hunt with bows and arrows. They have been called the lowest tribe in mentality on the islands.

It was a hot day, and having traveled from early dawn to avoid the intense heat, arrived at the habitat of the Negritos around two o'clock. Contrary to advice, I had not worn a sun helmet, and had a sunstroke just before we arrived at the top of the mountain. I was quite ill, and was forced to lie down in the shade of a tree while the others in our party ate the first meal of the day. I watched the others as they ate a picnic lunch, and also watched a circle of naked Negritos hunched down to stare at the Americans, too close for comfort, for they were a dirty lot.

About fifty of these unwashed people watched every bite of food that the members of our party put into their mouths, and you could see them drool as dogs often do when they see food. The Negritos crowded closer and closer, the circle closing in on the whites until they could almost touch them. One hideous old man was in the forefront of the circle. His repulsiveness made me nauseated when I looked his way.

"I've traveled among most of the wild tribes, and I have seen the lowest humans on earth, but I have never seen a type so low in the human scale as that old man," continued a photographer who had covered the earth in his time. We discussed the old man as we rested, but he did not know that we had consigned him to the lowest rung on the ladder of humanity. He stared at us, now and then turning his eyes from those who ate to watch me as I lay on the ground weak from illness.

When we had finished our luncheon a missionary handed the old man a sandwich because he seemed to be the oldest and the hungriest. Did he eat the sandwich? No. He handed it to a child standing near him. When another sandwich was handed to him, he took it over behind a tree, where another grisly Negrito was hunched on the ground and gave it to him. A third sandwich was handed to him, he presented it to an old woman near by. And so it continued, until the last bit of food was disposed of.

"It may be that he is not hungry," someone said.

"And it may be that he is generous, sacrificial, and kindly," was the reply of a woman in our party.

Then I noticed that the old man had disappeared. In a few moments he returned, carrying an armful of big broad palm leaves. He spread the leaves out on the ground under the shadiest tree and motioned in gestures of kindliness for me to roll over and lie down on the bed he had made for me.

Again he disappeared, and when he returned he was carrying a big bamboo tube of clear water slung over his scrawny shoulders. He brought it to where I was lying on the bed of palm leaves. Then, with a shrug of shoulders he swung the bamboo tube, and over my head and face I felt the cool refreshment of spring water, the first I had had in water in that day of intense heat. From the tube he poured some water into what looked to be a wild gourd cup and gave it to me to drink, did that old man whom we, in our infinite wisdom, had decided was the lowest type of human we had ever seen on earth. Yet in that kindly service I could hear faintly echoed: "Who so ever shall give you a cup of cold water in my name, I say unto you he shall not lose his reward."

I have never seen a cup of cold water given in His name to anybody, anywhere, at any time, which had in it more of the spark of God than I saw that hot afternoon. That native of the Philippines is one of the most unforgettable characters I have ever met. I often think of him and his kind as I hear firsthand stories of courage during the war, and remember the heroism these little brown brothers of ours demonstrated during the invasion of the Philippines by the Japanese.[6]

POEM:

> Vision of Truth that led the pioneers,
> Starring the dark and quieting their fears,
> Shine forth again upon the forward way
> Our feet must tread to meet the coming day.
>
> Give us their faith that sees the farthest good,
> Their never-failing zeal for brotherhood,
> Their strength that felled a wilderness to found
> Thy holy Church on high and holy ground.
>
> Winnow our spirits till they yield, as theirs,
> Thy golden grain unchoked by thorns and tares;
> Increase our talents till their shining store
> Builds on the rock thy kingdom evermore.
>
> Then shall we stand amid the rising towers,
> Sharing their reach toward higher realms than ours,

Finding along the trail our fathers trod
Our journey's end, the commonwealth of God.[7]
                                        —EARL MARLATT

PRAYER:

O thou, who art no respecter of persons, thou hast shown us through thy life and ministry the proper attitude toward the poor, the outcasts, and the oppressed. Thou knowest our unchristian attitudes toward the underprivileged, our failure to see their needs and to do something about it. Reveal to us something we can do to make their lot easier and to share with them the privileges and opportunities that we enjoy. Lead us into ways of ministering to them, of bringing relief from suffering, of lifting their burdens, and dividing with them the comforts of life which we enjoy. Forgive us for neglecting to give the cup of cold water, for failure to speak kindly or show concern for those who are doing the unskilled labor and bearing the heavy burdens. The only reward that we ask is that we may know that we are doing thy will. In Christ's name. AMEN.

HYMN: "We Thank Thee, Lord, Thy Paths of Service Lead," or "The Voice of God Is Calling."

BENEDICTION:

And now may the God of compassion watch over us all. AMEN.

SERVICE 14

LIVING AS BROTHER TO EVERY RACE

PRELUDE: "Berceuse" by Goddard.

CALL TO WORSHIP:

> My country is the world;
> My flag with truth impearled,
>   Fills all the skies;
> All the round earth I claim;
> Peoples of every name;
> And all inspiring fame
>   My heart would prize.
>
> And all men are my kin,
> Since every man has been;
>   Blood of my blood.
> I glory in the grace
> And strength of every race,
> And joy in every trace
>   Of brotherhood.
>
> —AUTHOR UNKNOWN

HYMN: "At Length There Dawns the Glorious Day," or "Where Cross the Crowded Ways of Life."

SCRIPTURE:

All ye are brethren. . . . One is your Father, who is in heaven. . . . [God] hath made of one blood all nations of men for to dwell on all the face of the earth. . . . They shall come from the east, and from the west, and from the north, and from the south, and shall sit down in the kingdom of God. . . . There is no difference between the Jew and the Greek: for the same Lord over all is rich unto all that call upon him. . . . God is no respecter of persons: but in every nation he that feareth him, and worketh righteousness, is accepted with him. . . . For whosoever shall do the will of God, the same is my brother.[1]

INVOCATION:

Thou perfect Master, who shinest upon all things and all men, as gleaming moonlight plays upon a thousand waters at the same time! Steadily and quietly sails the great ship of compassion across the sea of sorrow. Thou art the great physician for a sick and impure world, in pity giving the invitation to the "Paradise of the West." AMEN.[2]

POEM:

> Measure thy life by loss instead of gain,
> Not by the wine drunk, but the wine poured forth;
> For love's strength standeth in love's sacrifice,
> And whoso suffers most hath most to give.
> For labor, the common lot of man,
> Is part of the kind Creator's plan;
> And he is a king whose brow is wet
> With the pearl-gemmed crown of honest sweat.
> Some glorious day, this understood,
> All toilers will be a brotherhood,
> With brain or hand the purpose is one,
> And the Master-workman, God's own Son.
>
> —AUTHOR UNKNOWN

STORY:

THE TENTH JEW

THE shells were falling thick and fast. In the midst of it all were ten American boys of Jewish faith. One, fatally wounded, had asked that the Kaddish, the prayer for the dead, be said over his remains. Bound to the honor code of all soldiers, his buddies prepared to carry out his last wish. Tenderly they lifted his body into the closest shelter they could find. It was the bomb-shattered remains of a Catholic Church. Only three walls, two pillars and a cross, still stood. Suddenly one lad remembered that no Kaddish could be said without a Minyan (the minimum number required to be present for a service). A Minyan was ten. They were only nine.

The company had been ordered forward in twenty minutes. What could they do? They sat on the ruined slabs of stone that littered the church floor. They were dejected, unable to fulfill their buddy's last wish. His watch, his girl's picture, and dog-tag lay beside him, ready to be sent back to his loved ones. A simple burial prayer must be said. They would have to go. Just then came an ominous silence. The nine soldiers raised their heads to the sky and waited expectantly for something to happen. Then the battle broke forth with more fury than before. The men flung themselves on the ground as a mighty explosion caused the rest of the walls to cave in about them. The earth's trembling ceased. The air cleared. The men stood up to leave.

As they stood there in humble silence, they stared in amazement— now they were ten. The figure of Christ had slipped from the cross and stood among them, leaning against a pillar, erect—one of their number. The tenth Jew was in their midst. They said the Kaddish and went into battle. They had fulfilled their comrade's last wish.[3]

LEADER:

Here is another story of religious brotherhood.

It often occurs that when we have reached the end of our human resources and must depend upon God for help, we realize our spiritual kinship with people of other religious backgrounds.

After a night of fierce fighting on Guadalcanal, Barney Ross, the famous prize fighter, tells this experience that took place in the early morning, when he had fired his last shot in defense of three severely wounded buddies:

"We were praying; somehow you learn to pray out there whether you know how or not. And you don't care who hears you either. In a lull in that whistling inferno, I heard all our voices and realized we were all praying. I was praying to the Jewish God. Atkins, my pal with the mangled leg in the nearest foxhole, was praying to the Baptist God. The kid with a hole in his body and the middle finger of his right hand stuck into it to stop the flow of blood was praying to the Catholic God. The guy with the shoulder almost torn off, who was something else, was praying to his God.

"Suddenly I realized a strange thing: we were all praying to the same God. We were all using about the same words, asking for the same things—that if the Japs came, death would be quick, that our folks would be all right, and the rest of the company. And it struck me that there was no real difference between us at all; just a little on the surface. And I couldn't help but wonder if people have to come so close as that to death to realize that we are all on the same side and all trying to get to the same place." [4]

POEM:

Who is so low that I am not his brother?
　Who is so high that I've no path to him?
Who is so poor I may not feel his hunger?
　Who is so rich I may not pity him?

Who is so hurt I may not know his heartache?
　Who sings for joy my heart may never share?
Who in God's heaven has passed beyond my vision?
　Who to hell's depths where I may never fare?

May none, then, call on me for understanding,
　May none, then, turn to me for help in pain,
And drain alone his bitter cup of sorrow,
　Or find he knocks upon my heart in vain? [5]

—S. RALPH HARLOW

PRAYER:

O Thou who art the Father of all mankind, in deep shame we confess that we have not lived as Thy sons. Between us and Thy children of other races and colors we have raised walls of partition. In hardness of heart and callousness of soul we have assumed ourselves to be better than others. We have accepted privileges we have not been willing to share. We have been content to see those of darker skin denied the fruit of their land and labor. We have spoken much of freedom and equality while millions of our brothers, made in Thine own image, suffered grievously through our injustice. Forgive us, O Lord.

Help us, O God, to bring forth fruits worthy of repentance. Grant Thy continuing grace to those who are in bondage because of our sin. Give them patience to wait for the morning; implant in us a divine discontent that their night is so long.

We rejoice in the rich gifts of those of other races to our lives. We bless Thee for their power to endure in faith and hope, their laughter and song, their love of beauty and mellowed wisdom. Help us gratefully to receive what they offer, that all may be enriched.

We thank Thee, O God, that Thou hast made of one blood all nations of the earth. Help us to be one in Christ Jesus and in Him to labor together that Thy Kingdom may come. In His name. AMEN.[6]

HYMN: "In Christ There Is No East or West," or
        "O Brother Man, Fold to Thy Heart Thy Brother."

BENEDICTION:

And now to God the Father be honor and praise, dominion and glory, on earth as in heaven, this day and forevermore. AMEN.

SERVICE 15

REALIZING OUR WORTH

PRELUDE: "Finlandia" by Sibelius.

CALL TO WORSHIP:

      Our country hath a gospel of her own
      To preach and practice before all the world—
      The freedom and divinity of man,
      The glorious claims of human brotherhood,
      And the soul's fealty to none but God.[1]
                 —JAMES RUSSELL LOWELL

INVOCATION:

  We earnestly desire, O Lord, to know that which is worth knowing, to love that which is worth loving, to praise that which pleaseth thee best, to prize that which is precious to thee, and to hate all that is evil in thine eyes. We pray for wisdom and true judgment that we may search out and do what is well pleasing unto thee. AMEN.[2]

SCRIPTURE:

      O Lord our Lord,
         how excellent is thy name in all the earth!
         Who hast set thy glory above the heavens.
      Out of the mouth of babes and sucklings has thou
         ordained strength because of thine enemies,
           that thou mightest still the enemy and the avenger.
      When I consider the heavens, the work of thy fingers,
         the moon and the stars, which thou hast ordained;

107

What is man, that thou art mindful of him?
  and the son of man, that thou visitest him?
For thou hast made him a little lower than the angels,
  and hast crowned him with glory and honor.
Thou madest him to have dominion over the works of
  thy hands; thou hast put all things under his feet:
All sheep and oxen,
  yea, and the beasts of the field;
The fowl of the air, and the fish of the sea,
  and whatsoever passeth through the paths of the seas.
O Lord our Lord,
  how excellent is thy name in all the earth! [3]

HYMN: "Let All the World in Every Corner Sing," or
       "Now Thank We All Our God."
POEM:

> For man's unceasing quest for God,
> For God's unceasing quest for man,
> For records of his love and power
> Surrounding life since life began,
>   We thank thee, Lord most high.
>
> For ancient tales of long ago,
> Man's guesses when the world was young,
> For talks around the blazing fire,
> For stories told and stories sung,
>   We thank thee, Lord most high.
>
> For those great laws the Hebrews made,
> Among the greatest ever known,
> For early history wise men wrote,
> Engraved on parchment, skin, or stone,
>   We thank thee, Lord most high.
>
> . . . .
>
> For those most precious books of all,
> That show us Jesus Christ, our Lord,
> Seen through the eyes of faithful friends
> Who gave their lives to spread his word,
>   We thank thee, Lord most high. [4]

—ALICE M. PULLEN

THE OLD MAN AND THE RAM

AN AGING man sat cross-legged under the shadow of a great rock in the midst of the desert. He was watching an old ram whose black wool was burned brown by the pitiless sun, as it grazed on the bitter grass which grew up in tawny tufts between the rocks. A little distance away the flock, crowded under the shelter of another huge rock, was staring vacantly out into space and chewing cuds.

Huge of body, his massive features burned black by the relentless heat of the desert, there was something regal about the old shepherd. Exchange his rough goatskin coat for the purple and he would have graced a throne. In his black eyes, narrowed to a squint and peering out from under great craggy brows, there burned a fire which marked him as a man whose mind was on the march.

Jethro, the venerable sheik of Midian, was the only one who seemed to know much about the old shepherd, and he did not talk. All the desert really knew was that he had suddenly appeared out of the west and had attached himself to Jethro's establishment. In time a rumor of trouble in Pharaoh's court filtered out into the wilderness; but as is the custom of the desert, the past was not probed.

Behind those squinting, burning eyes, however, there raged at times a tumult. Memories of proud functions at court returned to the shepherd's mind to taunt him with contempt for his grubby role. As he stared out across the waste there were times when brilliant pageants paraded across the horizon, hosts of marching men appeared, rhythmic music pounded in his ears. But a hurried glance down at his rough goatskin cloak and out at his sunburned charges was usually sufficient to fetch him back to the desert and to reality.

This midday the tumult would not be tamed, and the aging shepherd's lips moved nervously as he conversed with himself in an undertone that reeked with bitterness.

"What's the difference between that old ram and me?" he asked himself, and his words squeezed out between lips drawn tight. "The sun vents its heat upon both of us alike. Each of us spends his days and his strength in search of food and water. In the evening time sleep comes to us to relieve us of the burden of the day.

"But no memories haunt him. He sees no rich palace with ivory couches when he stares out across the desert waste. No flute playing plaintive melodies ever awakens him in the night. He never feels the earth shaking under the feet of hosts tramping by. The pulse of power never throbs through his veins. He is a ram!

"I am a man! I have studied the stars and wondered. I have tasted the wine of authority. I have learned from the masters. I have sacrificed at the altars of the gods. And I have been tormented with long, long thoughts about the right and the wrong. I have sensed something strange and urgent in my heart, and I have struck out against a task master and in behalf of a slave.

"Nothing is wrong to that old ram, but many things are wrong to me. He is never driven by the good and the beautiful, but they will not let me rest. He knows no duty; I can never escape from duty. What makes the difference? What IS the difference?"

The aging shepherd ceased to stare out at the old black ram. His flashing, restless eyes were on the mountain top now, the fire within them burning even more intensely while he narrowed them just a little more tightly.

"Why must I go on thinking? Why is my spirit troubled within me? Why can't I graze and stare and in the evening time lie down to quiet rest as that old ram does, with no thoughts to torment me? Why don't water and grass and a goatskin cloak at night leave me content?" And his eyes shot down from the mountain top to the old ram and back up again in a twinkling.

It had been from Jethro, the aged and respected sheik, that he had learned about a mighty God who lived atop the craggy mountain with the sheer granite walls. Alone in the wilderness for days at a time, he had marshaled his mind before the mountain and strained to understand.

When the drifting clouds enshrouded its crest, he had had a sense of a vast loneliness, and had told himself that Jehovah could not see him, but had wrapped himself in obscurity. When the mighty thunders roared and the lightnings flashed far up along the granite walls, he had trembled at the sight of Jehovah's mighty power.

It was when the sky was clear, however, and when the giant granite crest stood out in contrast to the heavens that he seemed to feel a strange companionship. It was then that his spirit became calm and his thinking seemed to arrange itself. In hours like that he became confident that Jehovah, Jethro's god, spoke to him also. He could find no other explanation for the sense of peace and confidence that stole in upon him. It must be Jehovah!

As the aging shepherd lifted his eyes once more from the old ram to the mountain, it was shaking itself free from the clouds. The midday sun washed it clean of all obscurity and it stood out in sharp contrast against the blue. In that moment there dawned upon the mind of the shepherd a mighty concept, staggering in its implications and eternal in its significance.

"Jehovah made me different. He gave me something the old ram does not have and can never have. It is that which makes me a man."

Then, lowering his eyes as if in a desperate effort to understand, he said to himself, "And Jehovah breathed into his nostrils the breath of life and man became a living soul!" [5]

POEM:

What is man that Thou should'st mind him?
—The son of man that Thou should'st visit him?
In Thine own likeness, Lord,
Thy tender love designed him,
And was it not Thy word
That wrought the wonders of his frame,
And breathed in him the living flame
Of Thine own spirit?
—Didst bid him stand and walk upright,
Head to the heavens as in Thy sight:
—And of Thy magnanimity
Didst Thine omnipotence curtail
To crown him with free-will,—
The power to choose the great or small,
The high or low, the good or ill.
And sadly, sadly, has he used
That gift, and Thy great trust abused.
No more he follows Thy behest,
Nor sets Thee first, nor gives Thee best;
But goes his own way down the steep,
His own self-sown harvesting to reap,
And yet, without free-will, he were
But slave, and no more son and heir.
And so we thank Thee for Thy grace,
And pray Thee bear with us a space! [6]

—JOHN OXENHAM

111

PRAYER:

O God, we thank thee for a revelation of thyself through thy Son, for the record of his life and teachings in the Gospels. Speak to us through the Bible, through thy followers, and by the still small voice, that we may understand what it means to live as thy sons and daughters. We are grateful that thou didst create us in thy image. Forgive us for the times when we have placed our affections upon material things and have neglected spiritual values. We would seek first the kingdom of God, live by thy will and commit our lives entirely to thee. Suffer us not to be tempted beyond that which we are able to bear. In the words of Francis of Assisi, make us instruments of thy peace. Where there is hatred, may we bring love; where there is offense, may we bring pardon; where there is discord, may we bring harmony. May we replace error with truth; doubt with faith; despair with hope; darkness with light; sadness with joy. Make us not so crave to be loved as to love. Help us to learn that in giving we may receive, and in forgetting self, we may find life eternal. In Christ's name. AMEN.

HYMN: "My Soul, Be on Thy Guard," or
      "A Charge to Keep I Have."

BENEDICTION:

The God of peace be with you all. AMEN.

SERVICE 16

STANDING FIRM AND BOLD

Prelude: Hymn tune *"Ein' Feste Burg."*

Call to Worship:
Thou wilt keep him in perfect peace, whose mind is stayed on thee: because he trusteth in thee. Trust ye in the Lord for ever: for in the Lord Jehovah is everlasting strength.

Hymn: "Fight the Good Fight," or
"Go, Labor On!"

Leader:
In the Scriptures we read of those who lived by their convictions. who stood firm and bold regardless of the consequences.

Scripture:
Faith enabled Abraham to obey when God summoned him to leave home for a region which he was to have for his own, and to leave home without knowing where he was going. Faith led him to make a temporary home as a stranger in the land he had been promised, and to live there in his tents, with Isaac and Jacob, who shared the promise with him. For he was looking forward to that city with the sure foundations, designed and built by God. . . .
Faith led Moses' parents to hide him for three months after his birth, because they saw that he was a beautiful child and they would not respect the edict of the king. Faith made Moses, when he was grown up, refuse to be known as a son of Pharaoh's daughter, for he preferred sharing the hardships of God's people to a short-lived enjoyment of sin, and thought such contempt as the Christ endured was truer wealth than the treasures of Egypt, for he was looking forward

113

to the coming reward. Faith made him leave Egypt, unafraid of the king's anger, for he persevered as though he saw him who is unseen. . . .

For my time would fail me if I told of Gideon, Barak, Sampson, Jephthah, David, Samuel, and the prophets, who by their faith conquered kingdoms, attained righteousness, received new promises, . . . found strength in their time of weakness, proved mighty in war, put foreign armies to flight. . . .

Yet though they all gained God's approval by their faith, they none of them received what he had promised, for God had resolved upon something still better for us, that they might not reach the fulfilment of their hopes except with us. . . .

Therefore, let us too, with such a crowd of witnesses about us, throw off every impediment and the entanglement of sin, and run with determination the race for which we are entered, fixing our eyes upon Jesus, our leader and example in faith. . . .

Discipline is never pleasant at the time; it is painful; but to those who are trained by it, it afterward yields the peace of character. So tighten your loosening hold! Stiffen your wavering stand! And keep your feet in straight paths, so that limbs that are lame may not be dislocated but instead be cured.[1]

POEM:

        "I'll meet you in the morning," so
        The Christian heroes long ago
        Said when their final hour had come,
        As they went forth to martyrdom.

        In the white splendor of that dawn,
        What mattered their earthly years foregone?
        What were their transient agonies,
        In view of the eternities?

        Nor need we care, when our days are spent,
        How rough or brief the road we went,
        For life and love will be complete
        When in the morning we shall meet.[2]
                              —EFFIE SMITH ELY

RENEWAL

THE VAST arched hall was filled to its great oak doors. The Friars, swathed in black and gray cowls, all of them from Francis, the eldest, to Thomas, the youngest, the bishops, the learned men of the church were there. They sat tensely amid the splendor of satin, damask, ermine-trimmed purple, fine garments of the nobles and princes, the rich and powerful.

The ecclesiastics were alarmed, angry. The Friars were the most angry of all. A radical was to be tried, a man who defied them, declaring the church full of corruption, the Friars evil. But his worst crime was translating the Holy Book of the Scriptures from the Latin Vulgate into English. All men would be able to read without the clergy if this radical continued his work!

The Tribunal filed in with stern faces. John Wycliffe, former master of Balliol College, Oxford, stood alone before the judges, leaning on his staff, a bent and bearded figure in dusty garments. He remembered with bitterness and despair another day when these same men and women, rich and poor alike, stood at his side. He had been important to Parliament when he had access to the King's ear, when John of Gaunt, the richest nobleman in all England, Duke of Lancaster, had been his friend. He had once been sent to Bruges as ambassador of the crown. Princes and nobles had been patrons of his school at Canterbury, the finest and wealthiest of all Oxford Colleges. Even the Lord Marshal of England had sought his company then. That had been in a day before his enemies had succeeded in working up distrust against him, hatred of him because he endangered their evil schemes. Like the idol-makers of Paul's day they desired his destruction because he proclaimed truths which might empty their pocketbooks. His former friend, the King, had now turned against him. He was alone.

The row of judges seated themselves with a rustle of fine cloth. It looked to John as if each mouth in the line was sterner than the mouth before, and each pair of eyes harder and colder as they bored down on him. Twice his trial had been halted, making their eagerness to judge the greater.

"O Lord God," he prayed in the gloomy silence. "My God!"

He kept his eyes closed to shut out those faces, those eyes filled with loathing.

115

"Look up, fellow!" one of the justices roared in a rasping voice. "Show ye proper respect for ye Tribunal!"

John Wycliffe opened clear blue eyes, and waited. "Whereas," the charges began, "ye great arch heretike, John Wycliffe, hath fouled ye Holy Scriptures. . . ."

It happened suddenly. A swelling rumble sounded like mighty thunder rolling near. The judges moved uneasily in their high carved chairs. They cocked white wigs at one another. Their brows raised. The accuser paused, mouth wide. A shriek of terror arose. There was a stir throughout the room. Other cries lifted piercingly above the dismayed gathering. An earthquake was rocking the monastery!

"Shall the trial go forward?" one rabbit-faced judge arose nervously to demand.

"Indeed!" It was the sharp voice of Archbishop Courtney, who was on his feet in his corner. "Only an earthquake can purge such a one as this Wycliffe!" he shouted, waving a hairy hand, fisting it viciously. "It is the warning of God! Let the trial proceed!"

The judges settled back uncomfortably. The trial went on. At length the rumbling ceased.

John Wycliffe heard vaguely the words of accusation. With downcast heart he was remembering the day Archbishop Courtney had taken his arm, praised his scholarly attainments, asked him to dine, a day that seemed such a long time ago. He sighed. All so-called friends of earlier days had deserted. He knew now something he had not known then. All classes in all ages bow to power and money. People follow the popular, cater unashamedly to influence. Few men think for themselves, seek truth, dare to stand for the right against the opinions of men in high places.

It was dangerous to stand alone. He knew what standing alone meant. He would be excommunicated, a parson cast out of the Church. Somehow that didn't matter so much.

What John Wycliffe longed for most now was a friend, just one man who would be brave enough to risk the displeasure of the powerful, to have faith in him, to comprehend the issue, to take a stand for truth. If only he had that, he could undergo the persecution, the misery ahead. It would renew his faith in mankind. His dark unhappiness would not be without a light.

The Synod deliberated three days. The weather remained sultry. For three days John Wycliffe stood alone listening to accusation, denunciations of men whose selfish policy would deny the story of the selfless

116

Christ to be read by an upset world, by people who needed him as
their compass in an evil day. Misery sapped into his heart. And as the
hours dragged John's mind filled with disappointment at the blindness
of men, men's cruelty, that kept such a frail creature as man from
having the Scriptures in his own language to inspire him to great
living.

At last the time to announce the verdict came. In words that ac-
cused of corrupting the Holy Book, and maliciously purporting to
translate it, maliciously planting his own heresies, he was declared
guilty. Excommunication would indeed be swift. But his work was
not done. God would use him to go on proclaiming the evil works
of the Friars who infested England. He would go on with his trans-
lations. He was doing God's will.

It would be difficult. He could bear his agony if there was only one
man. . . . He turned from the Tribunal. There was no hope there.
His eager eyes searched the crowd of long, solemn faces, fat pampered
ones, faces filled with hatred wreathed in sneering triumph. He began to walk slowly toward the door. Under an arch he stood quite
still. Surely, he thought, here was one man. But not a man stirred.
Every eye seemed on him. Voices lifted in scorn, loud guffaws. Was
there no understanding here, no kindness? Tears blinded John Wycliffe.
He marched on alone, a disgraced and heartsick man.

Yet he had no regrets, for he had done no wrong. He had performed
a radical work by declaring that the Scriptures belonged to the common
people, and translating them for distribution to all.

There were slow, halting footsteps behind him. He lifted high his
head. There *was* someone! He stopped. He waited wonderingly.

"Organ of the Devil!" a voice hissed.

It was the voice of Brother Francis, Brother Francis whom he had
nursed through the Black Death until he had contacted it, himself, and
almost died. Francis spat savagely. His sloping brows contracted. His
tub-like abdomen shook with rage, flopping the heavy gold cross upon
his breast.

The fierce crowd closed in. "Heretic!" . . . "Enemy of the Church!"
. . . "Image of lies!" they shouted.

Rough hands whirled about him. A blow across his face sent him
reeling. Blood flowed red down his long beard onto his worn garments,
splattering against his bare ankles and the sandals on his feet. Laughter
sounded mockingly around him.

His legs were weak. Very weak. He staggered. He fell on his knees with a thud. He struggled to rise.

A strong arm lifted him, encircled his shoulders. Wonderingly John Wycliffe turned to look into the deep brown eyes of a portly young man.

"Move back!" the handsome gentleman said with authority. And his round face was stern. The crowd hesitated. "Move back!" he repeated.

The sun came out as John Wycliffe walked into the late afternoon with the steady right arm of a friend supporting him, a song in his heart, his faith in man renewed. Maybe the younger man understood everything he was trying to do. Maybe he didn't understand at all. Maybe he didn't approve. But there was the love of the Christ in his eyes. He had no fear of what Archbishop Courtenay would say! He was not worried about the King's displeasure. He saw life as something more than power and popularity. He thought for himself. Above all he loved his Lord and his fellow men.

"Beautiful day," the portly gentleman said, as the warmth of the May sun touched their faces.

John Wycliffe paused, looking up at his strong young companion.

"Aye," he said, and a smile lit up his thin, pallid face until it shone. "It's a *wonderful* day!"

Geoffrey Chaucer, poet beloved by the people, honored by kings and nobles, stood before Blackfriar's Hall in the City of London where John Wycliffe left him, watching the old scholar step slowly across the cobblestones.

And he thought of the dingy little homes of all the common people of England where one chamber sheltered a whole family existing on cheap meat, enjoying no luxuries. It was true what this Wycliffe said. These ignorant people did without the necessities like bedding and wheaten bread while the Friars peddled indulgences, fattened their own bellies on credulity and superstition, opening the door of eternal life only to those who would pay enough.

This Wycliffe was a very brave man, brave enough to denounce such robbery, to give up great influence and worldly possessions that such as these might be fed in body and soul.

Here, indeed, was a good parson full of love who sought no self-glory but only truth, happy in the virtues of a good life lived for others. Rhythm and music danced in Geoffrey Chaucer's mind as he watched. And a Canterbury Tale was born! [3]

STANDING FIRM AND BOLD

POEM:

O God most high, we thank Thee
   For the heroes Thou hast sent,
Strong souls who from their fellows
   Dared to be different;

Men who, through all the ages,
   Though slighted and defied,
Swam brave against the current,
   Nor drifted with the tide:

Tyndale, who from the gallows,
   Proclaimed the truth supreme;
Bunyan, in Bedford prison,
   Dreaming his deathless dream;

Columbus, with mutinous sailors,
   Venturing an unknown sea;
Lincoln, opposed and derided,
   Setting the bondslaves free.

We thank Thee for their courage
   Who wrought so well of old:
Help us in our day's conflicts
   To stand as firm and bold![4]

—EFFIE SMITH ELY

PRAYER:

O Lord, we lift our hearts to thee in the pure light of morning and pray that they be kept clean of evil passion by the power of forgiving love. If any slight or wrong still rankles in our souls, help us to pluck it out and to be healed of thee. Suffer us not to turn in anger on him who has wronged us, seeking his hurt, lest we increase the sorrows of the world and taint our souls with the poisoned sweetness of revenge. Grant that by the insight of love we may understand our brother in his wrong, and if his soul is sick, to bear with him in pity and to save him in the gentle spirit of our Master. Make us determined to love

119

even at cost to our pride, that so we may be soldiers of thy peace on earth.[5] AMEN.

HYMN: "Are Ye Able?" or
"March On, O Soul with Strength."

BENEDICTION:

Unto God's gracious mercy and protection we commit you; and the blessing of God Almighty, the Father, the Son, and the Holy Spirit, be upon you, and remain with you always. AMEN.

HELPING EACH OTHER

PRELUDE: Hymn tune "Dix."

CALL TO WORSHIP:

> For the joy of human love,
>   Brother, sister, parent, child,
> Friends on earth, and friends above,
>   For all gentle thoughts and mild,
> Lord of all, to thee we raise
>   This our sacrifice of praise.
>
> For each perfect gift of thine,
>   To our race so freely given,
> Graces human and divine,
>   Flowers of earth, and buds of heaven,
> Lord of all, to thee we raise
>   This our sacrifice of praise.[1]
>
> —FOLLIOTT SANDFORD PIERPOINT

HYMN: "Happy the Home When God Is There," or
    "Now in the Days of Youth."

SCRIPTURE:

Your love must be genuine. Hate what is wrong, and hold to what is right. Be affectionate in your love for the brotherhood, eager to show one another honor, not wanting in devotion, but on fire with the Spirit. Serve the Lord. Be happy in your hope, steadfast in time of trouble, persistent in prayer. Supply the needs of God's people, be unfailing in hospitality. Bless your persecutors; bless them; do not curse them. Rejoice with those who rejoice, weep with those who weep. Live in harmony with one another. Do not be too ambitious, but accept humble tasks. Do not be conceited. Do not pay anyone back with evil for evil. See that you are above reproach in the eyes of every one. If possible, for your part, live peaceably with everybody. Do not take your revenge, dear friends, but leave room for God's anger, for the Scripture says, "Vengeance belongs to me; I will pay them back says the Lord." No! If your enemy is hungry, feed him! If he is thirsty give him something to drink! For if you do, you will heap burning coals upon his head! Do not be conquered by evil, but conquer evil with good.[2]

PRAYER:

Infinite and eternal Spirit, our God and our Father, author of all good, and never far from any of thy children; we draw near to thee that in fellowship with thee we may receive of thy Spirit. May all the bonds of love and ties of friendship be made stronger and sweeter through him who in his mortal agony was not unforgetful that we need one another's love, even Jesus Christ our Lord. AMEN.[3]

POEM:

On the mighty mountain's rugged slope
    The glorious pine trees stand,
Drawing their greenness and their grace
    From barren cliff and sand:

So may my life, like the mountain pine,
From bleak surroundings grow tall and fine!

Upon them the storms relentless beat,
    The winds through their branches roar,
But the scars in their broken wood are rich
    And with healing resin pour:

So may my soul, like the mountain pine,
From its own harsh wounds give balm benign!

When, under the blight of November frost,
    The gayer trees loom bare,
Still the pines their changeless verdure lift
    Through snowy and songless air:

122

HELPING EACH OTHER

So may my faith, like the mountain pine,
In death's dark winter unfading shine![4]

—EFFIE SMITH ELY

LEADER:

We will hear the story of two young people who in trying times were able to help each other.

STORY:

THE MAN FROM SHUSHAN

"BETTER rest a little." Hashub set down his own load and Ephah let the unwieldy bundle slide from her back. "That is too heavy for you. It is almost as big as mine. You shouldn't have taken so much."

"The wood was there. And we had come so far for it. Besides—I am strong."

"I know. But why wear yourself out?"

"I am not wearing myself out, and if I were—what is strength for?"

"Sometimes I wonder. A man is born—lives—works—dies. Why?"

"Such questions are silly."

That morning, soon after sunrise, they had left the ruined city to go down the valley, seeking fuel for two tiny fires: the one in the rude shelter where Ephah lived with her father, grandfather, and two sisters; the other in the stone hut where Hashub lived with his Uncle Shebar.

Once wood could be gathered among the ruins of what had been palaces—wrecked during and after the siege—but that was now exhausted.

"Grandfather can remember," mused Ephah, "when every stone was in place, every tower had its watchmen, and he thinks he will live to see it built again. You do not think so?"

"No, I do not think so."

"Why will the walls not be rebuilt?"

"We are a little people, between the upper and nether millstones of two great peoples. One day we will be ground to powder and a wind will make us as other forgotten peoples."

"God will let them?"

He pointed to the ruined wall. "He let them do that."

Grandfather says that we forgot God—God did not forget us. He says other nations may be stronger but we are truly great, because

123

with us in his covenant and in us shall all nations of the earth b
blest. One day, he says, these walls will surely rise again and we, b
our obedience, may hasten that day."

"I have tried, but I cannot see things as he sees them."

"Hashub, you are always so—so sensible. And it was not sensibl
for David to go out with a sling against a giant, for Jonathan and hi
armor-bearer to attack a host."

He helped her adjust her load, then took up his own. Both seemee
lighter as they faced the steep climb.

From childhood, Ephah had known that one day she and Hashul
would marry. It had been arranged, as was the custom of their tim
and people, by their parents. Only, as the day came nearer, she a
times had doubts and misgivings.

Gone utterly was the ordered life of her grandfather's day. The
present was a time of upheaval and uncertainty. Only the faith o
her grandfather flamed like a beacon: from it her own had bee
kindled—hers, but not Hashub's. Hard for him living with poor, de
spondent Uncle Shebar; and yet, what if they could not share thi
great hope?

Sometimes she tried to answer that question. Was it possible tha
her grandfather's faith was but an old man's dream? Her own faith—
was she simply trying to make herself believe what she wished to be
lieve? That she refused to admit. All of which she forgot completely
when she reached home and heard the great news.

It was common knowledge that, a few day before, a man had arrivec
from the court of the great king. But until today his errand had re
mained a mystery. Today he had summoned the elders of the people
had shown credentials appointing him governor, and had told them
that his commission provided for the repair of the city wall and the re
building of its gates. Where new material was needed he had req
uisitions upon the keepers of the royal forests. The task was great
but he was prepared to undertake it upon one condition. The wall was
for the people. Would they rise up and build it?

Ephah was so excited she could hardly eat; and, as soon as she had
helped clear away the meal, she slipped down the street to Hashub's.
"Have you heard the good news?" she panted.

"About the man from Shushan? Yes," he said.

"Isn't it wonderful? That it has come at last—the time we have
waited for so long?

"If we could be sure." His face clouded.

124

"You are not going out tomorrow with the others?"

"Not until I know more. It—it all depends."

For a moment she looked at him steadily, then turned and walked way. She was wondering what it would mean to be married to a man who, to her, seemed a coward and a weakling.

Hashub spent an unhappy night, for the look in Ephah's eyes had ut deep. And yet—he could not shape his course only to please her. He must decide what was the best and wisest course. He tried not to be unduly influenced by Uncle Shebar, who always saw the dark side. But to see all the future as glittering with rainbow promises, as Ephah seemed to see it—! Surely that was silly. Yet she was dear to him; he had disappointed her sorely. He rose early next morning with one thing settled: he would not base his decision upon Uncle Shebar's judgment. He himself would go down to the Gate of the Fountain and there learn what he could.

He stood upon the threshold of their hut and noticed several groups moving toward the wall, among them were Ephah and her two sisters. About Ephah's slender waist was wound a plumb line. When they were out of sight, he turned back into the house. "I am going out with the others," he announced.

"Food will be ready when you return at noon," Uncle Shebar said.

There followed days never-to-be-forgotten by those who lived through them. The whole city was one flame of enthusiasm, burning ever brighter as, stone by stone, the wall arose about them. Hashub worked no harder than did his fellows, but for him the building of the wall came to absorb every other interest. He knew, with utter certainty, that this was the most important thing he would ever do and that, in comparison with it, life itself was a little thing. How had he learned it? Certainly not by sitting down and thinking. No; every hammer blow, every straining upon a lever to lift a stone made him feel sure that he was doing the right thing and for him the only thing.

Came disquieting rumors of plots against them, some apparently well founded, for prompt and efficient counter measures were taken. Their leader—! Some among them questioned whether he ever slept, for at any moment and in the most unlooked for places, he was likely to appear, his trumpeter at his side and a smile of encouragement in his eyes and upon his lips.

When the whole encircling wall had been raised to half its proposed height a plan to attack them was uncovered and an order given to arm

125

the laborers. Hashub worked with a tool of peace in his hands and tool of war at his side.

Simply amazing, how all responded to the magnetic appeal of their leader. Ephah's grandfather, with his crowding memories of other days, was with them, not indeed as a wall-builder but as a morale builder.

Every day now brought tidings of gates repaired and ruined tower restored. There were nights when Hashub went home so tired he could not eat; but always, with the first streak of dawn, he was at work again. When the wall was finished there was hardly energy left for a celebration, yet there was great rejoicing when all looked upon their completed work and saw that it was good.

Hashub and Ephah, as was natural, stood side by side, though they had seen little of each other during the crowded days just past. Hashub looked at her: clothing soiled and torn, hands calloused by the stone she had lifted, skin reddened and toughened by wind, sun, and rain, and to him she had never seemed more beautiful.

"When we are old as grandfather we can come to this, our wall, and put our hands on it—on the very stones we laid."

"And but for you," he said, "I might never have had a part in it."

"Oh, no!" she cried. "Why—"

He shook his head. "Yes: and it will be so always. These days have taught me more than to be a stonemason. You are quicker of perception than I am and in years to come, when we are married, you will see things I do not see, and I will hang back, and you will spur me on and—"

"Hashub!"

"Oh, yes; it's true."

"What makes you think foolish things like that?"

"I don't think them—I know them."

"Oh, Hashub!"

Their eyes, and then their hands met. At the moment, neither could speak but, against the background of the new wall, both stood smiling and happy.[5]

POEM:

> Every soul that touches yours—
> Be it the slightest contact—
> Gets therefrom some good;
> Some little grace; one kindly thought;

HELPING EACH OTHER

One aspiration yet unfelt;
One bit of courage
For the darkening sky;
One gleam of faith
To brave the thickening ills of life;
One glimpse of brighter skies
Beyond the gathering mists—
To make this life worth while
And heaven a surer heritage.[6]

—George Eliot

Prayer:

Our Father, help us to realize the importance of human contacts, that all of us need the inspiration coming from our friends which furnishes the incentive to spur us on to greater endeavor. Help us to demand of ourselves the best thought and action of which we are capable. Forbid that we should ever be a stumbling block to any who are striving to reach greater heights. Grant us wisdom, strength, and courage to withstand temptations and to live by the highest and best we know. Help us to live in such manner that our example will draw others to thee. In Jesus' name we pray. Amen.

Hymn: "O Son of Man, Thou Madest Known," or
"O Love Divine and Golden."

Benediction:

Let the beauty of the Lord our God be upon us: and establish thou the work of our hands upon us; yea, the work of our hands establish thou it. Amen.

SERVICE 18

TESTING OUR LIVES BY THINE

PRELUDE: Hymn tune "Serenity."

CALL TO WORSHIP:

> We may not climb the heavenly steeps
> To bring the Lord Christ down;
> In vain we search the lowest deeps,
> For him no depths can drown.

> .   .   .   .   .   .

> O Lord and Master of us all:
> Whate'er our name or sign,
> We own thy sway, we hear thy call,
> We test our lives by thine!

—JOHN G. WHITTIER

HYMN: "Beneath the Cross of Jesus," or
"When I Survey the Wondrous Cross."

SCRIPTURE:

And Pilate, when he had called together the chief priests and the rulers and the people, said unto them, Ye have brought this man unto me, as one that perverteth the people: and, behold, I, having examined him before you, have found no fault in this man touching those things whereof ye accuse him: no, nor yet Herod: for I sent you to him; and lo, nothing worthy of death is done unto him. I will therefore chastise him, and release him. (For of necessity he must release one unto them at the feast.) And they cried out all at once, saying, Away with this man, and release unto us Barabbas: (who for a certain sedition made in the city, and for murder, was cast into prison.) Pilate therefore, willing to release Jesus, spake again to them. But they cried, saying, Crucify him, crucify him. . . . And Pilate gave sentence that it should be as they

TESTING OUR LIVES BY THINE

required. And he released unto them him that for sedition and murder was cast into prison, whom they had desired; but he delivered Jesus to their will. . . .

And one of the malefactors which were hanged railed on him, saying, If thou be Christ, save thyself and us. But the other answering rebuked him, saying, Dost not thou fear God, seeing thou art in the same condemnation? And we indeed justly; for we receive the due reward of our deeds: but this man hath done nothing amiss. And he said unto Jesus, Lord, remember me when thou comest into thy kingdom. And Jesus said unto him, Verily I say unto thee, To-day shalt thou be with me in paradise. . . .

And when Jesus had cried with a loud voice, he said, Father, into thy hands I commend my spirit: and having said thus, he gave up the ghost. Now when the centurion saw what was done, he glorified God, staying, Certainly this was a righteous man.[1]

POEM:

> Where'er the face of Christ appears,
>   Men's hearts are drawn to Him.
> No other face so lights the years
>   When centuries are dim.
>
> The hungering ones fulfill their needs
>   In Him. The blind, the broken
> Find light and life, and mold their deeds
>   By what His lips have spoken.
>
> O soul, whoever you may be—
>   One deep look in those eyes
> Will thrill you for eternity,
>   And you will turn and rise;
>
> And none of life will be the same,
>   Nor earth the common place,
> For every leaf will burn with flame
>   When you have seen His face! [2]
>
> —ESTHER BALDWIN YORK

LEADER:

We will hear the story of Sergius Paulus, the Roman centurion, who witnessed the crucifixion of Jesus.

STORY:

I SAW A MAN DIE TODAY!

SERGIUS PAULUS was not a man to be upset easily, certainly not by the sight of blood. For twenty years he had carried a Roman sword and fought the battles of the empire. It had been his utter and complete brutality that had won for him his appointment as a centurion. And for several years now Sergius Paulus had been a most satisfactory executioner.

It is not the business of executioners to be curious. But this one today had been no ordinary crucifixion. The average man condemned to death was an outlaw, a bandit, or a plain cutthroat. But this one had been no everyday criminal. The hardened and coarsened centurion had recognized that fact the moment he laid eyes on his prisoner.

That Friday itself, with its terrifying three hours of blackness, had been awful enough. But in the midst of the darkness there had come a shaking of the earth that sent the soldiers reeling and tumbling. Even the stoutest of them were left unnerved. Their long years of discipline, however, were more than equal to the terror and they soon had the situation well in hand again. The man on the cross had died shortly before sundown.

It was over now, and as the powerful Roman centurion strode down the street and turned in through the narrow gate, he walked with all the dignity of an officer of the empire. Once inside his hired house, he relaxed a trifle. Rather noisily, as if to relieve his nerves a bit, he threw off his coat of mail and hung his short sword, clanking in its sheath, on a peg high up on the wall. A servant timidly fetched a basin of warm water and hastily retreated into the shadows of the outer court.

As the soldier plunged his arms into the water a gentle footfall was heard at the other side of the room, and the voice of a woman spoke. "What ails my lord?" she asked. "Hath the governor spoken ill of thee?" she added, a touch of banter in her voice.

On other occasions Sergius Paulus would have greeted her with gay affection, for he truly loved this renegade Jewess. Tonight, however, he was in no mood for jest. Even the beautiful Miriam could not take away his gloom.

"What meaneth this strange mood, Sergius?" she asked softly. "Thy countenance bespeaks something evil."

With that the great fellow turned about and, looking intently into the face of the girl, said, "Miriam, I saw a man die today." In his voice there was stark terror.

"But that is thy business, Sergius!" the girl exclaimed. "Hast thou not crucified men by the score?"

"But this one was different. I never saw a man die like he did." And Sergius's voice trailed off like the last low rumbling of a distant storm. There was something in it that forbade Miriam to speak further.

Sergius was silent for some minutes and then said: "Thou hast spoken truly, Miriam. Killing is my business. And I have watched full many a foul fellow die upon Roman crosses. But this was no ordinary man. May the gods protect me! I, who never quailed before, tremble to think of it!"

"Tell me about it, my lord. Trust me with thy heart."

"He was from Galilee. The people called him a prophet, and told strange tales about him." It was evident that Sergius was having some difficulty in making it plain even to himself.

"Six days ago he came down to the feast, raised a tumult in the Temple, drove the sheep and oxen out, overturned the tables of the money changers, and incited a riot. The priests say he preached some strange doctrine. But of that I know nothing, for no Roman can understand these things.

"I know not by what means they took him," the centurion went on, "but when I arrived at Pilate's judgment hall this morning his trial was on. It must have been about sunrise. Marcus, the high priest's servant, told me that his master had spent the whole night hearing evidence and plotting his death. When morning came they appealed to Pilate to confirm their sentence.

"He seemed a gentle fellow, and three times the governor examined him and could find no fault in him. But because of their tumult, and because there was a danger that the city might be incited to riot, Pilate gave them their will and delivered him over to me, along with two thieves, to be crucified.

"Miriam, I never saw a man die like he did. From the moment when first we stretched him out upon his cross and drove the nails through his hands, until the moment when he cried with a loud voice and died, not one curse or moan came from him. The thieves who hung, one on his right hand and the other on his left, split the very sky with their ravings and maledictions. But this man uttered not a cry.

"One never knows what to expect from these Jews. Today they were mad, shrieking and jeering like devils. I never saw such hatred.

131

Some of them spat upon him. They all railed at him. And then suddenly, as if one of the gods had wiped out the sun, that terrible blackness came over the earth, and the ground rolled under our feet like the waves of the sea. I can feel the sickness in my inward parts yet. The Jews told me afterward that the veil in their Temple was rent from top to bottom. But that man upon the cross spake scarcely a word that could be heard above the loud tumult.

"Only once he cried—then to say, 'I thirst.' But when they lifted up the sponge filled with vinegar and gall to deaden the pain, he shook his head and refused to drink.

"I tell you, woman, there was something majestic about him. I have heard the curses of the dying for twenty years, but I never saw a man meet death with such divine calm.

"The crowd made good sport of it. The priests taunted him. 'He trusted in God,' they cried. 'Let him deliver him now!' But he paid them no heed, save to say, 'Father, forgive them; for they know not what they do.' And I never expect to see such a light on another face again. Only once did he seem to weaken. That was when he cried out, 'My God, My God, why hast thou forsaken me?' But it was not long afterward that he was quiet, and before he died I heard him say, 'Into thy hands I commend my spirit.'"

Sergius dropped his head in his hands and his giant frame shook with emotion. "I cannot believe he is dead. Such a man cannot die."

"Who was he, Sergius?"

"All I know," he replied, "is what I read on the inscription which Pilate caused to be nailed to the cross above his head. The writing was: JESUS OF NAZARETH, KING OF THE JEWS.

At that Miriam shuddered. She could not trust herself to tell Sergius the strange tales she had overheard about the young prophet of Galilee who had shown himself a friend of sinners. Nor could she tell him about her friend who, not long ago, had been dragged through the streets and thrown at the Galilean's feet, and to whom he had spoken kindly, saying, "Go in peace. . . ."

Sergius watched her intently for a moment, and then dropped off into silence. But his breathing was labored, and now and then he whispered words—strange, disconnected words—as if bringing them up out of the deeps of his soul.

"Behold thy mother . . . thy son . . . Forgive them . . . they know not. . . . This day . . . with me . . . paradise. . . . My God, my God . . . forsaken. . . . Into thy hands . . . my spirit. . . . It is finished!"

At last he leaned toward the girl and spoke, and each whispered word was weighted with reverential awe: "Miriam, no man ever died like that before. No man ever prayed for the forgiveness of his enemies. He believed in God. You should have seen him die!"

Gathering himself and standing at his full height, with arms outstretched as if he were spanning his own cross, the centurion said—and there was the conviction of the ages in his words: "Surely ... surely ... *This man must have been the Son of God!*" [3]

POEM:

> I dreamed last night that the Christ was bound
>   To a whipping post. His head,
> Thorn-crowned, pressed hard against the wood,
>   While a whip with tongues of lead
> Lashed at His back, and struck and struck!
>   With every awful arc
> Of a soldier's arm, the quivering flesh
>   Received a bleeding mark.
> The patient face of the Lord was turned
>   Away, yet I could see
> In my heart the look of sorrow there,
>   Not for Himself, but me.
> Once more the soldier's whip was raised.
>   I sprang with a sudden cry
> To stay his hand! The soldier wheeled—
>   And the one who scourged—was I! [4]

—ESTHER BALDWIN YORK

PRAYER:

O God, whose beloved Son gave up his life on the cross that we might have life and have it abundantly; we who have known but refused his salvation appeal to thy mercy and seek thy help. Pardon and deliver us, we beseech thee, from tempers and ambitions that make for destruction and death, from all greed of gain, all lust for power, all pride of race or class, all contempt of others, all willingness to reap an advantage at the expense of the poor and the unprotected. Shame and arrest us by the pain of those who have been wounded for our transgressions and bruised for our iniquities. And direct our hearts to the steadfastness of Christ, who consented to suffer at the hands of others but never to inflict suffering upon any man or woman or little child. Give us grace to follow the example of his great devotion, and bring us to his trust and confidence in thee, that so we may be no longer the agents of death but of life and joy and peace. . . . Make us to desire with all our heart that thy holy will shall be done on earth as it is in heaven. Give us grace each day to ask what thou wouldst have us to do; and grant that we may follow thy leading, wherever it may take us, knowing that thou only art wise, thou only art good, thou only art able to lead us in the way everlasting; . . . through Jesus Christ our Lord. Amen.[5]

HYMN: "Rise Up, O Men of God," or
        "O Young and Fearless Prophet."

BENEDICTION:

So teach us to number our days, that we may apply our hearts unto wisdom. Amen.

SERVICE 19

SEEKING COURAGE AND CALMNESS

PRELUDE: Hymn tune "Consolation."

CALL TO WORSHIP:
The hour cometh, and now is, when the true worshippers shall worship
  the Father in spirit and in truth.
For the Father seeketh such to worship him.
God is a Spirit.
And they that worship him must worship him in spirit and in truth.[1]

HYMN: "Be Still, My Soul," or
     "When Morning Gilds the Skies."

POEM:
> Father, in Thy mysterious presence kneeling,
>   Fain would our souls feel all Thy kindling love;
> For we are weak, and need some deep revealing
>   Of trust and strength and calmness from above.
>
> Lord, we have wandered forth through doubt and sorrow,
>   And Thou hast made each step an onward one;
> And we will ever trust each unknown morrow—
>   Thou wilt sustain us till its work is done.
>
> . . . .
>
> Now, Father, now, in Thy dear presence kneeling,
>   Our spirits yearn to feel Thy kindling love;
> Now make us strong, we need Thy deep revealing,
>   Of trust and strength and calmness from above.[2]

—SAMUEL JOHNSON

INVOCATION:

O God, in whom there is perfect harmony, cast out the discords in our lives. Forgive our faults and weaknesses, and create within us clean hearts. Reveal thy will concerning us and help us to become the persons that thou wouldst have us be. Make us calm and quiet that we may hear thy still small voice speaking peace to our troubled minds. In Christ's name. AMEN.

SCRIPTURE:

Truly my soul waiteth upon God: from him cometh my salvation. He only is my rock and my salvation; he is my defense; I shall not be greatly moved. . . . My soul, wait thou only upon God; for my expectation is from him. He only is my rock and my salvation: he is my defense; I shall not be moved. In God is my salvation and my glory: the rock of my strength, and my refuge, is in God. Trust in him at all times; ye people, pour out your heart before him: God is a refuge for us. . . .

Trust in the Lord, and do good; so shalt thou dwell in the land, and verily thou shalt be fed. Delight thyself also in the Lord; and he shall give thee the desires of thine heart. Commit thy way unto the Lord; trust also in him; and he shall bring it to pass. . . . The steps of a good man are ordered by the Lord: and he delighteth in his way. Though he fall, he shall not be utterly cast down: for the Lord upholdeth him with his hand. . . . Wait on the Lord, and keep his way, and he shall exalt thee to inherit the land: when the wicked are cut off, thou shalt see it. I have seen the wicked in great power, and spreading himself like a green bay tree. Yet he passed away, and, lo, he was not: yea, I sought him, but he could not be found. Mark the perfect man, and behold the upright: for the end of that man is peace.[3]

HYMN: "Dear Lord and Father of Mankind," or
" 'Mid All the Traffic of the Ways."

LEADER:

We will hear a story of a man who in the face of persecution had courage and calmness.

STORY:

THE AWAKENING

THE Mermaid Tavern in Friday Street, London, was almost empty that cloudy morning in May, 1593. The poets and actors who whiled

136

away their free hours in the Mermaid had not yet risen. Only one guest sat at the long oaken table: John Donne.

He was writing his most romantic poem. He wanted to have it ready to read to his friendly critic, William Shakespeare, when he came later in the day.

John was studying law in Lincoln's Inn. In a few months when he became of age, he would inherit a fortune. Each day for several hours he wrote poetry. Scribbling eased the restlessness that beset him.

The door opened suddenly, and his brother, Henry, entered. He was wearing a gray doublet, white ruff, brown slashed breeches, and ash-colored hose. He strode forward, pulled out a chair, sat his frail body in it.

"John," he said, a frown puckering his pale, straight brow, "I need your help!"

John leaned forward. "What's the matter?" he demanded.

Henry looked around the large public room. He lifted his clear gray eyes to the gallery above, to the doors opening off it. The fat innkeeper was waddling about near the open fire, his broad back toward them.

"I have been hiding a Seminarist in my chambers," Henry divulged, "and I am under suspicion. A man trailed me here. If they discover him they will arrest him. You know what Clink Prison is like!"

John sighed. "What an age!" he said reflectively. "Everywhere a controversy is raging as to which is the true church! Protestants fight Catholics. Catholics fight Protestants. Everywhere reformers fight Anglicans. Even our good Queen Elizabeth persecutes men who seek God in their own way. I'm weary!"

Henry shoved forward to the edge of his chair. "John," he pleaded, "this is no time for contemplation. We cannot let them capture Brother William! All he is doing is pleading for tolerance!"

"That may be what you think," John said. "If Rome sent him, they also gave him a job to do. Rome, too, directs what a man must do and think!"

"This man is innocent of treason," Henry protested. "He is not an Anglican. That is his crime! You know I think the Humanists on the Continent, who have been shouting for a hundred years that Truth must be hauled out, that men think for themselves, and follow conscience, know what they're talking about."

"There must be something to this Protestant faith," John said thoughtfully.

"Take the Anabaptists," Henry continued. "Look at what Elizabeth does to them!"

"It is the same sin she strikes at in our priests. But she is not seeing clearly. Her reign is declining. England's best hope is a united country. Toleration is the only way. Not Acts of Uniformity!"

"Sh-h-h!" Henry placed a finger to his lips. "You will be judged an enemy of England!"

"That's just it!" John exploded. "No sovereign can legislate a man's conscience. No more can Rome!"

"But what are we to do about the priest?"

Before Henry could answer, the door behind him opened slowly. "Smile! Laugh!" John ordered tersely. "Do not look now! The man who just entered. . . . He is a queer-looking individual—red wig, narrow black eyes, hooked nose, black slashed breeches, yellow doublet."

"That's the man!" Henry said, tapping the table with his fingers. "I'm sure he followed me here!"

John raised his voice, rattling on about the latest affair of his heart, the foggy May weather. He was thinking as he talked, wondering desperately how he could help. Henry was in danger, too, if the priest should be captured.

John stood up. Henry looked at him with arched brows. "Come," he said casually.

They strolled leisurely across the room and out into the cool air. "What are you up to? Henry demanded as soon as the door had closed behind them.

"If your suspicions are correct, that man will follow us. If not, we have nothing to worry about. They don't know about your priest."

They made their way through the noisy, bustling streets. At the public fountain Henry tossed the usual coin to a ragged beggar squatting with outstretched palm. They rounded a corner, turned into the narrow alley where Will and his family lived. They paused. John looked back. He sighed. There was no one there.

"See!" he said. "You are overwrought, Henry. The man has not come after us!"

Henry gave a sheepish laugh. "I guess I have been studying too hard," he said. "A person's imagination can play foolish tricks."

"Let's go back to the Mermaid," John suggested. "We were seeing ghosts!"

"John!" Henry cried. "We were *not* seeing ghosts! Look!"

John looked. The red wig was sailing around the corner. John took his brother's arm. "To Will's," he said. "Will will think of something!"

A few minutes later they turned in at a gabled house in a row of gabled dwellings. Ann, Will's wife, greeted them, with her youngest hugging her full brown skirts. Will was in his study on the second floor, she told them. No, it was all right to interrupt him.

"Lock the door, Anne!" John said with urgency when they were inside. "I'll explain later." Leaving her gaping, he took Henry's hand and dragged him upstairs.

Will looked up as they entered. He had the face of one waking from a dream to reality. Indeed he lived in a world of dreams, of figures and characters who traipsed about in history and in their own age, of bad black-eyed maidens who did not exist but could be many maidens, murderous kings, helpless victims, witches, malicious vixens full of pranks.

Although Will was almost ten years John's senior, he was his most congenial friend. They often met at the Mermaid, where they read each other's works, and commented on them.

"Will!" John said quickly. "On the spur of the moment we came to you. You have an imagination. Henry has a priest in his chambers in Thavies Inn. He was trailed to the Mermaid. We were trailed when we left. The man must be outside now."

Will stroked his carefully trimmed beard. He stood up and came around the heavy oak desk. He sat on the edge of it, swinging his long legs. He motioned to some chairs. The Donnes sat down, facing him.

"Tell me, John," he said in his strong voice, "how deeply is Henry implicated?"

"I can answer that," Henry said, "I hate to see a man hounded, without a place to lay his head. I found him on the river bank. I shared my bed. That is all!"

"It will be difficult to make the Queen believe that! She has spies everywhere."

"But you have influence?" John pressed. "Your employer, Lord Strange, has influence?"

Will shook his handsome head slowly. "When it comes to Rome, nobody can influence her! Henry, you did a very dangerous thing. Why?"

Henry threw back his slim shoulders. "It was the only thing, Will,"

139

he said in a low voice. "The poor man had been cast out of every tavern in London!"

John looked at his young brother, at his good gray eyes, the sympathy written on his strong face. A lump welled up in his throat. Henry was one of the most unselfish people he knew. John had often envied him his calm, the peace he seemed to have; the way he lost himself in his interest for others. In his eyes now was the reflection of a light, as if Henry saw beyond the trouble he was in, to something of lasting value, the reflection of the illusive something he, himself, sought and could not find.

Will Shakespeare began pacing back and forth in his dark slashed breeches and white satin doublet. The ruff at his neck looked very white against the tan of his skin.

"Do you think they have searched your rooms?" he demanded suddenly.

"It will take several hours to get an order signed. I don't think they will do that until late afternoon. They are probably watching the rooms . . . and me," Henry said with a wry smile.

"I have an idea," Will said.

"A good one?" John asked.

"This afternoon Henry will have a party!"

"A party?" Henry echoed.

"He will entertain a band of minstrels in his rooms. I can get the costumes at the theater!"

"And?" John said.

"When they leave, the priest will escape with them."

At precisely four o'clock by the tower clock, a string of minstrels, in bright garments of red and green with hoods of tawny cloth, pranced into Thavies Inn. They moved in pairs, singing and tumbling through the public room. They danced up the stairs. Forty minutes later they were ready to start down again.

Will told them to wait while he peered from behind the heavy draperies onto the street below. John, looking over his shoulder, could not see the man in the red wig. People were hurrying along. Apprentices were calling their wares. The scene looked normal, safe.

After the band had gone, Henry held out his hand to Will. "I think you have kept two men out of the goal," he said.

John was still watching the street. A group of red-coated guards were circling the minstrels. He saw two of them take the disguised priest by the arms and lead him away.

Feet thundered on the stairs. There was a loud knocking at the door. Henry looked at Will. The door was thrown open. Three of her Majesty's guards stood there.

Henry stepped forward. "I'll come," he said. "I'm the one you want."

They started off, Henry was ahead of them. Will turned despairingly to John. "We tried," he said.

John did not answer for a moment. He was watching his brother being led away, across the busy street. The sound of the apprentices calling their wares drowned out the marching feet.

"What do you lack?" they shouted. "What do you lack?"

Will moved up beside John. "I know what I lack," John said slowly. "I lack courage and direction. Henry never has."

"I daresay he still has his calm," Will said with a sigh. "I wonder where he gets it?"

John Donne did not hear. He was staring unseeing at the people milling below. William Shakespeare saw his face kindle, heard his whispered words: "I must seek the Christ who gives a man courage like that. I need courage and calmness. I need Him." [4]

Poem:

> Beyond the war-clouds and the reddened ways,
> I see the Promise of the Coming Days!
> I see His Sun arise, new charged with grace
> Earth's tears to dry and all her woes efface!
> Christ lives! Christ loves! Christ rules!
> No more shall Might,
> Though leagued with all the Forces of the Night
> Ride over Right. No more shall Wrong
> The world's gross agonies prolong.
> Who waits His Time shall surely see
> The triumph of His Constancy;—
> When without let, or bar, or stay,
> The coming of His Perfect Day
> Shall sweep the Powers of Night away;—
> And Faith, replumed for nobler flight,
> And Hope, aglow with radiance bright,
> And Love, in loveliness bedight,
> *Shall greet the morning light!* [5]

—JOHN OXENHAM

PRAYER:

O Lord, who knowest our temptations, strengthen us wherein we are weak. If we have considered it an easy task to follow thee, if we have tried to serve other masters, if we have not taken thy promises seriously, forgive us. As we think of the great reformers, thy leaders who risked their lives to advance thy kingdom, we realize that we have not sacrificed as we should, we have not resisted evil, or stood firmly for the right. Strengthen us as we strive to walk in fellowship with thee, to live continually in thy presence, and to give our lives entirely in thy service. Give us sufficient courage to discipline ourselves: to turn from the wrong, to choose the right, and to live according to the highest and best that we know. Cleanse us from all unworthy desires, renew a right spirit before thee, and may we, like the disciples, rise up and follow thee. In Jesus' name we pray. AMEN.

HYMN: "Be Strong!" or
        "March On, O Soul with Strength."

BENEDICTION:

Watch ye, stand fast in the faith, quit you like men, be strong. The grace of our Lord Jesus Christ be with you. AMEN.

SERVICE 20

LIVING ON HIGHER LEVELS

PRELUDE: Hymn tune *"Laudes Domini."*

CALL TO WORSHIP:

> There is a tide in the affairs of men,
> Which, taken at the flood, leads on to fortune;
> Omitted, all the voyage of their life
> Is bound in shallows and in miseries:
> We must take the current when it serves,
> Or lose our ventures.[1]
>
> —WILLIAM SHAKESPEARE

AFFIRMATION OF FAITH:

I trust in the living God, Father Almighty, maker of heaven and earth and of all things and creatures visible and invisible. I trust in the kindness of his law and the goodness of his work. And I will strive to love him and keep his law and do his work while I live.

I trust in the nobleness of human nature, in the majesty of its faculties, the fullness of its mercy, and the joy of its love. And I will strive to love my neighbor as myself, and even when I cannot, will act as if I did. . . .

I will not kill nor hurt any living creatures needlessly, nor destroy any beautiful things, but will strive to save and comfort all gentle life, and guard and perfect all natural beauty upon the earth.

I will strive to raise my own body and soul daily into all the higher powers of duty and happiness, not in rivalship or contention with others, but for the help, delight, and honor of others, and for the joy and peace of my own life.[2]

HYMN: "Breathe on Me, Breath of God," or
       "Draw Thou My Soul."

SCRIPTURE:

Brethren, I count not myself to have apprehended: but this one thing I do, forgetting those things which are behind, and reaching forth unto those things which are before, I press toward the mark for the prize of the high calling of God in Christ Jesus. Let us therefore, as many as be perfect, be thus minded: and if in any thing ye be otherwise minded, God shall reveal even this unto you.[3]

PRAYER:

O God, to whom belong adoration and praise; prepare us through the active presence of thy Spirit, to come before thee worthily and to ask thee rightly; enlighten our understanding; purify our every desire; quicken our wills unto instant obedience to thy word; strengthen every right purpose; direct this hour of worship to the magnifying of thy name, and to the enduring good of us thy children and servants; through Jesus Christ our Lord. AMEN.[4]

STORY:

LAND OF THE ENEMY

THE clear Alaskan evening was crisp as Jim Brentwood and Ann Nelson came out of church. He was grateful that she had not refused when he asked to walk home with her. But he said his thanks silently for he did not want to be misunderstood. Since coming to Pine Cove, he had found that people expected the worst from him because he was the son of the late George Brentwood.

"Well, Jim, how do you like being home?" asked Ann.

"Doesn't seem like home," he said. "The fact is I feel like I've come into the land of the enemy."

"Then why do you stay?"

"Perhaps I won't. I had no idea my father was hated so much."

Ann maintained discreet silence and for a time they walked without speaking. Moonlight touched the water of Pine Cove with shimmering silver. White fishing boats bobbed peacefully at anchor, and at the right stood the Three Hawk Fish Cannery Jim's father had built and owned. Like the rest of his vast holdings, it had been grossly mismanaged during his long illness and after his death. Like everything else it had been sold by the estate and brought almost nothing.

"I suppose you heard," Jim said, "that the cannery has offered to sell me an eighth interest."

144

"I don't want to be cruel, Jim, but you should know the truth before you decide. They wouldn't have asked you if they weren't desperate for money. They can't get any more credit. They've had to swallow their pride to make you the offer, and they hate it."

"They didn't take pains to hide that," he said bitterly. "You'd think the name Brentwood was poison."

"They dread the idea of another Brentwood getting a foothold. Your father was like a small king. He bled them white. He brought in the Indians, uprooted them from the land where they belonged, and paid them the same wages he paid the whites."

"I know all that. I also know what my father was trying to do. He wrote me about his plans for this country, plans he never had a chance to complete."

"I suppose you will continue his work?" she asked.

"It always seemed logical that I should come back when I had finished my schooling. Now I'm here and the people don't want me, but they want my money. What should I do?"

"Loan them the money and leave town."

"It would be like throwing away money. The company is due to fail in a year or so."

After leaving Ann, Jim wandered about town and finally headed for the Indian section. His father had built the houses and sold them below cost to his Indian employees.

Dr. Charlie Whitehorse, a young Indian who had been educated on Brentwood money, offered a warm hand and invited him in. "I was beginning to wonder if you'd forgotten your promise to drop around," he said.

Jim sat down heavily and Charlie's expression changed suddenly. "What's bothering you, Jim?"

"Pine Cove isn't the place I thought it was," he said lamely. "I've been thinking of moving on."

"Why?"

"Oh, I don't know. I'm young. Might as well find some place with a future."

"That doesn't sound like a Brentwood," Charlie said.

"Why should I force my way in here where I'm not wanted?"

"You afraid, Jim?"

"Of course not. I'm trying to be practical."

"Then," said Charlie, "you won't mind my asking a question. What is it you want out of life, Jim—money?"

145

"Money helps, doesn't it?" he said.

"That doesn't answer my question," Charlie said firmly. "What is it you want?"

"I suppose I want what all men want—success, a home and family, happiness. All that takes money."

Charlie went to his desk, opened a drawer and drew out a bundle of letters. "From your father—I saved every one of them. He was like a father to me—one of the greatest men I ever knew."

Jim swallowed a lump in his throat. "I thought that, too, until I came back. Now they tell me he was a grasping money-maker."

"People have short memories. They choose to remember that he saddled the cannery with a mortgage which he intended to be temporary, but he died before he could lift it. All the economic ills we've suffered have been blamed on your father."

"Then why should I stay? What will it get me?"

"If you're thinking of money, very little, I should say." Charlie opened a package of letters. "Your father's philosophy, his plans are in these letters. I want to read what he says about money:

" 'I was thirty before I found out the truth about money. My wife died after the birth of our son, Jimmy. I remember those first nights alone. How foolish and vain my desire for money seemed then! Surely God intended life to be bigger than that. I looked into my son's eyes and saw the helpless trust, and then I knew what I wanted more than anything else. I wanted his life to be filled with beauty and significance, and I determined to make this wilderness in Alaska a better world for him.

" 'You know the rest of the story; how I set up the bank, the lumber mill, the cannery, and all the rest. I set them up, not to make money, but because they were needed. Every penny I made went back into the land. Right now the cannery at Little Horse cannot survive without help. The whole area would suffer if it fails. I shall find money for it if I have to mortgage our cannery here. Then, perhaps, I can turn to such things as hospitals, schools, and libraries.

" 'It is my hope, Charlie, that you will fill your life with a purpose that is above selfish interests.' "

Charlie looked up. "There's nothing I can add to what he said, Jim. Don't leave town until you have decided what you want out of life."

Jim nodded. His father had built for a better world, and left a harvest of hate.

The next day when he inquired of Ann whether she wanted him

to leave, she replied, "I was merely passing on what I knew to be public opinion. All you've said to the people here seems to indicate that you expect this place to be your personal gold mine. There were some, like myself, who hoped you'd be like Dr. Charlie Whitehorse. He's afraid the cannery will fail and the Indians would scatter and all of your father's work would be wasted. He has organized the Indians and each one contributes one day in work or in wages each month and the hospital is half finished. He's asked for no help from the whites, but he is making it clear that their help would be appreciated."

Jim recalled that his father had once said about the Indians: "The greatest thing we can do for them is to give them an opportunity to help themselves."

"Let's go, Ann. There's something I have to tell Charlie."

Taking Charlie's hand, Jim said, "I've decided to stay. I don't know how we're going to do it, but things will work out. My money is going for the cannery and your hospital. It's a start and the money will come somehow."

Charles smiled. "The only money your father ever took out of this place was for your education and mine. He always thought of that as an investment in the future of Pine Cove. It was part of his plan that you and I should come back and continue his work."

"He must have been a wonderful person," Ann said. "Maybe you'd let me help with his plan."

Jim smiled, "You will, Ann."

She was already far more a part of those plans than she realized." [5]

POEM:

There are three lessons I would write—
    Three words as with a burning pen,
In tracings of eternal light,
    Upon the hearts of men.

Have Hope. Though clouds environ now,
    And gladness hides her face in scorn,
Put thou the shadow from thy brow—
    No night but hath its morn.

Have Faith. Where'er thy bark is driven—
    The calm's disport, the tempest's mirth—
Know this: God rules the host of heaven,
    The inhabitants of earth.

Have Love. Not love alone for one,
　　But man as man thy brother call;
And scatter like the circling sun
　　Thy charities on all.

Thus grave these lessons on thy soul—
　　Faith, Hope, and Love—and thou shalt find
Strength when life's surges rudest roll,
　　Light when thou else wert blind.[6]
　　　　　　　—JOHANN CHRISTOPHER FRIEDRICH VON SCHILLER

PRAYER:

O God, the source of all wisdom, who knowest our needs before
we ask, grant us knowledge and understanding to face our problems
in the spirit of Christ. Grant us patience to wait in thy presence until
thy will concerning us is made known. May we not set our affections
on material gain, but may service to others be the motive of our lives.
Make us channels through which thy truth is revealed to the world
and messengers of love and good will to all we meet. Help us to uproot
the sins of greed and selfishness and to be more interested in helping
others. In Jesus' name we pray. AMEN.

HYMN: "Lord, Speak to Me, That I May Speak," or
　　　"A Charge to Keep I Have."

BENEDICTION:

May thy Spirit lead us into wider fields of service. AMEN.

SERVICE 21

SHARING IN HIS NAME

PRELUDE: "Allegretto" by Beethoven.

CALL TO WORSHIP:
> He gives nothing but worthless gold
>   Who gives from a sense of duty;
> But he who gives a slender mite,
> And gives to that which is out of sight,
>   That thread of the all-sustaining Beauty
> Which runs through all and doth all unite,—
> The hand cannot clasp the whole of his alms,
> The heart outstretches its eager palms,
> For a god goes with it and makes it store
> To the soul that was starving in darkness before.[1]
>
> —JAMES RUSSELL LOWELL

HYMN: "We Thank Thee, Lord, Thy Path of Service Lead," or "O Master, Let Me Walk with Thee."

INVOCATION:
> O Lord of life, lead our lives
>   In thy way of Wisdom and Truth,
>   In thy way of Goodness and Love,
>   In thy way of Beauty and Peace,
>   In thy way of Humility and Power,
>   In thy way of Service and Joy
>   Unto Life Everlasting. AMEN.[2]
>
> —CHAUNCEY R. PIETY

149

SCRIPTURE:

Will a man rob God? Yet ye have robbed me. But ye say, Wherein have we robbed thee? In tithes and offerings. . . . Bring ye all the tithes into the storehouse, that there may be meat in mine house, and prove me now herewith, saith the Lord of hosts, if I will not open you the windows of heaven, and pour you out a blessing, that there shall not be room enough to receive it. . . .

Upon the first day of the week let every one of you lay by him in store, as God hath prospered him, that there be no gatherings when I come.[3]

OFFERTORY SENTENCE:

Give of thy bread to the hungry, and of thy garments to them that are naked; and according to thine abundance give alms; and let not thine eye be envious, when thou givest alms.

OFFERING.

POEM:

> And the voice that was softer than silence said,
> "Lo it is I, be not afraid!
> In many climes, without avail,
> Thou hast spent thy life for the Holy Grail;
> Behold, it is here,—this cup which thou
> Didst fill at the streamlet for Me but now;
> This crust is My body broken for thee,
> This water His blood that died on the tree;
> The Holy Supper is kept, indeed,
> In whatso we share with another's need;
> Not what we give, but what we share,
> For the gift without the giver is bare;
> Who gives himself with his alms feeds three,
> Himself, his hungering neighbor, and Me." [4]
> —JAMES RUSSELL LOWELL

STORY:

THE CUP

IN THE light issuing from a low window, Jeremiah the Potter held a finished cup in his hands, turning it before his eyes. He scrutinized it carefully, frowning with displeasure.

150

"A very poor article," he thought. "There must have been an inferior clay mixed into the last pot." He shook his head. The cup was indeed an awkward-looking specimen. The flanges at the lip were too thick, and the body was squatty, not the usual graceful work of art he turned out.

"It is no good," he mused, "in fact, it is very poor."

The potter placed the cup on a shelf beside the other cups and flasks already there. It stood out like the ugly lump of earth that it was. The clays had not mixed properly; it was streaked, and there was no shape to the body. Just a poor cup, results of working when the mind was turned to other channels. He decided not to waste time and material glazing it.

Jeremiah stood in the doorway of his home and shop combined, which faced the main thoroughfare leading from Jerusalem to Bethany. There were many people on the road today, although it was early in the morning.

He sighed and slapped gray, drifted road dust from his smock. Today was a great day for some. It was an infinitely sad day for others.

A young man, close to his early twenties, came around the corner of the house and paused before him, bare brown feet washed in the warm dust. "Father, do you know what Marcus, the leatherman, is telling?"

"Eh? No, Joel. What is Marcus saying that causes you such excitement?" He answered absently, his thoughts far afield. The young man came into the room.

"Marcus said Pilate released Barabbas, the robber, and gave the Teacher to the people to do with as they please! That was last evening . . . today he is being crucified on the hill Golgotha, along with two thieves!"

"Aye, my son," Jeremiah turned and walked to the door of his shop. "See all those travelers on the road." He pointed to the crowd that scurried past, hurrying toward the city gates. "They are going to see the Crucifixion. People are drawn to acts which they do not understand . . . acts of pain and violence."

The potter drew close to the young man and looked steadily into the clear, young eyes. "Joel, my son, I knew Jesus. . . . He is good and wise and kind. The people who will put him to death are mistaken. He will never die. Instead, he will live in the hearts and minds of us who love and believe him, as a plant grows in good soil."

Joel walked restlessly to the doorway and watched the crowd. Finally he turned. "Father, I am going out into the city. May I have a cup to catch a drink at the fountain by the gate?"

The potter looked around from the work he had taken again into his hands. "Aye . . . take the cup on the end of the shelf by the door. It is no good. The clay is poor. Leave it at the fountain so others may have a drink when the hour is hot."

Joel took the cup in his hands and tucked a small water bag in the sash at his waist. In a moment he was gone, his stalwart form swallowed by the crowd that moved through the city gates toward the hill Golgotha.

The cross loomed high and crude against the lowering sky.

For hours the man had hung there in agony, yet no cries for mercy had passed his gray lips. A group of bearded, gray-robed men stood a little distance away from him with some weeping women. Roman soldiers, resplendent with plumed helmets and gleaming lances, strolled here and there, and one group had split up the clothes of the Teacher and were noisily casting lots for them.

Joel, the son of Jeremiah, the potter, crept close to the cross. His young eyes, used to brutality from the Roman soldiers, had never witnessed such a scene as this. He was pale and his lips trembled, but he felt an urge to get closer to the Teacher whom his father had known.

Suddenly the Teacher spoke from where he hung upon the cross. "I thirst," he said.

Joel suddenly thought of the cup he had failed to leave at the gate well. Taking it from his sash, he filled it to the brim with sparkling water from his small water bag.

Slowly he pushed through the crowd to the foot of the cross, and touched a bearded, robed man on the arm.

"He thirsts. I have water here . . . but I cannot reach it to him." The man looked down into his earnest eyes.

"Aye. You are a good lad." And the man, taking the cup of water from Joel, filled a sponge with the sparkling liquid and started to lift it to the parched lips of the Nazarene.

"Here! What are you doing, Jew dog?" A burley soldier thrust his way through the crowd and, flinging the bearded man aside, seized the cup of water.

"Ha! So he is thirsty, eh? Well—" He flung the water from the cup and, pulling a gourd from his belt, filled the cup with a brackish, evil-smelling fluid.

"He shall have a drink! Here, you whom men call King of the Jews! Does this not suit your regal taste?" And the soldier filled the sponge, pressed it upon the point of his lance and, leaning up, thrust the vile thing against the Teacher's pale lips.

The deep eyes closed; the lips compressed, but there was no change of expression upon the pain-twisted features.

Roaring with mirth, the Roman soldier smeared the sponge over the face of the man on the cross, but when he turned to refill the sponge, he found an empty cup.

The soldier gave the empty cup to a Greek slave, who stood quietly by holding his master's shield.

"Here, dog, take this cup and scrub it well. Scour it with sand and stone it until the taste is clear of gall and vinegar. I shall drink from it this night. If a King can drink from it, then I, Flavius Galio, can also quench a thirst from it!"

The slave nodded, bowed, and left the hill. In the barrack of the Roman guards, he scoured the ugly cup. With sand and smooth stones he polished it, until when he tasted water from it, there was no tinge or smell of gall or vinegar.

The day became stormy. Thunder rolled; across the brow of Golgotha lightning darted brilliant fingers.

Flavius stamped into his barrack and flung the heavy helmet upon his cot. Sitting down, he unbuckled the mesh armor and sighed gustily.

"What a day," he muttered. "Dry season it is, and yet it thunders and storms, and the heavens are like a great fire licking at the evils of a world." Turning his head toward the servant quarters, he yelled,

"Dog of a slave—where are you? Bring your master a drink. A cool, sweet draught of wine!" The Greek slave entered in a moment, carrying a cup filled with wine.

"Ah, the cup. Did you scrub it well?"

"Yes, my master, with sand and pebbles until the water tasted clear and sparkled to the very bottom."

"Very well." The soldier raised the cup and sipped the wine. His face clouded and he spat the wine from his mouth with a wry grimace. "Gall!" he roared, "gall and vinegar! You lazy scoundrel, I'll scourge your hide, disobeying my orders! The slave paled and cowered, his eyes wide with fright.

"Take and scour it again, Greek dog, and bring it to me during my evening meal. And if there is one taste of gall or vinegar, I'll—" The slave took the cup and ran from the room.

The day advanced and finally, with tapers alight and smoking the Roman guard entered their dining hall, remarking noisily of the strange day. Flavius sat down at the head of the long table in the position befitting a centurion in charge of a full platoon of guard. The meal progressed through the usual courses until the wine was served.

The Greek slave approached Flavius and placed the cup before him, an anxious expression upon his face. He had scoured the cup until the grains of clay were worn thin. Water and wine had he drunk from it, and the taste was clear and sweet.

Flavius arose, "Guards, I have here," he raised the cup on high "the vessel from which drink was given a King of the Jews. I propose a toast to our emperor, and my lips shall drink from this same cup." The entire guard arose. Raising their cups, they shouted a toast "Long live Caesar!" and they drank.

As Flavius raised his cup, the red gleam of the wine darkened before his eyes and swirled into a brackish mess. The thick, bitter stink of gall seized his nostrils; and as he sipped, the sour tang of vinegar made his throat contract, and a nausea arose in his stomach.

With a roar of rage, he turned and struck the slave to the floor. Rushing to the door, he flung the ugly cup into the darkness of the night, his face twisted with a deep and penetrating fear. . . .

In the cool dawn a beggar shambled along the dusty road paralleling the Roman barracks. Jerusalem lay before him; and there, within the gates, was a cool spring where he could quench his heavy thirst.

His weary eyes swept the road before him. Sometimes he found scraps of bread or fruit, and sometimes even coins where travelers had lost them.

Suddenly he saw an article glinting dully on the ground before him. Stepping closer, he bent over and saw a cup lying on the sand. It was a plain, crude thing, so scoured that the clay seemed very fragile.

He picked the cup from the ground and put it away in his clothes, plodding on his way. The gates of Jerusalem passed, he paused at the well.

Taking the cup from the clothes, he filled it to the brim with clear sparkling water. Greedily he drained it of the cool liquid, filled it again, and drained it to the last sweet drop.

He started to put the cup away in his clothes, then paused momentarily. "If I leave the cup," he muttered to himself, "some thirsty one like myself will come along and be able to drink from the spring

Otherwise they might have to pass on and remain thirsty. Who knows?" he continued to muse, as he placed the cup on a cool, mossy edge, "someday it may press the lips of a king who happens this way."

The cup, moistened and cool, received the gleam of early morning sun and reflected a soft, golden light.[5]

POEM:

I gave a beggar from my scanty store
Of hard-earned gold. He spent the shining ore
And came again, and yet again, still cold
And hungry, as before.

I gave the Christ, and through that Christ of mine
He found himself, a man, supreme, divine,
Fed, clothed, and crowned with blessings manifold,
And now he begs no more.

—AUTHOR UNKNOWN

PRAYER:

Our Father, touch our hearts that we may be willing to give of our time, talents, and possessions to help carry on thy work in the world. Make us humble, patient, and co-operative as we strive to advance thy kingdom. Help us to feel the importance of the ordinary tasks near at hand: the giving of a cup of cold water in Jesus' name, being kind to the lonely, sharing the burdens of the poor, and bringing joy to the sorrowing. May we give not grudgingly or of necessity, for praise or vainglory, but may we do all within our power to live as Christians and share the good news of the gospel with all people, and thus hasten the coming of thy kingdom. In Jesus' name we pray. AMEN.

HYMN: "True-hearted, Whole-hearted, Faithful and Loyal," or
"O for a Heart to Praise My God."

BENEDICTION:

The Lord bless you, and keep you: the Lord make his face shine upon you, and be gracious unto you: the Lord lift up his countenance upon you, and give you peace. Amen.

SERVICE 22

GIVING—NOT SEEKING

Prelude: "Morning Hymn" by Haydn.

Call to Worship:

> God—let me be aware.
> Stab my soul fiercely with others' pain,
> Let me walk seeing horror and stain.
> Let my hands, groping, find other hands.
> Give me the heart that divines, understands.
> Give me the courage, wounded, to fight.
> Flood me with knowledge, drench me in light.
> Please—keep me eager just to do my share.
> God let me be aware.[1]

—Miriam Teichner

Hymn: "Saviour, Thy Dying Love," or
"The King of Love My Shepherd Is."

Scripture:

Remember now thy Creator in the days of thy youth. . . . Commit thy way unto the Lord; trust also in him. . . . Trust in the Lord with all thine heart; and lean not unto thine own understanding. In all thy ways acknowledge him, and he shall direct thy paths. . . . Lay not up for yourselves treasures upon earth, where moth and rust doth corrupt, and where thieves break through and steal: but lay up for yourselves treasures in heaven, where neither moth nor rust doth corrupt, and where thieves do not break through nor steal. . . .

He which soweth sparingly shall reap also sparingly; and he which soweth bountifully shall reap also bountifully. Every man according as he purposeth in his heart, so let him give; not grudgingly, or of necessity: for God loveth a cheerful giver.[2]

GIVING—NOT SEEKING

PRAYER:

O Lord, our Saviour, who hast warned us that thou wilt require much of those to whom much is given; grant that we, whose lot is cast in so goodly a heritage, may strive together the more abundantly . . . to extend to others what we so richly enjoy, and as we have entered into the labors of other men, so to labor that in their turn other men may enter into ours, to the fulfillment of thy holy will. Through Jesus Christ our Lord. AMEN.[3]

LEADER:

We will hear a story of a young couple with limited means who worked out the problem of tithing according to Christian principles.

STORY:

COUNT ME IN, TOO

"YES, you're probably right," Lester Dutton heard himself saying to his wife, Velma, as he deftly flicked off his stubborn black whiskers with his new electric razor. "It's right to be a tither. Still, it's just like I've told you a hundred times already—we positively can't do it this year. Prices are too high! Next year, perhaps—"

"But our faith, Lester," Velma cut in, her soft blue eyes casting a reproving glance at her handsome young husband. "Where's your faith?" she queried.

"Oh, bother my faith!"

"But why wait until next year, Lester? The church needs money this year. Needs it now! Oh, Lester, please."

"No." He tossed his wavy, black hair impatiently and grew adamant. The tone of his voice sounded final.

Velma knew she could proceed no further. To argue longer would be futile. Nor was this, indeed, the first argument they'd had. Each Sabbath morning for a month now, ever since their pastor had announced Budget Sunday and appealed for a larger number of tithers, this dispute had flared in the Dutton apartment. Funny that they never discussed this question, though, except when they dressed for Sunday school each Sunday morning.

Lester Dutton, finishing his shaving, cleaned his electric razor and put it away. Going into the bedroom, he cast a sidelong glance at his petite, brunette bride who sat combing her hair before the vanity.

"Feeling as pretty as you're looking?" he teased evasively as he moved over to playfully pull a lock of her shining hazel hair. H felt a slight twinge of conscience that he had disagreed with her sharply. Still, what could a bride of a month know about finances?

Velma rose quickly in response to his banter. Her gaze measure the depths of his dark brown eyes, tried to fathom what lurked behi them. "Yes, I am," she retorted, "but if you really loved me—"

"I'd give in and follow like Mary's little lamb, I suppose," I finished for her. Then averting his eyes, he began industriously shini his shoes. If he thought he had delivered the knockout punch, howeve he was soon to learn his mistake.

The trim, young brunette drew herself up to her full five-foot-s and countered firmly: "If you really loved me, Lester Dutton, you listen to reason. You'd listen to our pastor. You'd listen to God. You walk in the light. You'd do it now—not next year!"

A deep, studied silence ensued. Lester, continuing to shine his sho briskly long after they had a gleaming luster, did not look up. H seemed to be weighing her words with solemn mien. However sharp he might disagree with her, he knew he loved her dearly, and that w bound to complicate the situation. Moreover, had she not led him Christ, and subsequently into the church, less than a year ago? Whe would he be had he not met her?

Looking up at last, his eyes met hers. "Velma, I owe a great deal you," he said, as if he felt compelled to make vocal his thought "I'm sorry if I've hurt your feelings. On the other hand, I simply not see how I can contribute a tenth this year. With prices so hig my forty-a-week won't even go around, much less have a tenth left f the church. If you can suggest a plan—"

"Excuse me, Lester, it's quite time we were off to Sunday school Velma said, glancing hurriedly at her wrist watch. Drawing on h new red hat with the wispy black veil, she continued, "As for a pla I have one. It works when you know nothing else to do or try. I' ready to go now if you are. I hope we get there on time—I hate to late."

Outside in the car, she revealed her plan as they sped through th city traffic. Her plan, she confided, was prayer. She firmly believed prayer. She believed that God could make their remaining nine tent go farther than the whole ten tenths. She dared him to put God t the test, insisting that he could not outgive God!

Lester Dutton reached the church far from a submissive moo Capitulation had not entered his head. He'd not give in.

GIVING—NOT SEEKING

A wise teacher, who had apparently tarried long in the place of prayer, rose before the young Homebuilders' Class. Lester and Velma Sutton listened raptly to her words.

What was that she was saying? The subject today is "God's Priorities." During World War II, we grew accustomed to priorities. Well, God has some priorities, too. For instance, God has a priority on our finances. We owe him the first tenth of our income.

Lester leaned forward, turning pale. Here it was again! Was there no escape from this nagging question? Velma haunted him at home—now the teacher. Had Velma tipped off the teacher? Were they in league together?

Her spiritual earnestness recaptured Lester's attention. What? Had he ever read Malachi 3:8-10? No. Would he take her Bible then, opened to that passage, and read it to the class? He reached out a trembling hand, took the open Bible, and, trying to keep the inner conflict from creeping into his voice, read aloud:

"Will a man rob God? Yet ye have robbed me. But ye say, Wherein have we robbed thee? In tithes, and offerings. . . . Bring ye all the tithes into the storehouse, . . . and prove me now herewith, saith the Lord of hosts, if I will not open you the windows of heaven, and pour you out a blessing, that there shall not be room enough to receive it."

Lester's voice grew husky in spite of himself. Handing the Bible back to the teacher, he sank dumbly into his chair. Did he just imagine that the eyes of the class were boring into him? Or was he just suddenly becoming self-conscious?

As one in a daze, he heard the teacher continuing. "Lester has read to you God's word. Malachi raises a startling question: 'Will a man rob God?' There are those who will rob the government, the city, their brothers, their parents, their children, but surely no one would stoop so low as to rob God! How shall we answer this question? Our first impulse is to answer an emphatic, 'No.' No man would be so mad as to rob God. But we are wrong. Men will rob God! Friends, you are on dangerous ground if you've been stealing or withholding God's tenth. The people of Malachi's day were required to tithe. Think you less is required of us with our far greater light?"

But Lester had quit listening. He squirmed restlessly in his chair, the chair squeaking each time he turned. If only he could force himself to sit still and appear unconcerned. Strange, that his chair was the only

159

one that squeaked. He knew he couldn't endure this much longer. He'
go mad!

The teacher went on relentlessly: "This passage lays emphasis o
bringing our tithes now—not a year from now. Today, friends, i
Budget Sunday. Our pastor has implored more of our members t
become tithers. Our pastor must have a better salary to meet the hig
cost of living. The Homebuilders' Class represents a large segmen
of the salaried strength of our church. I'm asking the class to mak
a decision this morning. All who will be tithers, stand."

The class stood as one man. Only Lester and Velma remained seated
It was a poignant moment! Lester felt a tug at his arm. Velma wa
trying to persuade him to stand with the others. He noticed hot tear
trembling upon her long, dark lashes. Her chin quivered. Somehow
he managed to shake off her persuasions. Outwardly he appeared
adamant, as he had at the apartment, but inwardly he was shaken
Luckily he had led Velma to the back row of seats. Peradventure, hi
failure to stand would not be discovered.

Then he suddenly remembered his wife's words en route to church—
praying he'd become a tither. Abruptly Lester began to feel he coul
not continue to disappoint her. Not if he loved her.

In the car, on the way home after the morning sermon, Leste
finally broke the strained silence that engulfed them. "Dear, you
prayers have been answered," he announced.

"Really?" she retorted curtly, remembering her humiliation in th
class.

"Yes, I'm a tither!" he exclaimed with unconcealed animation
"After church—while you were shaking hands with friends—
slipped around to the pastor and told him to count me in, too. I
may be a little rough for us for a while, but we can make it if we try
There are lots of places we can save. And like you said this morning
God will help us if we do our part."

The car hummed leisurely through the light homeward traffic
Her hand slipped gently into his, as she snuggled up close besid
him. "Oh, darling, I'm so proud of you," she said softly.[4]

Poem:

      It is in loving—not in being loved,—
        The heart is blest;
      It is in giving—not in seeking gifts,—
        We find our quest.

If thou art hungry, lacking heavenly food,—
    Give hope and cheer.
If thou art sad and wouldst be comforted,—
    Stay sorrow's tear.

Whatever be thy longing and thy need,—
    That do thou give;
So shall thy soul be fed, and thou indeed,
    Shalt truly live.

—AUTHOR UNKNOWN

PRAYER:

O Lord, help us to have a right attitude toward our possessions. May we realize we are only stewards of the things which we think we own, and that we shall eventually have to give an account of our stewardship. Lead us into an understanding of thy will and purpose concerning all that we have, and strengthen us that we may have courage to use everything as thou dost direct. Help us to resist every influence which would make us more self-centered or draw us away from thee. Be thou our guide and counselor in every thought and action of our lives as we now strive to commit all that we have and are to thee. AMEN.

HYMN: "Take My Life, and Let It Be," or
      "My Jesus, as Thou Wilt."

BENEDICTION:

My God shall supply all your need according to his riches in glory. AMEN.

SERVICE 23

PRACTICING HIS PRESENCE

PRELUDE: "Arioso in A" by Bach.

CALL TO WORSHIP:

Of all the prizes
That earth can give,
 This is the best:
To find thee, Lord,
A living Presence near
 And in thee rest!

Friends, fortune, fame,
Or what might come to me—
 I count all loss
If I find not
Companionship
 With thee!

—AUTHOR UNKNOWN

HYMN: "Still, Still with Thee," or
 " 'Mid All the Traffic of the Ways."

SCRIPTURE:

Whither shall I go from thy Spirit? or whither shall I flee from thy
 presence?
If I ascend up into heaven, thou art there:
If I make my bed in hell, behold, thou art there.
If I take the wings of the morning, and dwell in the uttermost parts
 of the sea;
Even there shall thy hand lead me, and thy right hand shall hold me.
If I say, Surely the darkness shall cover me; even the night shall be
 light about me.

Yea, the darkness hideth not from thee; but the night shineth as the
day: the darkness and the light are both alike to thee. . . .
How precious also are thy thoughts unto me, O God! how great is the
sum of them!
If I should count them, they are more in number than the sand:
when I awake, I am still with thee. . . .
Search me, O God, and know my heart: try me and know my thoughts:
And see if there be any wicked way in me, and lead me in the way
everlasting.[1]

LEADER:

Do we have a time set aside for devotions, for daily communion
with God? Is God real to us as we pray? What is the purpose of
prayer? Do we use it to try to bend God to our will, or to try to
discover God's will concerning us? Do we use prayer to confess our
shortcomings, to seek forgiveness, to make amends, and to lead a
better life? Are we ready that God's will may be done in our lives?
Let us ask God to reveal his will and purpose and to give us the
courage to follow the impressions which come from him. God's power
is available to all who seek to know and to follow him.

SCRIPTURE:

Ask, and it shall be given you; seek, and ye shall find; knock,
and it shall be opened unto you: for every one that asketh receiveth;
and he that seeketh findeth; and to him that knocketh it shall be
opened. Or what man is there of you, whom if his son ask bread,
will he give him a stone? Or if he ask a fish, will he give him a
serpent? If ye then, being evil, know how to give good gifts unto your
children, how much more shall your Father which is in heaven give
good things to them that ask him? [2]

LEADER:

In the following poem a suggestion is given by which we may
live continually in the presence of God.

POEM:

> I met God in the morning
>   When my day was at its best,
> And his presence came like sunrise,
>   Like a glory in my breast.

All day long the Presence lingered,
  All day long he stayed with me,
And we sailed in perfect calmness
  O'er a very troubled sea.

Other ships were blown and battered,
  Other ships were sore distressed,
But the winds that seemed to drive them
  Brought to us a peace and rest.

Then I thought of other mornings,
  With a keen remorse of mind,
When I too had loosed the moorings,
  With the Presence left behind.

So I think I know the secret
  Learned from many a troubled way:
You must seek him in the morning
  If you want him through the day! [3]

—Ralph S. Cushman

PRAYER:

O Lord, thou hast promised thy presence where two or three are met in thy name. Make us aware of thy presence, speak to each of us, and give us courage and determination to follow thy guidance. Give us more of the spirit of him who came not to be ministered unto but to minister and give his life for us. In his name we pray. AMEN.

POEM:

O Love divine, that stooped to share
  Our sharpest pang, our bitterest tear!
On thee we cast each earthborn care,
  We smile at pain while thou art near!

Though long the weary way we tread,
  And sorrow crown each lingering year,
No path we shun, no darkness dread,
  Our hearts still whispering, Thou art near!

PRACTICING HIS PRESENCE

When drooping pleasure turns to grief,
　　And trembling faith is changed to fear,
The murmuring wind, the quivering leaf,
　　Shall softly tell us thou art near!

On thee we fling our burdening woe,
　　O Love divine, forever dear!
Content to suffer while we know,
　　Living and dying, thou art near!
　　　　　　　　　　　　　—OLIVER WENDELL HOLMES

STORY:

"THE GOD IN YOUR HOME"

SHE was a dainty slip of a Japanese girl. Her bright, wondering almond eyes looked out in interested query at all the things in this great, wonderful America. Eagerly she studied at the American University. The girls called her Cherry Blossom, for she seemed like a bloom from her favorite cherry tree, blown across the ocean from her own Sunrise Land.

Ethel Clarkson, one of the college girls, wrote home to her mother, begging permission to bring Cherry Blossom home with her for the holidays. "She fairly absorbs knowledge and adopts our American customs in the most charming way," wrote Ethel.

When Christmas time came, dainty little Cherry Blossom was all aglow over the thought of spending Christmas in the beautiful American home of her friend. She had been inside the great schools and colleges in America. She had seen their art galleries and public buildings. She had been in many churches. But the thing she longed most to see, on the inside, was a Christian home.

That first Christmas time in America was a wonderful holiday season to little Cherry Blossom from Japan. But soon vacation time was over. Mrs. Clarkson stood in her library with her hands on the shoulders of the little Japanese girl she had learned to love deeply.

"Now tell me before you go, you dear little Cherry Blossom," she asked playfully, "how you like the way we American folk live? Are you homesick for a real, genuine bow? Are you weary of sitting in chairs and sleeping in beds—and wearing shoes all day long—and being bothered with knives, forks and spoons?"

The little girl laughed merrily.

"I love it," she said clapping her hands. "It is such fun trying to see which spoon to take up next. Your home is wonderful." Then her eyes grew suddenly wistful—"But," she said, and hesitated.

"But what," said Mrs. Clarkson, encouragingly.

"There is one thing I miss," said the girl with a far-away look in her eyes, "that makes your home seem queer to me. You know I have been with you to your church and I have worshipped your God there, but I have missed the God in your home. You know, in Japan we have a God-shelf in every house with the gods right there in our home. Do not Americans worship God in their homes?"

All during the afternoon Mrs. Clarkson was strangely silent. The innocent question of her departing guest had gone straight to her heart, with an overwhelming accusation. Her thoughts flew back over the busy years to those days when she first had a home of her own, and a time and a place for the worship of God in her home.

Then the thousand distractions of a large household and a busy life crowded in, and the God in her home had been crowded out. She had not meant that it should be so. And as she thought of it all a great longing filled her heart and the light of a firm conviction filled her eyes. That evening she talked with each member of her household.

Thus it was that little Cherry Blossom from Japan, on her next vacation visit to the Clarkson home, found the God in that home she had missed, and gave her heart to him.[4]

POEM:

> More things are wrought by prayer
> Than this world dreams of. Wherefore, let thy voice
> Rise like a fountain for me night and day.
> For what are men better than sheep or goats
> That nourish a blind life within the brain,
> If, knowing God, they lift not hands of prayer
> Both for themselves and those who call them friend?
> For so the whole round earth is every way
> Bound by gold chains about the feet of God.[5]
>
> —ALFRED TENNYSON

PRAYER:

O God, our understanding Friend whose lovingkindness never fails us, we confess in shame that too often we have forgotten Thee. Through self-concern we have set up walls to shut Thee out. Through

166

absorption in the details of our lives and the duties of the hour, we have allowed our vision of Thee to fade. Even in the doing of Thy works, we have let slip from our lives the awareness of Thy presence. Forgive us, O Lord.

We rejoice that where Thou art, there is power. Where Thou art, life is rich with meaning. Where Thou art, nothing is common or unclean. Show us Thyself, O Lord, in our daily living.

Help us today to open the eyes of our souls to Thee. Show us Thyself in the splendor of Thy world, the joys of human fellowship, the infinite richness of the persons whose lives touch ours. Reveal to us Thy yearning heart even in the tribulation and turmoil of a stricken world. Let each joy and sorrow, each task and each moment of relaxation from toil, be illumined by Thy presence.

So shall we go to rest when the day is done, weary in body but refreshed in soul. When we wake no more to see Thee here, may we enter into the joy of our Lord to praise Thee anew as we behold Thy glory. In the name of our Lord Jesus Christ, in whom we see Thee as Thou art. Amen.[6]

Hymn: "Be Still, My Soul," or
"We May Not Climb the Heavenly Steeps."

Benediction:

May we go from this service with an awareness of thy presence. Unto God's loving care we commit ourselves. Amen.

SERVICE 24

LIVING ABUNDANTLY

PRELUDE: Hymn tune "Sicilian Mariners' Hymn."

CALL TO WORSHIP:

> Teach me to live! 'Tis easier far to die—
>   Gently and silently to pass away—
> On earth's long night to close the heavy eye,
>   And waken in the glorious realms of day.
>
> Teach me that harder lesson—how to live
>   To serve thee in the darkest paths of life.
> Arm me for conflict, now fresh vigor give,
>   And make me more than conqu'ror in the strife.
>   —AUTHOR UNKNOWN

HYMN: "Dear Lord and Father of Mankind," or
      "'Mid All the Traffic of the Ways."

SCRIPTURE:

Then said Jesus unto them again, Verily, verily, I say unto you, I am the door of the sheep. All that ever came before me are thieves and robbers: but the sheep did not hear them. I am the door: by me if any man enter in, he shall be saved, and shall go in and out, and find pasture. The thief cometh not, but for to steal, and to kill, and to destroy: I am come that they might have life, and that they might have it more abundantly.[1]

PRAYER:

Cleanse us, O merciful Lord, from our secret faults and from those sins that most abuse us.

Wash off the strains our malice has caused in others and those which our weakness has received of them.

Let them not perish by our occasions nor us be undone by theirs.

But let our charity assist one another and thy clemency pardon us all.

Pardon, O gracious Jesus, what we have been; with thy holy discipline correct what we are.

Order by thy providence what we shall be, and in the end crown thine own gifts. AMEN.[2]

POEM:

> God of the spirit wind, whose rushing quickened
> Men of all nations to faith in thy word,
> Waken our courage as theirs was awakened,
> Breathe out thy spirit on us, O Lord.
>
> Touch us with cloven flame, forging forgiveness,
> Fusing our hearts into fervent accord,
> Steeling our wills with the faith that thou livest,
> Temper our souls with thy fire, O Lord.
>
> God of the glowing love, making men brothers,
> Burn out the dross of belief in the sword;
> Fashion one vision more golden than others;
> Peace ever more through thy mercy, Lord.
>
> Then shall thy spirit sons, purged of all hatred,
> Spurning all envy and martial reward,
> Stand a world—nation, united and sacred,
> Pledging eternal good will, O Lord.[3]

—EARL MARLATT

STORY:

THE GREATEST GIFT

"DO COME back to earth, Kyle," said Janice. "I had something to tell you."

"Sorry," he said. "Everything seems so new, and yet so familiar. It's wonderful to be back and see you."

"Don't you want to hear what I have to tell you?"

"I know already," he said. "You're going to tell me I've been given the lookout job at Bailey's Peak by the Forest Service. Pretty lucky

169

for me, since I'm studying forestry at the university. But I really didn't expect to get it."

Janice said, "People never forgot that you were the one who started that drive for the new high-school gym. They believe in you, Kyle."

"We simply needed a new gym and I happened to think of a way to get it. Say! Did you have anything to do with my getting that job?"

"No," she smiled. "You don't need that kind of help, Kyle. Why do you always underestimate yourself?"

"It doesn't help my confidence any to think that you were the one responsible for my going to the university. You insisted that I could go down there, get a job and work my way through."

"All of which proves that you can do a great deal more than you think you can."

"But that isn't what I wanted to tell you," Janice said. "My Uncle John died while you were away at school, and his son, Tommy, has gotten completely out of control."

"Seems to me he's given nothing but trouble for the last couple of years."

"Aunt Kate has had her hands full just caring for Uncle John. Tommy had just turned sixteen and he thinks he's a man. He's run away from home three times during the last year. No one in town will give him a job."

"I suppose you've talked to him," Kyle said.

"Everyone's talked to him. Father tried it. Tommy simply won't listen to older people any more. I thought you might be able to do it."

"Oh, I'll talk to him if you wish, Janice. But what good will talking do? He's had too much of that already."

"Exactly what I think. I happen to know that Mr. Small over at the Ranger station has given you a free hand to choose an assistant lookout for Bailey's Peak. If you gave Tommy that job—"

"Now wait a minute," Kyle said. "Mr. Small made it clear that he's allowing me to pick my own assistant because he has confidence in me. He said he wanted me to have experience in hiring men, and a man is judged by the people he hires. Bailey's Peak will be my responsibility, and I don't intend to risk my job and my reputation by taking on a lazy, unreliable boy like Tommy."

"What will happen to Tommy?" Janice asked grimly.

"He'll go from bad to worse, I suppose. That's tough, but it isn't my responsibility."

"Someday Tommy will get into real trouble, then everyone in town will condemn him and say it was his fault. It won't be. It will be the fault of those who never gave him a chance. It will be your fault, mostly, Kyle, because there's no one in town who'd have a better chance with him."

He groaned inwardly, wondering how he had become involved.

"Think it over tonight," Janice said. "Tommy is interested in the job. He's coming over to see you about it in the morning."

As Tommy stepped into the living room where Kyle indicated, he had a sullen set to his lips.

"What makes you think you want to work at Bailey's Peak?"

"I'd just like to get out of town."

"There'll be lots of work besides watching from the tower for fires. There will be wood to chop, dishes to wash, the cabin to clean. You might have to go on errands once in a while."

"Well," he said, "it would be better than hanging around town."

Kyle's terrier came bounding into the room at that moment and Tommy began playing with it.

"You might find it lonesome at Bailey's Peak."

The boy glanced at him sharply. "I guess you don't want me to work for you. That's all I want to know. I'm not asking any favors from anybody."

The boy had suddenly put him on the defensive and Kyle resented it. For an instant he was tempted to let the boy go. It would be good riddance. But he said, "Get your things packed, Tommy. We'll drive up at two o'clock."

All the pleasure of living in the wilderness was dashed to the earth during that first miserable week at Bailey's Peak. Tommy resented taking orders, and he rarely carried them out. He could not be trusted in the lookout tower for more than a few minutes without falling asleep. After the first few days, Kyle accepted Tommy's failings with patient silence. Talking to him only made things worse. Kyle did his own duties and Tommy's as well. Fortunately, the boy proved useful in one respect at least. He liked driving to town for supplies, though it took a day to do it, instead of three hours.

"I'll put up with him another week," Kyle told himself. "If he doesn't show improvement by then, I'll get rid of him and get someone else."

Kyle was alone in the lookout tower one morning. White fingers of morning mist hung in the hollows, and far to the south he could see Lake Mantoc. He went to the phone in the glass tower room.

"Mantoc Ranger Station," an assistant ranger said at the other end of the line.

"This is Baily's Peak lookout calling. All clear except for a smudge on the horizon above Oak Ridge. I think it's a cloud."

"It is," agreed the ranger. "Say, I've got a message for you. Janice Hooker and some friends are driving out to your place next Sunday. Mr. Small wants to talk to you."

"Hello, Kyle," said Mr. Small. "What is this I hear about your hiring Tommy Hooker as assistant. Are you sure that was wise?"

"I've known Tommy's people for years. He comes from a very nice family. I'm sure he's going to be all right."

"They don't speak very highly of him in town."

"That's true," Kyle admitted. "Tommy's got good stuff in him and a sharp mind. He's going to be all right."

"I hope you are right, Kyle. If you people didn't spot a fire simply because of your misplaced confidence in someone, thousands of acres of timber and many lives might be lost."

"Don't worry about Tommy. He's all right."

As Kyle turned he saw Tommy standing a few feet away. "I—I didn't really mean to be listening," he said.

"That's all right. You didn't know I was talking about you."

"I've been listening almost every day. I figured you were going to report how bad I was. Why did you say I was good, Kyle?"

"I told what I thought was the truth. I know you've been putting on an act. You thought I didn't like you like the others. I don't, but I keep remembering you're the son of John Hooker. He was as fine a man as I ever met. You're the same way inside, Tommy."

Without answering, Tommy turned and fled down the steps. Kyle had made a dent in Tommy's armor, a small dent, but it might be important. It occurred to him that now he was stuck with Tommy for the rest of the summer. It was time he did something about him. On sudden impulse he went to the phone and called the assistant ranger.

"I've changed my mind about having you send me one of those pups. My assistant is crazy about dogs. I think it would be good company for him."

So it happened that Tommy found himself the owner of a little dog, the first he had ever had. But the pup came first with Tommy.

Nothing else seemed to matter. Tommy had something of his own to love and he was happy. The sullen expression had gone from his face.

Kyle continued to do the work of two people for he never knew when Mr. Small might show up for inspection. Sunday was only three days away when Kyle suddenly came down with chills and fever. On wobbly legs he tried to climb the lookout tower—and failed. He went back to bed.

"Tommy, get up and phone the ranger station to send a doctor. You'll have to keep watch today in the lookout tower. I can't make it."

In the twilight haze between naps Kyle was aware that the doctor had been there and left. The fever broke during the following night, and he slept soundly. The next day he wanted to get up but Tommy forced him to stay in bed. In his own mind he felt sure that Tommy was making a mess of things. It was all the fault of Janice. He should never have listened to her.

On the following day Tommy fixed breakfast for both of them, and Kyle noticed with approval that everything in the kitchen was exactly as he would have kept it. An hour later Mr. Small's car drove up.

"Glad to see you up. Say, you were perfectly right about Tommy. He's all business. He spotted three campfires in the last two days."

Kyle shook his head. "I'm glad to know that. To tell you the truth, I've been plenty worried."

"You weren't fooling us any," Mr. Small said. "We knew you were doing all the work. The boy never called in a report once. You've done a miracle with him. How did you do it?"

"Well I guess I made him like me. I got him that dog because that was what he had always wanted. He loves that dog and I figured that love would drive the bitterness out of his mind. I made the same mistake with him that everyone else did. I didn't trust him with anything. I kept watching him. I guess that's why he wouldn't work. He wanted to be trusted on a job, and I never gave him that chance. I've learned a bigger lesson than Tommy. He was the one that showed me."

Mr. Small beamed with pleasure. "I'm glad you feel that way. Now I can tell you that Janice Hooker came to me before she spoke to you about Tommy. She told me that Tommy respected you. She believed you could do something for him. But she wasn't thinking of Tommy as much as she was thinking of you. She knows me well enough to know that I want men around me that can handle people.

She wanted to prove to me that you were capable of dealing with a difficult problem.

"But I haven't proven anything," Kyle protested. "Whatever has happened to Tommy has been an accident, not anything I did. I took a cold—"

"You would have in time," Mr. Small said. "You'd made a fine start. Tommie's changed—he's grown up—willing to work."

He placed his hand on Kyle's shoulder and gave him an affectionate pat.

"You've made the boy, Kyle," he said with genuine warmth, "and you've made me proud of you." [4]

PRAYER:

Our Father, thou knowest our weaknesses and the sins which doth so easily beset us. Since at best we are unprofitable servants, guide us into ways that are pleasing to thee, that we may render a more acceptable service. Forgive our mistakes, lift our affections to things above, and grant us strength to withstand all temptations. Help us to get rid of attitudes which are harmful, unworthy thoughts, and degrading actions. Deliver us from the cares of the world, vain hopes and foolish desires. Grant that through the help that comes from thee, we may take whatever comes to us and make it contribute to our growth in character. We commit our lives to thee, in all our ways we acknowledge thee, vouchsafe to direct our paths and lead us into abundant life. In the name of the Master of us all we pray. AMEN.

HYMN: "Awake, My Soul, Stretch Every Nerve," or
"God of Grace and God of Glory."

BENEDICTION:

Grant that we may always do what is acceptable in thy sight, through Jesus Christ our Lord. AMEN.

SERVICE 25

CHOOSING WORTHY GOALS

PRELUDE: Hymn Tune "Ton-y-botel."

CALL TO WORSHIP:

> Life is a leaf of paper white
> Whereon each one of us may write
> His word or two, and then comes night.
>
> . . . .
>
> Greatly begin! though thou have time
> But for a line, be that sublime,—
> Not failure, but low aim, is crime.[1]
> —JAMES RUSSELL LOWELL

HYMN: "Go Forth to Life, O Child of Earth," or
"He Who Would Valiant Be."

SCRIPTURE:

Rejoice in the Lord always: and again I say, Rejoice. Let your moderation be known unto all men. The Lord is at hand. Be careful for nothing; but in everything by prayer and supplication with thanksgiving let your request be made known unto God. And the peace of God, which passeth all understanding, shall keep your hearts and minds through Christ Jesus. Finally, brethren, whatsoever things are true, whatsoever things are honest, whatsoever things are just, whatsoever things are pure, whatsoever things are lovely, whatsoever things are of good report; if there be any virtue, and if there by any praise, think on these things. These things, which ye have both learned, and received, and heard, and seen in me, do: and the God of peace shall be with you. . . . I can do all things through Christ which strengtheneth me. . . . But my God shall supply all your need according to his riches in glory by Christ Jesus.[2]

LEADER:

As we meditate on our aim or goals that we have set for ourselves, let us try to decide on some of the things that we are going to demand of ourselves.

POEM:

> Great God, I ask thee for no meaner pelf
> Than that I may not disappoint myself,
> That in my action I may soar as high
> As I can now discern with this clear eye.
>
> . . . .
>
> That my weak hand may equal my firm faith,
> And my life practice more than my tongue saith;
>   That my low conduct may not show,
>   Nor my relenting lines,
>   That I thy purpose did not know,
>   Or overrated thy designs.[3]
>
> —HENRY DAVID THOREAU

HYMN: "We May Not Climb the Heavenly Steeps," or
        "A Charge to Keep I Have."

LEADER:

We will hear the story of a young man who was led to consider the greatest values of life, to place first things first, before deciding upon his goals.

STORY:

STRIVING AFTER THE WIND

ATTORNEY Guy Saunders hurried out of his office with a new spring in his step, his young face beaming, his eyes twinkling. He caught up his Panama hat, and was about to clap it over his head when his secretary looked up with a start.

"Going so soon, Mr. Saunders? I meant to tell you Mayor Catero called while you were in conference. He wants to see you."

"He did? One of these days, Helen, it'll be the governor calling."

"Well, today," she said flatly, "it was only a small-town mayor. What shall I tell him?"

"Got to go over to Smith Construction Company about that contract.

176

If they retain me, Helen, it will be the biggest step-up in my career. I'll have a client with real money for a change, instead of running my head off for peanuts and buttons."

"What shall I tell the mayor?"

"See him first thing in the morning." Then he was on his way.

At six that evening, when he finally left the imposing offices of the Smith Construction Company with a year's contract almost in his pocket, he was positive that this was his lucky day.

At eight he went over to call on Karen Wise. Three weeks had passed since they had last been together. But this night, surely, he felt, it would be different. Luck was with him. He had something to tell that would make her appreciate him. He joined her on the front porch and began telling her about it at once.

"Think of it!" he said. "Smith Construction offers to pay me two thousand a year just for small routine work that won't average an hour a day. I'll get all their big cases, too. They'll pay me regular fees for them. That should mean two or three thousand more!"

"That's fine," Karen said. "You're going to accept, of course."

"I'd be crazy if I didn't. But I'm holding out for twenty-five hundred. Can't let them think I'm getting a bargain."

Karen's silence had frost on it.

The old uneasiness seeped back into his heart like drops of ice water. It seemed to him that she didn't quite see the significance of it. He tried again. "With all that money, Karen, I'll be in a position for the first time in my life to settle down and—well, think about getting married."

"Will you?"

It was a coldly impersonal question that needed no answer. The silence closed down over them, held them mute, and vaguely, Guy was aware of the crickets in the front yard and the frogs in the reedy marsh at the edge of town. The haunting whisper was back in his mind.

"You see?" it whispered. "You've lost her, Guy. Can't you see Karen has changed? Can't you see she wasn't happy to be with you again? She's sitting here now only because it's the polite thing to do."

Guy glanced at her uneasily. A milky radiance of moonlight brushed the delicate line of her throat. It gleamed like slow fires in the auburn mass of her hair. It seemed to him that there was a little upward tilt to her chin.

"Just what are you thinking, Karen?" he asked.

She turned her head slowly, as if drawn reluctantly from her thoughts. "Ecclesiastes," she said. "All is vanity and a striving after the wind."

Guy frowned. There was a dry feeling in his mouth, and for a moment he completely forgot about the Smith Construction Company. "You know," he said reflectively, "sometimes that describes pretty well how I feel."

"Yes, I know. That's why I happened to be thinking about it."

They were sparring with words, not getting anywhere. Guy decided to face her honestly. They couldn't go on like this. His best, apparently, was not enough for her. "Karen, something has been happening between us. What is it? I want you to tell me honestly. Have I done anything to—to make you act like this?"

"Is it only in me that you notice the change, Guy?" she asked. "How about the rest of the people in Dalton?"

He nodded. A slow change had come over everyone in his home town. He had noticed it growing slowly over the last two or three years and he had been helpless to do anything about it. "I feel it most when I'm with you," he said. "Is—is there something wrong with me, Karen?"

"It's not easy to say." She spoke slowly, deliberately, searching her mind. "For one thing, you're really not happy. You scramble too hard after the mighty dollar. It shows on you. It might do you good to talk about it."

He shrugged. "I don't see what there is to talk about."

"Talking things over sometimes makes you see them more clearly, Guy," she said patiently. "Why do you sometimes feel that all is vanity?"

"Maybe it goes back to the scholarship the Dalton Council gave me for college. It always gave me a terrible feeling of personal responsibility. I had to make good in a big way, or I'd let them down."

"Not much danger of that. You made a straight A average in college."

"But it doesn't end there!" He made a hopeless gesture with his hand. "I won that scholarship on brain power. I was able to live up to it in college. Now I'm a lawyer and it's up to me to make the most of what they've given me."

"For one whose only been practicing a couple of years, you've been doing all right," she reminded him tartly. "You've had more business than you could take care of."

"Small stuff that doesn't amount to a hill of beans." He threw himself disconsolately back in the swing. "You say I've been doing all right. Then what is wrong with me? Why do most of you get that distant look when you talk to me? You think things about me, things that show in your face, but you never put them into words. Why?"

"Perhaps," Karen said, looking down at her hands, "perhaps we keep remembering what you were like before the scholarship."

"If I've changed," Guy went on doggedly, "I'd like to know about it. I've done the very best I could. I've tried to justify people's faith in me."

For a time Karen said nothing. She turned her head and looked thoughtfully at the rambler roses on the trellis. It was as if she were trying to shape unpleasant thoughts into words as soft as rose petals. She gave up suddenly and turned to him.

"You asked for an honest answer, Guy. It may hurt. You won that scholarship for a number of reasons. People liked you. They liked your thoughtfulness, the cheerful and generous way you helped others. You were in the choir, a real church worker among the young people. Those are the things people remember. Those are the things they liked—and now they're wondering what's happened to them."

"Starting up a law practice is a full-time job, Karen."

"That is not it. You're striving after the wind."

Guy shook his head. "Well, there's no use talking about that. It's impossible to make women understand anything about business."

"The change I'm talking about, Guy, began long before you went into practice. You center yourself completely in your work. You forget about being a person. It was the same in college. Study, study, study, so that you could make a record. Nothing else mattered."

"I didn't enjoy it," he said heavily. How could he make her see the emptiness in him, the hollow ache, the frustration, the self-doubts? How could a man give himself to others when he had shriveled to a dry husk inside and had nothing to give? "I can't explain how I feel, but law hasn't given me much satisfaction either. I get spite cases, hate cases, cases instituted for revenge, all the petty things that no other lawyer will handle. I've got to take some of them."

Karen stood up. "If you won the friendship and respect of some of the good people in town, instead of turning your back on them, you'd be getting better cases. As it is, you're too intense. Be your own real generous self again and you won't have to worry. You've forgotten about your real self, Guy."

He awoke the next morning still feeling depressed from the weight of her words. Then he remembered the Smith Construction Company contract and felt better. It would give him a fresh start, put him on his feet.

The first order of business, Helen reminded him, was his conference with the mayor. Mayor Catero sat tall and spare behind his desk when Guy came in.

"Glad to see you, Mr. Saunders. I'll come right to the point. How would you like to be the city attorney?"

The suddenness of it took Guy off his balance. "Wh-hy," he stammered. "It would be a great honor. I—"

The mayor chuckled. "Don't blame you for being surprised. You see our present city attorney, Mr. Henderson, has been ill much of the time lately and wishes to resign. He hasn't been able to care for things for some time. A lot of work is piling up that needs to be done.

Guy swallowed. He had difficulty finding his voice. The city attorney's job was obviously going begging. There was a lot of detailed, time-wasting work, and only one thousand dollars a year; hardly the sort of thing that would interest an attorney with a good practice. Guy felt almost certain the job had already been offered to the three top attorneys in town and that they had refused. Now it was his for the asking.

"What I was going to say," Guy began uncertainly, "I don't see how it would be possible for me to accept."

"It's a good opportunity for you, son. Most of us working for the city have been in a long time. We're all getting old. Things are running down. We were looking forward to having a young man with us, someone who had plenty of fight and some good ideas. There's a lot of hard work to be done to set things right."

"It isn't the work," Guy said. "The truth is, I've had an offer from the Smith Construction Company. They've got a case against the city, as you know, which would make it impossible for me to take both jobs. I couldn't work on both sides of the same case. If I became city attorney the Smith Construction Company would withdraw their offer."

"I understand. Under the circumstances, I suppose I shall have to look elsewhere. I'm very sorry about this, Mr. Saunders. A man of your energy could put some real life in the city government."

The interview was closed and Guy returned to his office.

180

Along about noon, the skies darkened with angry clouds. Wind whipped up the dust, caught up papers in the street, rattled the windows. A sudden gust scattered the sheets and letters on Guy's desk and he leaped up to close the windows. He was scarcely back in his chair when he heard the fire-alarm bell at the city hall.

"Mr. Saunders!" Helen came into the room. "Mr. Saunders, it's in the Mexican shanties! I can see it from my window. The whole sky is red out there."

Guy took one look at the angry smudge of smoke and fire. So far as he could tell, all three of the dilapidated wooden row-house structures were ablaze. They housed thirty or forty families of Mexicans who had come several years ago to work sugar beets. Now it was the only home they knew.

"Come along, Helen," Guy said briskly. "They'll need all the help they can get. Must be a hundred kids in that village, and with this wind, the fire's liable to spread into town."

The hopelessness of it became apparent as soon as they stepped from the car. The row-house structures were already half-consumed by the flames. The fire department made little effort to fight it. With the help of gathering townsmen, they cleared the Mexicans and their children from the danger area and went to work wetting down near-by houses. For an hour they worked in the blistering heat. And then it rained. In the confusion people stood for a moment in the downpour. It was almost as if a prayer had been answered.

Guy took several loads of women and children in his car to the church basement, and then suddenly Mr. Aims and Karen got into the front seat with him. There were two women and one child in the back seat.

"That's all," said Mr. Aims. "Every last one of them. That's what comes from having a bunch of old men running the town. Those houses should have been condemned long ago."

"It's the town's responsibility," Karen said, "and you can be sure they've got no funds for anything like this."

No one spoke until they had brought their charges to the church basement. Guy and Karen canvassed the town for extra bedding. It was almost nine before they stopped for a cup of coffee and a sandwich. There were smudges of dirt on her cheeks. But Guy saw only the tightness of her lips, the deep burning in her eyes. She seemed on the verge of tears.

"What's going to become of these people, Guy?" Karen tightened

181

her fists. "If I were a man—" She stopped suddenly and looked at him. A flush of excitement came to her face. "There's no reason why I can't do it anyway! I will!"

"What are you talking about? You will what?"

"I'm going to organize a community drive. There isn't a man down at city hall that can—"

"Wait! I won't be long." Guy hurried to the telephone booth.

"When he returned a few moments later, a mysterious little smile played on his lips. He sat down and looked at her. "Now, what were you saying?"

"I'm going to organize a community drive."

"You mentioned the city hall."

"I said there wasn't a man there who was capable of doing a real drive."

He grinned. "You're wrong, Karen."

"All right. You name him."

He hadn't planned to tell her like this. It had happened so suddenly. He hardly knew himself what had gotten into him that made him get up and rush toward the telephone booth. But he had made the call and Karen was sitting there now looking at him with a kind of vague wonder and mistrust. "Well," she said again, "go on, name him."

"I was just talking to the mayor. You are now looking at the new city attorney. We're going to put on that drive, Karen!" His words had an exultant ring, though they barely suggested the fullness within him. "We can do this together."

From the look in her eyes, he felt sure that there would be many things they would be doing together. But this seemed to him hardly the moment to say it.[4]

PRAYER:

Our Father, as we decide on our goals, help us to find in the life of Jesus the principles by which we shall live. Help us as we make the basic decisions of life to choose the path that leads to thee. Guide us into a proper sense of values. Help us to overcome fear, get rid of tension, and to build our lives upon enduring truths such as faith and honor, truth and goodness, love and service. Take away from us any desires that are not in accordance with thy will, help us to resist all forms of evil, the customs which degrade and the lower tendencies which defeat. Create within us a clean heart and a pure mind, and may we have right attitudes toward all persons and things. Take away the dimness of our sight that we may catch a vision of the heights we can reach as we strive to live more like Jesus each day. AMEN.

HYMN: "Dear Master, in Whose Life I See," or
"My Jesus, as Thou Wilt."

BENEDICTION:

The God of peace make you perfect in every good work to do his will, working in you that which is well pleasing in his sight; through Jesus Christ. AMEN.

SERVICE 26

GIVING CHRIST FIRST PLACE
(*Christmas*)

PRELUDE: "Adoration" by Borowski.

CALL TO WORSHIP:

> God wills that peace shall be on earth,
>> And holy exultation:
> Sweet Babe, I greet thy spotless birth
>> And wondrous Incarnation.
> Today in Bethlehem hear I
>> Even the lowly singing:
> With angel-words they pierce the sky;
>> All earth with joy is ringing.[1]

—John of Damascus

HYMN: "It Came upon the Midnight Clear," or
"O Come, All Ye Faithful."

SCRIPTURE:

And there were in the same country shepherds abiding in the field, keeping watch over their flock by night. And, lo, the angel of the Lord came upon them, and the glory of the Lord shone round about them: and they were sore afraid. And the angel said unto them, Fear not: for, behold, I bring you good tidings of great joy, which shall be to all people. For unto you is born this day in the city of David a Saviour, which is Christ the Lord. And this shall be a sign unto you; Ye shall find the babe wrapped in swaddling clothes, lying in a manger. And suddenly there was with the angel a multitude of the heavenly host praising God, and saying, Glory to God in the highest, and on earth peace, good will toward men.

And it came to pass, as the angels were gone away from them into heaven, the shepherds said one to another, Let us now go even unto Bethlehem, and see this thing which is come to pass, which the Lord hath made known unto us. And they came with haste, and found Mary and Joseph, and the babe lying in a manger. And when they had seen it, they made known abroad the saying which was told them concerning this child. And all they that heard it wondered at those things which were told them by the shepherds. But Mary kept all these things, and pondered them in her heart. And the shepherds returned, glorifying and praising God for all the things that they had heard and seen, as it was told unto them.[2]

POEM:

> May we not squander in reckless mirth
> The holy day of the Christ-child's birth,
>   Father, we pray Thee!
>
> Let us darken not with hate or scorn
> This time when the Prince of Peace was born,
>   Father, we pray Thee!
>
> When at bountiful tables we laugh and feast,
> Help us remember Thy poorest and least,
>   Father, we pray Thee!
>
> May lesser guests not crowd all space,
> But Christ in our lives have foremost place,
>   Father, we pray Thee! [3]

—EFFIE SMITH ELY

LEADER:

We will hear the story of the birth of the Christ-child as one of the shepherd boys remembered it.

STORY:

THE SHEPHERD BOY'S TALE

THE long, slanting rays of the morning sun were just beginning to tint the topmost tiles of Bethlehem's whitewashed towers as little Nathan ben Zerah, breathless from running and wide-eyed with wonder, pushed back the heavy gate and hurried through the shadows of the courtyard to a narrow door set deep in the wall at the rear. A mangy dog, whining sleepily, scrambled up from an angle in the wall, and slunk away into deeper darkness. Somewhere, back behind the cattle sheds, a cock crowed lustily.

Pulling vigorously at the rough leather latchstring, the boy opened the door and stepped inside. Feeling his way along the wall, through the darkness of the windowless room, he reached some stone stairs and started climbing up to the family quarters above. Picking his way as quickly as possible to the top landing, he let himself into a room through the latticed windows of which the morning light was filtering.

As he opened the door a young woman arose hastily from her straw mat in the corner, and hurried across the room to meet him. It was very evident that his arrival was a great surprise to her.

"Why, Nathan, what are you doing here at this hour of the morning?" she demanded. "Is anything wrong? Have the wolves been among the sheep? Where is your father?"

Merab, the beautiful young wife of Zerah ben Gera, had married the quiet-mannered shepherd as soon as she had come of age, and had always been inordinately proud of him. His towering strength, his great fidelity, and his deep piety marked him out as an unusual man in any company. His great love for the girl was something holy and splendid, and their joy had known no bounds when God looked with favor upon them and gave them a man-child for their first-born. Their regret that he was their only child was tempered by the fact that he was unusually brilliant, pious, and obedient.

If Merab's pride in her husband had been great before, it almost overwhelmed her that evening in the month of Sivan when Zerah returned from the Temple in Jerusalem, where he had gone to offer sacrifices, with the news that he had been appointed by the High Priest to tend the flocks, designed to be slain on the Temple altars, which grazed on the plains just east of Bethlehem. Only the devout and eminently honorable were esteemed worthy of so serious a responsibility, and even the modest Zerah ben Gera could not keep the light of pride out of his eyes as he told his beloved of the high distinction that had come to him.

It was a task that called for the rarest skill and the utmost faithfulness. The Judean hills, only a little more than a mile away, were infested with wolves, and the slightest damage to any sheep would render it unfit as an altar offering. By day the flock fed on the lush grass along

186

the gentle slope at the south side of the valley, and by night the shepherds watched over their sleeping charges with all diligence. At least one was always awake and on guard.

Little Nathan was never so happy as on those rare occasions when he was permitted to spend the night on the hillside with his father, who was master of the flock, and in company with the shepherds who assisted him. Devout men all, they regaled the lad with stories of David the shepherd king, of Ruth the Moabite, and of little Samuel who grew up in the Temple at the side of Eli the priest. Under the tutelage of these righteous and just men, chosen because of their loyalty to the ancient faith of Jehovah, the boy had developed a reverence in the presence of the animals so soon to be sacrificed for the sins of the people. He did not understand, but he felt it all.

It had been little Nathan's custom at sundown to hurry away to the fields, carrying food and drink to his father and the shepherds. Sometimes, when the chill of winter was in the air, he carried his father's great cloak wrapped around his narrow little shoulders. When morning came he returned across the plains with the empty water jug and food basket—tired, sleepy, and happily quiet. Some day, he dreamed, he would himself be a shepherd, chosen by the High Priest for this holy task.

This morning it was different. He was back at least two hours ahead of his usual time, without water jug, food basket, or great cloak, and the excitement in his eyes indicated the great emotional strain under which he labored. But, child of the East as he was, he masked his feelings under an ill-feigned calm.

"Tell me, child, what has happened. It is not yet light! And where is the jug and the basket?" Merab was struggling to be stern, but her anxiety softened her rebuke into something like a caress.

"Oh, Mother!" the boy exclaimed. And with the utterance of his first word all his poise and calm were gone; his words poured out in a torrential, at times almost incoherent, flood.

"It has been a wonderful night. No one ever has known another like it. Everyone says so. The shepherds are wild with joy. I have heard music—heavenly music—and an angel spoke to father and the shepherds. And I saw the baby! Think of it! I saw him!" He paused in his excitement, then asked, "Mother, did you hear the angels sing?"

Merab looked deep into the eyes of her son as if trying to determine whether or not he was mad. Certainly, some strange spell possessed

187

him. What did these wild words mean? Angels . . . heavenly music . . . a baby!

Dropping to her knees that she might better see her boy's face in the dim light, and seizing him sharply by the shoulders as if to shake him into his senses, she cried: "Nathan, my son, where have you been, and what does this strange talk mean? Tell me, whose baby is it? Where is he? Who saw the angels and what was the music? Where is your father?"

"It was in the fields, and we were keeping watch over the flocks, and all at once a great light burst upon us and it was as light as day, only it wasn't daylight. It was the light of a glory such as no day has ever known."

The boy was looking straight into his mother's eyes and speaking with a forthrightness that admitted of no doubt, and an excitement that gave no time for any questions.

"And suddenly, out of the glory, a voice spoke—it was the voice of an angel. I never heard an angel before, but this voice had to be one. Father and the shepherds all say so.

"And the angel said, 'I'm bringing great, good news—for you and for everybody. There is born, this day, in Bethlehem, a Saviour. He is God's chosen. God sent him. And if you will go into the city you will find him all wrapped up and lying in a cattle stall."

"Just then the sky seemed full of angels and they all sang the most beautiful music you ever heard, Mother. I don't know whether I was on the earth or in the sky, it was so beautiful. I just thought I was out of myself, it was so wonderful."

Merab herself was trembling by now. Seizing the child and holding him tight, she said: "What did they say? What were they singing about? Tell me!"

"I didn't understand it all, I was so happy," the lad said, and his voice was shaking. "But they kept singing, 'Glory to God in heaven, and peace on earth among men of good will.' I don't know how long they sang, for I seemed to lose track of things, but when I came to, they were gone and the shepherds were so amazed they couldn't say a word.

"Father was the first to speak. He seemed to forget all about the sheep, and he said: 'Let's go to Bethlehem and see what has happened. This is something the Lord has made known to us." We ran as fast as we could. We didn't know exactly where we were going—that is, none of the rest of us did, but Father seemed to know. When we came

188

to the inn he rushed in, and from the cattle sheds there streamed a light, and we hurried over.

"And, oh, Mother, I have never seen such a baby. And his mother—she seemed to be just a girl! Maybe there was a light there, but I didn't see it. But it was light, just as if light came from the baby himself. I was so frightened and so glad that I could not speak. Everybody from the inn was there—the rich grandees, and soldiers, and merchants, and travelers. Father crowded in ahead of a big rough soldier with a heavy sword, and when he saw the baby he fell down on his knees and worshiped.

"And when we got outside, Father told all the people—wise and rich—about what we had seen in the fields, and they were so astounded they couldn't seem to get things straight, and Father had to tell it over and over. Some of them even asked me, Nathan, if I had seen it too, and I told them that I had."

Merab touched her son's tousled hair, and dreamily she murmured, "Tell me, son, about the baby's mother."

At that Nathan's voice sank to almost a whisper. "Mother," he whispered into her ear, "she was very young—and very, very beautiful. And a light shone out of her eyes like the stars. But she never said a word. She just listened—and smiled—and looked at her baby. But she was thinking!"

Now Merab was very intent. "What was her name, did you hear?" she asked.

"Someone said her husband called her Mary."

Mother and son turned their faces toward the high, latticed window, and the early morning light streamed in upon them.

"And Mother," the boy said, finally, "there was a soldier there with his big sword and Roman cloak. He seemed so big and rough. But there was kindness in his face, and his voice was tender when he spoke. He seemed to be thinking.

"When we got outside, and Father told him about the angels and the song and the words about 'men of good will,' the soldier said, in a strange sort of voice, 'Maybe I am mad, but somehow I feel that that child may save us all.'

"Mother! I know! I'm just a boy. But I believe God was there at the manger. I believe I have seen him."

The eyes of Merab were moist and tender as she ecstatically folded her trembling child to her heart.[4]

189

POEM:

> Let not our hearts be busy inns,
>   That have no room for Thee,
> But cradles for the living Christ
>   And his Nativity.
>
> Still driven by a thousand cares
>   The pilgrims come and go;
> The hurried caravans press on;
>   The inns are crowded so!
>
> .   .   .   .
>
> Here are the rich and busy ones,
>   With things that must be sold,
> No room for simple things within
>   This hostelry of gold.
>
> Yet hunger dwells within these walls,
>   These shining walls and bright,
> And blindness groping here and there
>   Without a ray of light.
>
> Oh, lest we starve or lest we die
>   In our stupidity,
> O come, Thou Child, within and share
>   Our hospitality.
>
> Let not our hearts be busy inns,
>   That have no room for Thee,
> But cradles for the living Christ
>   And His Nativity.[5]

—RALPH S. CUSHMAN

PRAYER:

Father in heaven, giver of light in thine Eternal Son, we adore thee!

O thou, who long ago didst prove thy covenant with us—and from eternity didst come to us in tenderness and in compassion—we give thee thanks for the continuing signs of thy gracious presence with us; for the daily reminders of thy redeeming deeds; for the return of Christmas; for the gift of thyself.

Thou, who in the long ago didst come to the shepherds and all who were humble, come to us now that we may be taught humility the shepherds knew—and then, having been taught, may be renewed in the faith, the hope, and the love of the Christmas everlasting. . . .

Thou, who in the long ago didst take up our life in the humble guise of human existence, come to us again amid the scenes of family and friendship we know. . . . Bless our homes. Inspire them to sing thy praises and to reflect thy love and light into all the dark places of earth.

Thou, who didst long ago teach us the things that belong to thy peace, so come to us now, that our hearts may be freed from sin; our nation redeemed from evil and injustice; and our world led by thy wonderful counsels into a righteous peace. Amen.[6]

Hymn: "As with Gladness Men of Old," or
"Silent Night, Holy Night."

Benediction:

May love and peace which came into the world through the Christ child remain with us forever. Amen.

SERVICE 27

BRINGING OUR GIFTS
(*Christmas*)

PRELUDE: Hymn tune *"Adeste Fideles."*

CALL TO WORSHIP:

> How silently, how silently
> The wondrous gift is given!
> So God imparts to human hearts
> The blessing of his heaven.
> No ear may hear his coming,
> But in this world of sin,
> Where meek souls will receive him still
> The dear Christ enters in.[1]

—PHILLIPS BROOKS

HYMN: "The First Noel," or
"The Kings of the East Are Riding."

SCRIPTURE:

Now when Jesus was born in Bethlehem of Judea in the days of Herod the king, behold, there came wise men from the east to Jerusalem, saying, Where is he that is born King of the Jews? for we have seen his star in the east and are come to worship him. When Herod the king had heard these things, he was troubled, and all Jerusalem with him. And when he had gathered all the chief priests and scribes of the people together, he demanded of them where Christ should be born. And they said unto him, In Bethlehem of Judea: for thus it is written by the prophet, And thou Bethlehem, in the land of Juda, art not the least among the princes of Juda: for out of thee shall come a Governor, that shall rule my people Israel. Then Herod, when he had privily called the wise men, inquired of them diligently what time the star appeared. And he sent them to Bethlehem, and said, Go and search diligently for the young child; and when ye have found him, bring me word again, that I may come and worship him also. When they had heard the king, they departed; and lo, the star, which they saw in the east, went before them, till it came and stood over where the young child was. When they saw the star, they rejoiced with exceeding great joy.

And when they were come into the house, they saw the young child with Mary his mother, and fell down, and worshipped him: and when they had opened their treasures, they presented unto him gifts; gold, and frankincense, and myrrh. And being warned of God in a dream that they should not return to Herod, they departed into their own country another way.[2]

POEM:

> There is a hush that comes on Christmas Eve—
> Life's hurry and its stress grow far away;
> And something in the silence seems to weave
> A mood akin to sadness, yet we say
> A "Merry Christmas" to the friends we meet,
> And all the while we feel that mystic spell,
> As if the Christ Child came on noiseless feet,
> With something old, yet ever new, to tell—
> The eyes grow misty, yet they shed no tear,
> And those that we have lost, somehow seem near.[3]
>
> —MARGARET E. BRUNER

LEADER:

We will hear the story of the wise men written by Lew Wallace when he was governor of New Mexico Territory:

STORY:

THE VISIT OF THE WISE MEN

THE eleventh day after the birth of the Christ-child in the cave in Bethlehem, three wise men approached Jerusalem by the road from Shechem. The approach to Jerusalem from the North is across a plain which dips southward, leaving the Damascus Gate in a vale or hollow. This road is narrow, but deeply cut by long use. On either side are olive-groves, which must, in luxurious growth, have been beautiful especially to the travellers fresh from the wastes of the desert. On thi road the three wise men stopped before a party in front of the Tombs

"Good people," said Balthasar, "is not Jerusalem close by?"

"Yes," answered a woman into whose arms a child had shrunk. "I the trees on yon swell were a little lower you could see the towers o the market-place."

Balthasar gave the Greek and Hindoo a look, and then asked "Where is he that is born King of the Jews?"

The women gazed at each other without reply.

"Have you not heard of him?"

"No."

"Well, tell everybody that we have seen his star in the East, and ar come to worship him." Whereupon the three wise men rode on. . . They came at length to a tower of great height and strength overlook ing the Damascus Gate. A Roman guard kept the passage-way.

"I give you peace," the Egyptian said in a clear voice. . . . "We hav come great distances in search of one who is born King of the Jews Can you tell us where he is?"

The soldier raised the visor of his helmet, and called loudly. Fron an apartment at the right of the passage an officer appeared. "Wha would you?" he asked of Balthasar, speaking in the idiom of th city.

Balthasar answered in the same idiom: "Where is he that is bor King of the Jews?"

"Herod?" asked the officer confounded.

"Herod's kingship is from Caesar," answered Balthasar, "not Herod.

"There is no other King of the Jews," answered the officer.

"But we have seen the star of him whom we seek, and have com to worship him."

The Roman officer was clearly perplexed. "Go farther," he sai at last. "Go farther. I am not a Jew. Carry the question to the Doctor in the Temple or to Hannas, the priest, or, better still, to Herod him self. If there is another King of the Jews, he will find him." There upon he made way for the strangers and they passed through the gate and on into the city in quest of information as to the place where thi new-born King of the Jews might be.

Later that evening, about the beginning of the first watch, there wa an assemblage in the palace on Mount Zion, of probably fifty people who never came together except by order of Herod, and then only when he had demanded to know some one or more of the deepe mysteries of Jewish law and history. This company sat upon the divan after the style of Orientals, in costume singularly uniform, except as to color. They were mostly men advanced in years. Their demeanor was grave, dignified, even patriarchal. In brief their session was that of the Sanhedrin. On the table before them lay out-spread a scroll or volume of parchment inscribed in Hebrew characters; and behind the leader of the Sanhedrin, stood a page richly habited.

Without moving, Hillel, the venerable, called the page: "Hist! Go tell the King we are ready to give him answer." The page hurried away.

After a time two officers entered and stopped, one at each side of the door: after them slowly followed a most striking personage—an old man clad in a purple robe bordered with scarlet and girt to his waist by a band of gold linked so fine that it was pliable as leather. He walked with halting step, leaning heavily on his staff. Not until he reached the opening of the divan did he pause or look up from the floor; then, as for the first time conscious of the company, and roused by their presence, he raised himself and looked haughtily round, like one startled and searching for an enemy—so dark, suspicious and threatening was his glance.

Such was Herod the Great—a body broken by disease, a conscience seared with crimes, a mind magnificently capable, a soul fit for brotherhood with the Caesars; but guarding his throne with a jealousy never so vigilant, a power never so despotic, and a cruelty never so inexorable. Herod moved on until at the tripod opposite the venerable Hillel, who met his cold glance with an inclination of the head and a slight lifting of his hands.

"The answer!" snarled the King with imperious brevity—"The Answer! Where is this King of the Jews to be born?"

Hillel glanced at the parchment on the tripod; and pointing with a tremulous finger, said: "In Bethlehem of Judea, for thus it is written by the prophet, 'And thou, Bethlehem in the land of Judea, art not least among the princes of Judah; for out of thee shall come a governor that shall rule my people Israel.'"

Herod's face was troubled; and his eyes fell upon the parchment while he thought. Those who beheld him scarcely breathed; they spoke not, nor did he. At length he turned about and left the chamber.

Later that evening the wise men were summoned by the King's

messenger, who said: "I bring you a message from Herod, the King, which will not be put off."

The wise men arose, put on their sandals, girt their mantles about them and followed the messenger into the presence of Herod. Suddenly the guide halted, and pointing through an open door said to them, "Enter, the King is there. . . ."

Herod, sitting upon the throne to receive them, clad as when at conference with the doctors and lawyers, claimed all their minds.

"Who are you? and whence do you come?" he asked. "Let each speak for himself."

In turn they gave him account referring simply to the cities and lands of their birth, and the routes by which they came to Jerusalem. Somewhat disappointed Herod asked them directly: "What was the question you put to the officer at the Gate?"

Balthasar answered: "We asked him, Where is he that is born King of the Jews?"

"Is there another King of the Jews," asked Herod, trying to trap them.

"There is one newly born," answered another of the wise men.

"Tell me all you know about this newly-born King, and I will join you in the search for him. But tell me first how, so widely separated by seas and deserts, you all came to hear of him?"

Balthasar raised himself erect, and said, solemnly: "There is an Almighty God. He bade us come hither, promising that we should find the Redeemer of the World; that we should see him and worship him, and bear witness that he was come; and, as a sign, we were each given to see a Star. His Spirit stayed with us, O King; his Spirit is with us now!"

The monarch touched a bell, and an attendant appeared. "Bring the gift," said the King. The attendant went out, but in a little while returned and, kneeling before the guests, gave to each one an outer robe or mantle of scarlet and blue, and a girdle of gold. They acknowledged the honors with Eastern prostrations.

"A word further," said Herod, when the ceremony was ended. "To the officer of the Gate, and but now to me, you spoke of seeing a star in the East. . . ."

"What time did it appear?"

"When we were bidden to come hither."

Herod arose, signifying the audience was over. Then stepping from the throne toward them, said, with all graciousness:

196

"O illustrious men, you are indeed the heralds of the Christ just born. Know that I have this night consulted with the wisest in things Jewish, and they say with one voice that he should be born in Bethlehem of Judea. I say unto you, go thither; go and search diligently for the young child, and when you have found him bring me word again, that I may come and worship him. To your going there shall be no let or hindrance. Peace be unto you. . . ."

Directly the guide came and led them back to the portal Gate. Then the Greek said impulsively, "Let us go to Bethlehem, O brethren, as the King has advised."

They gave gifts to the steward . . . and departed. And as they came out of Hinnom, lo! the star appeared, perfect as any in the heavens, but low down and moving slowly before them. And they folded their hands reverently and exclaimed with exceeding great joy: "God is with us! God is with us!" And they followed the star to Bethlehem and until it came and stood over where the young child lay.

As the strangers neared the house, the star rose, and when they were at the door, it was high up overhead; and when they entered, it went out lost to sight. The apartment was lighted by a lantern enough to enable the wise men to find the mother and the child awake in her lap.

"Is this child thine?" asked Balthasar of Mary.

And she who had kept all the things in the least affecting the little one, and pondered them in her heart, held it up to the light, saying: "He is my Son!"

And they fell down and worshipped Him.

In a little while they arose and, returning to their camels, they brought gifts of gold, frankincense, and myrrh and laid them down before the child, abating nothing of their worshipful speeches. Then, their search completed, and being warned of God in a dream, they departed by another route to their homes in distant lands, having borne witness that this Child was the Christ, sent of God for the redemption of all nations.[4]

PRAYER:

Our Father, grant that our approach to Christmas may be a heart-searching time for each of us. We confess our sins and beg thy forgiveness. May the spirit of Christ be born anew in our lives that they may radiate good will and peace toward all people. We commit to thee all our hopes and plans for this holiday season, asking thy blessing on all our activities. Enter into our lives, make us living temples of thine, and grant us strength to follow faithfully in the footsteps of thy Son our Lord. AMEN.

HYMN: "Silent Night, Holy Night," or
    "Angels, from the Realms of Glory."

BENEDICTION:

May we go from this service strengthened in every good purpose to live according to God's will. AMEN.

SERVICE 28

OBSERVING EASTER

PRELUDE: "The Palms" by Faure.

CALL TO WORSHIP:

      Oh, let me know
The power of thy resurrection!
      Oh, let me show
Thy risen life in clear reflection!
      Oh, let me soar
Where thou, my Saviour Christ, art gone before!
      In mind and heart
Let me dwell always, only, where thou art.

      Oh, let me give
Out of the gifts thou freely givest;
      Oh, let me live
With life abundantly because thou livest;
      Oh, make me shine!
In darkest places, for thy light is mine,
      Oh, let me be
A faithful witness for thy truth and thee.
            —FRANCES RIDLEY HAVERGAL

HYMN: "Joyful, Joyful, We Adore Thee," or
      "Come, Ye Faithful, Raise the Strain."

SCRIPTURE:

    And the angel answered and said unto the women, Fear not ye: for I know that ye seek Jesus, which was crucified. He is not here: for he is risen, as he said. Come, see the place where the Lord lay. And go quickly, and tell his disciples that he is risen from the dead; and, behold, he goeth before you into Galilee; there shall ye see him: lo, I have told you. And they departed quickly from the sepulcher with fear and great joy; and did run to bring his disciples word.[1]

LEADER:

What does Easter mean to each of us? Does it mean getting rid of our doubts and fears, finding new hope and faith, and at last achieving victory and newness of life? Is it a time when we check up on ourselves, set new goals, and rededicate ourselves to Christ's way of life and to service in the church?

INVOCATION:

Forgive us, O Lord, for the times when we have doubted thy word and have lacked faith to follow thee; when we have been bound down by fears and have lacked courage to believe thy promises. We are sorry for the times when we have been too occupied to hear thy voice, or to follow thy leadership. Forgive us for the times when we have held back the progress of thy kingdom. Attune our ears to hear thy voice, strengthen us when our faith is weak, and make us eager to follow thy will. In Christ's name. AMEN.

POEM:

> He stood at the tomb's black entrance
> Where the stone was rolled away.
> The air was sweet to His nostrils;
> The light of early day
> Flushed His pale cheeks faintly.
> His luminous shadowed eyes
> Held dark wonder calmly
> In depths grown sorrow-wise.
>
> A cock crew in the distance.
> The Man stepped slowly down
> The grassy slope of the Garden.
> From an olive tree a brown
> Songster praised the morning;
> Again the cock crew—twice.
> Pierced hands drew close the mantle
> White and scented with spice.

OBSERVING EASTER

The field flowers, bright and dewy,
Waved banners in the grass.
The spring world, sun-awakened,
Lay shimmering as glass.
He heard a woman weeping
For One she counted dead.
Life burned like fire within Him.
"Why weepest thou?" He said.[2]

—ESTHER BALDWIN YORK

STORY:

THE EMPTY TOMB

AS THEY climbed the slope to the sepulcher, the four women went, in unspoken accord, more slowly. The journey through Jerusalem's narrow and deserted streets had been black and desolate beyond the telling. They had reached the outskirts of the city when a sharp earthquake occurred and the sky over head took on a queer unfamiliar color. They had huddled together for long frightened moments, rolling eyes upward at the great heaped clouds and feeling the road tremble as if with palsy. Salome had suggested turning back, but Mary Magdalene would have none of it. With resolution now she led the way up the twisting path to the garden of Joseph of Arimathea, a dark silent figure in the gloom. Salome and Mary, the mother of James, wept and moaned a little as they mounted the incline, their grief steady and resigned. All rebellion had gone out of them when they had watched with Jesus' mother at the foot of the cross. Only the sorrow, deep and beyond human stemming, remained.

Joanna, like Mary Magdalene, could not weep. A great heaviness was upon her, the weight of spirit and of body and of the night. Her thoughts were slow as words thickly spoken in alien tongue. Her feet dragged as if shackled. The jars of spices which she bore were an almost intolerable burden. She could go no farther. She could not. Yet—she must. She, with those faithful others, must minister to the broken body of her Master.

"But who will roll us away the stone from before the sepulcher?" wailed Salome in sudden anxiety.

"Perhaps the guards will help us when they see we mean no trouble," said Mary, the mother of James.

Joanna thought of the size of the boulder. "It will take at least three score."

Only Mary Magdalene said nothing. Rounding a group of thick-leaved trees, they stopped. There were lights in the garden ahead, and much confusion. Nay, there was one light, a strange radiance from the sepulcher. Soldiers were running toward them, away from the tomb. Others stood huddled together in groups. Some knelt with faces covered, sobbing like children.

Joanna was stricken with consternation. The stone was rolled away from the cave's mouth. Father in heaven, what had happened? She started forward with her companions. No voice challenged them. None of the guards made any attempt to halt them.

Mary Magdalene was first at the sepulcher. Joanna followed her, stooping down to look into the cavern. She heard Mary Magdalene's quick intake of breath, and then she herself felt the quickening of her startled heart. The body of Jesus was not there!

The jar of sweet ointment fell from Joanna's nerveless hands with a crash. She looked down blindly at the shattered pieces on the cave's floor, and fragrance drifted up to her slowly. Her throat was painfully tight. Her two fists ached. Was it not enough that they had crucified him? Could they not let the dead rest in peace?

Beside her, she heard Salome breathe: "Behold!"

She lifted her head and through eyes blurred with moisture saw, in the dimness of the tomb, two white figures, one at the head and one at the foot, where the body of Jesus had lain.

For the shaking of her lips, Joanna could utter no sound. Nor could she look longer upon the figures, for the strange glistening of their raiment.

There came a voice from the sepulcher, and it was like no voice which Joanna had ever heard.

"Fear not: for I know you seek Jesus which was crucified. He is not here, for he is risen, as he said. Go quickly and tell his disciples that he goes before you into Galilee. There shall you see him. Lo, I have told you."

When Joanna came to herself she was with Salome and Mary the mother of James hastening along the road back to Jerusalem. How or when she had left the sepulcher, she knew not. Only one thing she knew. They must find Peter and John and the others. They must tell them of the astounding events.

Salome said suddenly: "But—but where is Mary Magdalene?"

"Is she not with us?" asked Joanna. She turned her head, half expecting to see a figure hurrying to overtake them. But there was nought upon that road but the pale dawn.

Mary Magdalene could not leave. She stood without at the sepulcher and the tears she could not shed before, fell now. She was frightened, bewildered and, above everything, desolate. In her agony, she knew not what to think. Were those gleaming figures in the sepulcher part of a dream or vision, or were they representatives of evil men who had robbed the tomb of the body of her beloved master? She walked blindly in the garden, not able to see her way because of tears. She stumbled into bushes. Branches caught at her garments, and she bruised her sandaled feet on sharp, upthrusting stones. Dimly, she was aware of a man approaching and turned a little away from him, bowing her face in her hands.

"Woman," said the stranger, "why do you weep?"

She did not answer. Why did she weep? There was reason in plenty. None, she moaned inwardly, had ever known such cause for grief. She had been thrust from a height into a pit where no light came and out of which she could never climb.

"Whom do you seek?"

The man's voice seemed to her far away, and she wished that he would go away and leave her with her sorrow. Yet, he might know something of what had occurred here. Perhaps he was the gardener.

"Sir," she said pleadingly, "if you have borne him hence, tell me where you have laid him, and I will take him away."

"Mary!"

That voice! That voice of infinite compassion. That tone of tender rebuke. Father in heaven, who was it spoke thus to her—who? She turned, shaking from head to foot, and blinked the tears from her eyes.

"Rabboni!"

It was he! It was her Master! It was Jesus of Nazareth. Joy crowded into her heart. There was room for nought else. She flung herself forward to touch him, to hold him. . . .

Jesus said to her: "Touch me not, for I am not yet ascended to my Father: but go to my brethren, and say to them that I ascend to my Father and your Father; and to my God and your God."

Mary Magdalene sank to her knees in the dew-wet grass, and her prayer had no words, for it needed none. . . . When she lifted her head, Jesus had disappeared. Nevertheless, she doubted not that she had indeed seen him, and returned to Jerusalem with rejoicing to seek out the disciples.[3]

POEM:

>What shall we be like when
>We cast this earthly body and attain
>To immortality?
>What shall we be like then?
>Ah, who shall say
>What vast expansions shall be ours that day?
>What transformations of this house of clay
>To fit the heavenly mansions and the light of day?
>Ah, who shall say?
>
>But this we know. . . .
>We drop a seed into the ground,
>A tiny, shapeless thing, shrivelled and dry,
>And, in the fullness of its time, is seen
>A form of peerless beauty, robed and crowned
>Beyond the pride of any earthly queen,
>Instinct with loveliness, and sweet and rare
>The perfect emblem of its Maker's care.
>
>This from a shrivelled seed? . . .
>Then may man hope indeed!
>
>For a man is but the seed of what he shall be,
>When, in the fullness of his perfecting,
>He drops the husk and cleaves the upward way,
>Through earth's retardings and the clinging clay
>Into the sunshine of God's perfect day.
>No fetters then! No bonds of time or space!
>But powers as ample as the boundless grace
>That suffered man, and death, and yet, in tenderness,
>Set wide the door and passed Himself before . . .
>As He had promised . . . to prepare a place.
>
>Yea, we may hope!
>For we are seeds,
>Dropped into earth for heavenly blossoming.

Perchance, when comes the time of harvesting,
His loving care
May find some use for even a humble tare.

We know not what we shall be . . . only this . . .
That we shall be like Him . . . as He is.[4]

—John Oxenham

PRAYER:

Our Father, who through the resurrection of thy Son from death hath delivered us from the power of sin and darkness, and hath given us life eternal, grant unto us a sense of victory, that we too shall not be bound by death. Make us aware of thy presence in our lives, that through the help coming from thee, we may conquer evil and walk daily in newness of life. Help us to begin living now the quality of life which is worthy to endure throughout eternity. Make us perfect in every good thing to do thy will, working in us that which is well pleasing in thy sight, through Jesus Christ. AMEN.

HYMN: "Jesus Christ Is Risen Today," or
"Sing, Men and Angels, Sing."

BENEDICTION:

Now unto him that is able to keep you from falling, and to present you faultless before the presence of his glory with exceeding joy, to the only wise God our Saviour, be glory and majesty, dominion and power, both now and ever. AMEN.

HONORING OUR MOTHERS
(*Mother's Day*)

PRELUDE: "Ave Maria" by Bach-Gounod.

CALL TO WORSHIP:

> We search the world for truth. We cull
> The good, the true, the beautiful,
> From graven stone and written scroll,
> And all old flower-fields of the soul;
> And, weary seekers of the best,
> We come back laden from our quest,
> To find that all the sages said
> Is in the Book our mothers read.[1]
>
> —JOHN GREENLEAF WHITTIER

INVOCATION:

O Lord, we thank thee for our mothers, for their watchful care over us, for their love for us expressed in so many ways, for their teaching and guidance, and for the ideals which they have had for us. May we demand of ourselves the very best in thought and action, so that we may make real the dreams which they have had for us. In Christ's name. AMEN.

SCRIPTURE:

> Who can find a virtuous woman?
>   for her price is far above rubies.
> The heart of her husband doth safely trust in her,
>   so that he shall have no need of spoil.
> She will do him good and not evil
>   all the days of her life.
> She seeketh wool, and flax,

and worketh willingly with her hands. . . .
Strength and honor are her clothing;
  and she shall rejoice in time to come.
She openeth her mouth with wisdom;
  and in her tongue is the law of kindness.
She looketh well to the ways of her household,
  and eateth not the bread of idleness.
Her children arise up, and call her blessed;
  her husband also, and he praiseth her.
Many daughters have done virtuously,
  but thou excellest them all.
Favor is deceitful, and beauty is vain:
  but a woman that feareth the Lord,
  she shall be praised.
Give her of the fruit of her hands;
  and let her own works praise her in the gates.[2]

HYMN: "O Happy Home," or
  "Happy the Home when God Is There."

LEADER:

Let us meditate on the sayings of great men concerning mother:
"A man never sees all that his mother has been to him till it's too
late to let her know that he sees it."—WILLIAM DEAN HOWELLS.
"Unhappy is the man for whom his own mother has not made all
other mothers venerable.—JOHANN P. F. RICHTER.
"The love of a mother is never exhausted, it never changes, it never
tires. A father may turn his back on his child, brothers and sisters become inveterate enemies. But a mother's love endures through all; in
good repute, in bad repute, in the face of the world's condemnation, a
mother still loves on, and still hopes that her child may turn from
his evil ways and repent; she can never be brought to think him unworthy.—WASHINGTON IRVING.

POEM:

Lord who ordainst for mankind
  Benignant toils and tender cares,
We thank thee for the ties that bind
  The mother to the child she bears.

We thank thee for the hopes that rise
    Within her heart, as, day by day,
The dawning soul, from those young eyes,
    Looks with a clearer, steadier ray.

. . . .

Such thanks the blessed Mary gave
    When from her lap the Holy Child,
Sent from on high to seek and save
    The lost of earth, looked up and smiled.

All-Gracious! grant to those who bear
    A mother's charge, the strength and light
To guide the feet that own their care
    In ways of Love and Truth and Right.[3]
        —WILLIAM CULLEN BRYANT

STORY:

THE MOTHER OF BOOKER T. WASHINGTON

THE mother of Booker T. Washington was a slave and without education. She was unable to tell her boy the date of his birth, in fact she was not sure whether he was born in 1858 or 1859. Of his father the boy knew nothing; the only parent that he knew was the patient, overworked mother, whose chief ambition in life was to see that her children had a happier time than she had known.

The mother was the plantation cook. All the cooking for the whites and the slaves had to be done over an open fireplace, mostly in pots and skillets. Even as a small boy Booker Washington knew that his mother worked harder than any woman ought to work. From early morning till night she toiled, and could give her children attention only when her heavy day's work was over. At this time there came to Booker an ambition—one which spurred him on for many years—it was to earn sufficient money to make his mother comfortable.

Often Booker saw and overheard his mother praying. Many times he heard her pray for freedom, and for some time he did not understand what she meant. Later, a great moment in his life came, when, with his brother, sister, and mother, together with many other slaves, he heard a proclamation read, and his mother explained to him that they were no longer slaves; they were free.

Although quite illiterate herself, Booker's mother was anxious that he should learn to read and write. Somehow she got a copy of Webster's spelling book; the first book he had ever had in his hands, and he almost devoured it. At that time not a single Negro that he knew could read, and he was too timid to ask any white person to give him lessons. In his ambition to secure an education it was his mother who always encouraged him and urged him on. In later life Booker said: "My dear mother had a large fund of good, hard common sense which enabled her to meet and master every situation. If I have done anything in life worthy of attention, I feel sure that I inherited the disposition from my mother."

Freedom did not bring immediate prosperity to the Negroes by any means. After a terrific struggle, Booker's mother managed to send him to school, at least for some time daily. He had to work both before and after school, and there were difficulties of which he had not thought. All the other children were well dressed and this made Booker uncomfortable. When he told his trouble to his mother, she tried to find some way out of the difficulty. To make a cap for him, she sewed two pieces of homespun together, and her boy was the proud possessor of a homemade cap. When he became a man he said: "I have owned many hats and caps in my life, but never one of which I have felt so proud as of that cap made of two pieces of homespun cloth, sewed together by my mother."

Encouraged by his mother, Booker made steady progress at school. Then he heard about a school for Negroes where there were opportunities for work, so that pupils could pay part of their board while they were in attendance. By strict economy he managed to save enough money to reach this school, which was known as Hampton Normal and Agricultural Institute. Here he remained for three years, and made such progress that when his course was completed he was given a position on the staff as a teacher. Just before this appointment came he paid a visit to his people at Malden, West Virginia. He had not been home for two years, and his mother rejoiced greatly to notice his development in every way. He spoke before the church and Sunday school and his mother's pride in him was almost pathetic.

During this vacation Brooker's mother was taken ill and died. In his struggle to gain an education he had overcome many obstacles. Whenever he felt discouraged, the thought that some day he would be able to take care of his mother spurred him on. Now, when his ambition was about to be realized, she was taken from him. It was the saddest moment of his life.

Many honors came to Booker T. Washington in later life. He became the friend of many distinguished people, among them president Grover Cleveland. On several occasions he was invited to be a guest at the White House. He was welcomed by Queen Victoria and other great personages of Great Britain. He received the degree of Master of Arts from Harvard University, and was recognized as the foremost educator of his people. Could his mother have looked into the future and seen her son honored and respected throughout the entire world, how happy it would have made her! But all who study the career of this great man recognize how much he owed to his mother.[4]

POEM:

One who has known through childhood days and youth
    A mother who has been a guide and friend,
Will have a firm foundation, strong as truth
    On which to build, and yet not comprehend
In early years the greatness of its scope;
    And still, this guiding power will ever be
A staff of courage when the heart would grope—
    A beacon light glimpsed from a stormy sea.

And so when one looks back in after years,
    And thinks upon the many kindly deeds
True mothers do, dispelling hurts and fears,
    Administering to childish wants and needs,—
      The care bestowed will leave its pure impress,
      And fill the heart with grateful tenderness.[5]

—MARGARET E. BRUNER

PRAYER:

Our God, we thank Thee for the mothers of this and every generation. In their love and fidelity we see that which on earth is closest to Thy nature.

As each of us turns in thought to his own mother, may we be loyal to the best she taught us. We thank Thee that in her we have the gift of God.

Be with all mothers. Help them to rear the children entrusted to them in health of body, mind, and soul. Show them how to open the eyes of the young to the rich beauties of Thy world; the treasures hid in great books; the richness of soul in all Thy people of whatever color, race, or nation. May their children, looking to them, see Thee and be led to follow Thee.

Grant thy special blessing to those on whom the burdens of our time rest most heavily. We pray Thee for anxious mothers whose sons are at war or suffering for conscience' sake, for destitute mothers whose homes have been shattered by war, for refugee mothers who have no homes. We pray Thee for those among the poor and the downtrodden of the earth who, because of the sin of our society, must live every day in fear and in want. Forgive us that we are ever complacent before these evils, and stir in us the determination that these things shall no longer be.

Hasten the day, O Lord, when all families in Thy great family shall dwell together in peace and security upon earth. We ask it in Christ's name. AMEN.[6]

HYMN: "O Perfect Love," or
          "O Love Divine and Golden."

BENEDICTION:
May thy love and peace be with us in all our homes evermore. AMEN.

SERVICE 30

DECIDING FOR CHRIST
(*Decision Day*)

PRELUDE: "Sonatina in F" by Clementi.

CALL TO WORSHIP:

Let us search and try our ways, and turn again to the Lord.
And ye shall seek me, and find me, when ye shall search for me with all your heart.

HYMN: "Draw Thou My Soul," or
" 'Mid All the Traffic of the Ways."

SCRIPTURE:

Ho, every one that thirsteth, come ye to the waters, and he that hath no money; come ye, buy, and eat; yea, come, buy wine and milk without money and without price. Wherefore do ye spend money for that which is not bread? and your labor for that which satisfieth not? hearken diligently unto me, and eat ye that which is good, and let your soul delight itself in fatness. Incline your ear, and come unto me: hear, and your soul shall live: and I will make an everlasting covenant with you. . . . Seek ye the Lord while he may be found, call ye upon him while he is near: let the wicked forsake his way, and the unrighteous man his thoughts: and let him return unto the Lord, and he will have mercy upon him; and to our God, for he will abundantly pardon. For my thoughts are not your thoughts, neither are your ways my ways, saith the Lord. For as the heavens are higher than the earth, so are my ways higher than your ways, and my thoughts than your thoughts. . . . But seek ye first the kingdom of God, and his righteousness; and all these things shall be added unto you.[1]

DECIDING FOR CHRIST

INVOCATION:

O Lord, whose way is perfect; help us, we pray thee, always to trust in thy goodness, that walking with thee and following thee in all simplicity, we may possess quiet and contented minds, and may cast all our care on thee, for thou carest for us. AMEN.[2]

POEM:

> Along the roadway of my days,
> I need a song to sing:
> A song of life, a song of joy,
> A melody to ring
> Triumphant with a mighty theme.
> Earth's harmonies go wrong.
> God stirs new music in my soul
> And gives to me that song
>
> Deep in the darkness of my nights,
> I need a star to shine—
> A ray of hope, a light to guide
> These stumbling feet of mine,
> Something to make my eyes look up
> When joy seems faint and far.
> God sets a beacon in the dark
> And gives to me a star.
>
> Among the luring lanes of sin,
> I need a Saviour's love—
> A Hand to help, a Voice to speak,
> A Friendship from above.
> I need One glad to die for me
> To bear my guilt and shame.
> God has a Saviour for my soul
> And Jesus is His name.[3]

—ESTHER BALDWIN YORK

STORY:

THE UPPER ROOM

MARY had come the two miles from Bethany to assist in serving supper to Jesus and his disciples who had gathered in the upper room

213

of the house of young Mark and his mother. Mary Magdalene and the mother of Mark looked up in surprise as she burst into the kitchen.

"Mary, is something wrong?" Mark's mother stopped stirring the young herbs she was boiling.

Mary looked about her. The familiar scene. The smell of warm food. Nothing different. Nothing to fear.

She laughed unsteadily, "I was afraid I might be too late!"

The face of Mark's mother crinkled into a relieved smile. "Too late? Nay, you are come in good season. My son has not yet returned with the wine he was sent to buy."

"But—Jesus—is he—?"

"He and the disciples are all gathered upstairs," said Mary Magdalene. She bent down to look into the oven. Mary crossed to stand beside her, glad of the fire's warmth, as if somehow it might take from her a thin foreboding, like a physical chill, which would not leave her.

She looked up at the sound of the anxious voice of the mother of Mark. Jesus had come quietly down into the kitchen.

"Master! Is something lacking?"

"I would have a basin of water," he said. "My disciples are weary and their feet dusty."

"I will wash them," said Mary of Bethany eagerly.

Jesus smiled slightly, shook his head. "Nay, Mary, tonight that is my task."

She started to protest but could not speak against the gentle determination in his manner. Yet she rebelled at the thought of Jesus ministering to those who rightfully should have ministered unto him in such a menial task.

She returned to the kitchen to find John Mark entering with a keg of wine, which she took and carried upstairs. It was heavy, but she took no thought of that. Little enough burden to bear for Jesus, who bore so much for others. Jesus who had raised Lazarus, her beloved brother from the tomb with sure authority, divine authority. This had been to her the final proof that he was more than a righteous mortal—he was, as he said, the Son of God. The Messiah!

In the upper room Jesus was indeed washing the disciples' feet. They were permitting it. Bewilderment, even consternation, sat on every face—but, yea—they were permitting it.

Jesus finished with the drying of the feet of Judas Iscariot, whose face alone was expressionless, and turned to Peter who was next.

Peter, unable to control himself, said violently: "Master, do you wash my feet?"

Jesus paused, looking at him quietly. "What I do you do not now understand. But you will hereafter."

Peter pressed his lips together and said righteously: "You shall never wash my feet." He looked about at the others rebelliously, critically.

Jesus' answer was swift. "If I wash you not, you have no part with me."

On Peter's face the inner struggle was written in line and muscle. At last he said humbly: "Lord, not my feet only, but also my hands and my head."

Pondering deeply, Mary of Bethany went down the stairs. She told Mary Magdalene what she had seen. The latter nodded but said nothing.

The bread and herbs were now ready, and Mary and young Mark took them upstairs. The washing of the feet was finished, and all were seated around the long table. Jesus was in the center with John on his right hand and James on his left. Judas Iscariot sat next to James. Peter had chosen to sit on the end seat at the left.

As Mary picked up the water jug and basin to take them down to the kitchen, Jesus was speaking gravely to the disciples: "If I, then, your Lord and Master, have washed your feet; you also ought to wash one another's feet. For I have given you an example, that you should do as I have done to you."

Mary went downstairs again, grateful that she had heard these words, and came back shortly with vinegar for the herbs. This time, she became aware of a change in Jesus' expression and tone.

"He who eats bread with me has lifted up his heel against me," he said sorrowfully.

Mary stood still. She was halfway to the stairs, but could not take a step, nor lift her hand. It was as if all the evil, all the revenge, the lust, the greed of Jerusalem had settled like a great brooding shadow upon this upper room. Yet it was a feeling that came to her, as before in the streets, rather than the words he spoke. For often he spoke in terms not easy to comprehend, and what he meant exactly by these words, no one could tell with certainty.

The disciples looked around the table at one another, and back at Jesus, uneasily.

Jesus said: "I tell you this before it comes to pass, that afterward, when all is fulfilled according to the scripture, you may believe that I am he."

"Master," said Andrew, "speak plainly. We know not what you mean."

There was silence—thick and impenetrable. No voice ventured into the dark stream of it. Then Jesus lifted his head. "Even that I must tell you, that afterward you may believe." His eyes went slowly from one to another, dwelling at last upon Judas Iscariot. Then his eyes lifted upward, away from them all.

"Verily, verily, I say unto you, that one of you shall betray me."

Immediately there were protestations.

"Nay, not I!"

"Master, do not believe it!"

"Never!"

But Mary saw that each looked doubtfully at the others, suspicion and incredulity mingled in his countenance. Now, uncertainly, the disciples were asking, each in turn: "Is it I?"

The Master, after a moment when he seemed to be in prayer, broke off a piece of unleavened bread and, dipping it into the vinegar, handed it to Judas.

Judas, after a moment's hesitation, took the bread, crushing it in his fist. He did not look at Jesus whose eyes were upon him, stern—but somehow compassionate. Later, with awe, Mary was to remember that look and marvel at it.

Jesus said: "What you do, do quickly."

None seemed to know what Jesus meant, save John alone, upon whose face a strange expression dawned. Mary, trying to evolve some clear thought from her chaotic emotions, argued that no doubt Judas had neglected some important errand for the Master, as lately he was wont to do. This seemed plausible, for Judas rose at once and, brushing by her without a word, went down the stairs.

Mary followed, but when she reached the kitchen he had gone. Mary Magdalene was standing with a stranger, a young girl in rags. Tears had furrowed her dirty cheeks. Her hair was a dark tangle and dry as baked hay.

Mary Magdalene said: "This is Drusilla, whose father Jehu is imprisoned in the Tower of Antonia. She has been tending sheep near the Master's birthplace of Bethlehem in order to raise the two hundred shekels necessary to release her father from the dungeon. At night her bed was a pile of dried grasses in a cave—"

"But I didn't mind that!" burst out Drusilla. "Little by little I was saving money to save my father, and when the lambs are born this spring—ah, but then it will be too late!" She began to sob, the weary rhythmical weeping of one who had done much mourning, and sank upon the floor.

"What does she mean—too late?" asked Mary of Bethany.

"She has received word that her father is to—is to be executed tomorrow," said Mary Magdalene.

"I have saved one hundred and fifty shekels. Only fifty more would save him!"

Mary said swiftly: "My sister has gone to Ephraim with Lazarus to sell some sheep. There should be enough from the sale when she returns—"

"You mean you will let me borrow fifty shekels from you? Then I shall not have to bother the Master after all. When will your sister return?"

"I expect her any time. She should be back soon now. Even if she were to come tonight, though, the prison wouldn't be open, would it?"

"Not after dark," said Drusilla.

"Then nothing can be done until tomorrow, I fear," said Mary.

"Then I'll come back early tomorrow morning," she stood, her chin quivering. "I—I cannot tell you!" She fled out into the darkness before either of the Marys could protest.

"But where will she stay the night?" asked Mary of Bethany in concern.

"Perhaps she will return to Bethlehem and her flock," said Mary Magdalene, "or it may be that she knows of a nearer cave. Indeed, this daughter of the outcast Jehu, is a little like the birds of the air which the Master speaks of. She will find a nest, and our Father will watch over her."

The eyes of the two women met in deep understanding. Mary felt reassured. Mary Magdalene was always so sure, so certain that God

WORSHIP SERVICES FOR LIFE PLANNING

would take care of His own. There was in her a strength of conviction hard won and fast held to.

Mary, thinking she might be needed to serve, returned again to the upper room with young Mark.[4]

POEM:

> Jesus, whose lot with us was cast,
> Who saw it out, from first to last:
> Patient and fearless, tender, true,
> Carpenter, vagabond, felon, Jew.
>
> . . . .
>
> Who, as your hour neared, did not fail—
> The world's fate trembling in the scale—
> With your half-hearted band to dine,
> And chat across the bread and wine:
> Then went out firm to face the end,
> Alone, without a single friend:
> Who felt, as your last words confessed,
> Wrung from a proud, unflinching breast
> By hours of dull, ignoble pain,
> Your whole life's fight was fought in vain:
> Would I could win and keep and feel
> That heart of love, that spirit of steel.
>
> —AUTHOR UNKNOWN

PRAYER:

Our Father, we are grateful that thy plan of salvation includes every person of every race and condition of life, and that thy love embraces the least and most unworthy ones of us. We are thankful that thy Son has demonstrated and made plain through his life and teachings the Christian way of living. As we come to thee making our own decision and dedication to thy cause, we renew our vows of loyalty to thee and to the church. Help us to uproot old ways of thinking and acting which are not pleasing to thee; strengthen us wherein we are weak, forgive our mistakes and shortcomings as we strive to live on a higher level. Forgive our lack of love, understanding, and concern for others, and make us steadfast as we strive to follow in the way which Jesus has exemplified. AMEN.

HYMN: "Are Ye Able?" or
"Just as I Am, Thine Own to Be."

BENEDICTION:

The peace of God, which passeth all understanding, keep your hearts and minds in the knowledge and love of God, and of his Son Jesus Christ our Lord. AMEN.

SERVICE 31

FOLLOWING CHRIST
(*Dedication Day*)

PRELUDE: "My Heart Ever Faithful" by Bach.

CALL TO WORSHIP:

> Jesus, thou Joy of loving hearts!
>   Thou Fount of life! Thou Light of men!
> From the best bliss that earth imparts,
>   We turn unfilled to thee again.
>
> .   .   .   .
>
> O Jesus, ever with us stay;
>   Make all our moments calm and bright;
> Chase the dark night of sin away,
>   Shed o'er the world thy holy light!
>   —BERNARD OF CLAIRVAUX

INVOCATION:

Give us, O Lord, steadfast hearts, which no unworthy affection may drag down; give us unconquered hearts, which no tribulation can wear out; give us upright hearts, which no unworthy purpose may tempt aside. Bestow on us, also, O Lord, my God, understanding to know thee, diligence to seek thee, wisdom to find thee, and a faithfulness that may finally embrace thee. AMEN.[1]

AFFIRMATION OF FAITH:

I affirm my faith in the reality of the spiritual world, in the sacred voice of duty, in the compelling power of truth and holiness, in prayer, in the life eternal, in him who is the life of my life and the reality behind all things visible. I rejoice to believe in God.

I reaffirm my discipleship and the dedication of my body and mind

220

to Jesus Christ, my Lord. I claim anew a share in his redemption and full salvation. As he has been my Saviour to this day, so shall he be my Saviour to the end. I merge all the power of my life in his redemptive purpose and stand ready to bear the cross after him.

I affirm my faith in the kingdom of God and my hope in its final triumph. I determine by faith to live day by day within the higher order and the divine peace of my true fatherland, and to carry its spirit and laws into all my dealings in the world that now is.

I make an act of love toward all my fellow men. I accept them as they are, with all their sins and failures, and declare my solidarity with them. If any have wronged or grieved me, I place my mind within the all-comprehending and all-loving mind of God, and here and now forgive. I desire to minister God's love to men and to offer no hindrance to the free flow of his love through me.

I affirm my faith in life, I call life good and not evil. I accept the limitations of my own life and believe it is possible for me to live a beautiful and Christlike life within the conditions set for me. Through the power of Christ which descends on me, which besets me behind and before, and which dwells in the innermost fastnesses of my spirit, I know that I can be more than conqueror.[2]

HYMN: "Once to Every Man and Nation," or
        "O Young and Fearless Prophet."

POEM:

> O Thou best gift from heaven,
> Thou who thyself hath given,
> For thou hast died—
>
> This hast thou done for me,—
> What have I done for thee,
> Thou crucified?
>
> I long to serve thee more,
> Reveal an open door
> Saviour, to me.
>
> Then counting all but loss,
> I'll glory in thy cross,
> And follow thee.

—AUTHOR UNKNOWN

SCRIPTURE:

If any man will come after me, let him deny himself, and take up his cross daily, and follow me. For whosoever will save his life shall lose it: but whosoever will lose his life for my sake, the same shall save it.[3]

HYMN: "I Heard the Voice of Jesus Say," or
"Hark, the Voice of Jesus Calling."

LEADER:

We will hear the story of one who for material gains sought to follow Jesus.

STORY:

THE UNDERSTUDY

WE WERE returning from a highly profitable journey through the Decapolis and were coming to our own city of Sebaste, lying serene beneath the light of the stars. But within, all was not as quiet as it looked to be, and I had hardly exchanged greetings with the servants ere I heard the news. Later the master sent for me.

"What is all this gossip?" he asked.

As I reported what I had heard, he gave close attention.

"These men come from Jerusalem? Odd they should come here and should have been able to gather such a following. What is their game?"

"I have heard no report of their taking money from anyone."

He chuckled. "Wise men—they are waiting. Not ordinary, ranting dervishes, I take it. Such could hardly have made so much talk."

"They are not dervishes. It is said they have healed Adin."

"Adin! That can hardly be. You know all we have done for him."

I knew well. Adin was a cripple, who in times past had often sought my master's help. I had compounded drugs for him and had had part in incantations, which both my master and I knew to be mere gibberish.

"Perhaps tomorrow you had best look about a little."

"Yes, Master."

The next morning I went forth as a sort of scout. I heard one of the men from Jerusalem, and his manner was direct and simple, though some of their claims were amazing enough. And I saw Adin, running and leaping, just to show that he was healed. I went home and reported. When I had finished, my master said, "Perhaps I myself had better study this."

Sometimes, in thinking back upon it all, I have wondered why my master was so gravely concerned about the newcomers. He valued money, but this I am sure was not a mere question of money. He looked upon them as competitors, but in Sebaste there was business enough for all. What chiefly troubled him, I think, was professional pride. That here, in his home city, these men should be able to outdo him—that was unendurable.

Afterward I learned that my master's unbelief was at the bottom of his failure to understand the men. He simply could not see them as anything other than what he was—clever tricksters, working only for their own advantage. That morning he did not try to see the men themselves, but he sought out certain friends and learned all they could tell him. In the evening he attended one of their meetings. He returned long after midnight and a light burned in his room until near morning.

I had counted upon his sending me to some of the meetings. When he attended regularly, and nothing was said of my going, I made bold to ask if I could serve him. He replied, "Thank you. So far, you would make nothing of it. I can make nothing of it myself—yet."

When one day I heard that he himself had become one of their followers, I was surprised. I had talked little with him of late, but I had seen enough to know that inwardly he was perplexed and annoyed. When a second time I had hinted that I would like to attend one of their gatherings, he cut me short. "Such talk is not for youth. Youth is too impressionable."

Today I understand his meaning, as I did not then. I had learned that the men from Jerusalem spoke much of a religion not of forms and ceremonies but of the heart and hand, a religion that bids men do justly, love mercy, and walk humbly, and such ever makes strong appeal to all that is bold and generous in youth.

My master's joining them did not for one moment mean that he had accepted such teachings, but merely that he had decided that his only way of penetrating their secrets was to become one of their brotherhood. After that I was more reconciled to missing the meetings.

Then came the night I shall never forget. My master was attending all their meetings. He never missed one. That night as usual he came in late and, passing him, I chanced to catch a glimpse of his face, so contorted and ashen that I sprang forward to help him, sure he must be ill. He brushed me aside and passed to his room without a sign of recognition. I stood wondering if I ought to follow him but finally did not. Yet I could not sleep, and twice I stole to his door to listen. Once I heard him groaning as if in pain, and again I heard him muttering charms to avert evils, charms at which we both had smiled a hundred times when selling them.

When I saw the gardener, I suddenly recalled that he too, like the master, had joined the strangers. "Were you at last night's meeting? Was the master there?" The gardener was greatly disturbed; that I saw at once. A simple-minded man, he would never have thought of deceiving anyone. I pressed him with questions and this was his story.

The master had stayed after the meeting to talk with the leaders. The gardener had stayed but in the background, being minded to attend him home—at a distance. At night the streets of our city are not always safe. The master spoke with the chief man from Jerusalem.

For long, he said, he had watched them, and he confessed freely that he was quite baffled, some of the things they did were to him still a mystery. Now he was ready to pay them money, much money, if they would tell him their secret.

"And then—?" I asked.

The gardener shuddered. "The man from Jerusalem," he said, "laid a curse on him."

Having heard his story, I stood for a long time silent. Finally, in desperation at what to do, I went to the cook and bade him prepare such food as we all knew the master loved best. I myself took it to him but stopped upon the threshold, scarce recognizing the face of him who had always been so poised, so confident. Out of eyes like those of a man in torment he looked at me, saying: "Who bade you bring food? Know you not I am fasting?"

"Master—," I stammered.

"Take it away. And you also—begone. Begone forever."

"Master!" I cried. "What have I done to anger you?"

"Have you no sense of danger? Fly, I tell you. I am a man accursed. Fly lest the wrath to come overtake you too."

There were more wild words. When I tried to answer him, he seemed ready to do me violence. At last I turned and left the room, taking the food with me. It was the last time I ever saw him.

As if in a dream, I treaded the streets of Sebaste and passed out the gate. Beyond the wall I sat down upon a stone at the roadside, perplexed and troubled as I had never been before. Youth, health, certain skills, and a little gold—all these I had. Many would have called me fortunate. But I had no plan, no guide, no friend. The only secure world I had ever known lay about me in ruins. A man was coming down the road and, as he drew nearer, I thought I recognized him.

"Are you not one of those from Jerusalem?" I asked.

"I am," he answered, "and am now returning thither. After that, something tells me I shall be sent to Gaza."

I yielded to a sudden impulse. "May I go with you a little way? I am not a runaway slave," I added.

"Who then are you?"

"Until an hour ago, I was apprenticed to the great Simon, known to all our city."

"You are with him no longer?"

"He has sent me away, with harsh words. He is unfit, he said, to be the guide of any youth."

"Perhaps he was right. He had been kind to you?"

"He was my only friend. As a child I knew neither father nor mother but was like a dog on the streets, sleeping where darkness overtook me, eating what refuse I could find or steal. One day he came, asking me questions, looked at my hands, took me with him. Since then I have had a place to sleep and enough to eat. This coat upon my back, these sandals upon my feet, everything I have came from him."

He knew my master. "Yet," he said softly, "he trained you to deceive men, to take their money for that which was not bread, their labor for that which could never satisfy. He taught you too that money could buy anything. That of course is not true. I think he knows it now."

We walked on a little way in silence. Then smiling once more, he said: "Last week you heard Drusilla and saw Caius?"

They had come to Sebaste with a traveling troupe: the woman with a voice of wondrous beauty, the man having strength surpassing that of any I had ever seen before.

"Yes," I said.

"Strength and beauty are two things gold cannot buy—not all the gold in the world. They are gifts of God, to be used for him and for his children. And better gifts than these has he given us. Gifts so precious that to think they may be bought with money is utter folly and blasphemy. Do you understand," he asked, "what I am saying?"

"Partly—I think."

Again for some little distance we walked on in silence, coming a
last to a spring where we stopped to drink.

"Now that your master has sent you away," he asked, "what wil
you do?"

"I do not know," I said.

"Why not follow my Master?"

"Who is he, that I might follow him?"

As we walked on, he told me. So it was that I came to be one o
the new brotherhood, a believer in him who is called the Christ.[4]

POEM:

> Lord, I would follow, but—
> First, I would see what means that wondrous call
> That peals so sweetly through Life's rainbow hall,
> That thrills my heart with quivering golden chords,
> And fills my soul with joys seraphical.
>
> Lord, I would follow, but—
> First, I would leave things straight before I go,—
> Collect my dues, and pay the debts I owe;
> Lest when I'm gone, and none is here to tend,
> Time's ruthless hand my garnering o'erthrow.
>
> Lord, I would follow, but—
> First, I would see the end of this high road
> That stretches straight before me, fair and broad;
> So clear the way I cannot go astray,
> It surely leads me equally to God.
>
> Lord, I would follow,—yea,
> Follow I *will*,—but first so much there is
> That claims me in life's vast emergencies,—
> Wrongs to be righted, great things to be done;
> Shall I neglect these vital urgencies?
>
> *Who answers Christ's insistent call*
> *Must give himself, his life, his all,*
> *Without one backward look.*
> *Who sets his hand unto the plow,*
> *And glances back with anxious brow,*

His calling hath mistook.
Christ claims him wholly for His own;
He must be Christ's, and Christ's alone.[5]

—JOHN OXENHAM

PRAYER:

Have mercy upon us, O God, after thy great goodness; and after the multitude of thy mercies do away our offenses. Let thy unspeakable mercy free us from the sins we have committed and deliver us from the punishment we have deserved. Oh, save us from every work of darkness and cleanse us from all filthiness of flesh and spirit, that for the time to come we may with a pure heart and mind follow thee, the only true God.

O Lamb of God, who both by thy example and precept didst instruct us to be meek and humble; give us grace throughout our whole lives in every thought, word, and work to imitate thy meekness and humility. Mortify in us the whole body of pride.

Grant, O Lord, that we may look for nothing, claim nothing, and resent nothing; that we may go through all the scenes of life, not seeking our own glory, but looking wholly unto thee and acting wholly for thee.

O thou Giver of every good and perfect gift, if at any time thou pleasest to work by our hands, teach us to discern what is our own from what is another's and to render unto thee the things that are thine. As all the good that is done on earth, thou doest it thyself, let us ever return to thee all the glory. AMEN.[6]

HYMN: "Arise, My Soul, Arise," or
"Jesus Calls Us, o'er the Tumult."

BENEDICTION:

Be perfect, be of good comfort, be of one mind, live in peace; and the God of love and peace shall be with you. . . . The grace of the Lord Jesus Christ, and the love of God, and the communion of the Holy Ghost, be with you all. AMEN.

SERVICE 32

MINISTERING TO OTHERS
(*Missions Sunday*)

PRELUDE: "Andante" from *Sonata in G* by Beethoven.

CALL TO WORSHIP:

> Jesus, stand among us
> In thy risen power;
> Let this time of worship
> Be a hallowed hour.
>
> Breathe the Holy Spirit
> Into every heart;
> Bid our fears and sorrows
> From each soul depart.
>
> Thus with quickened footsteps
> We pursue our way,
> Watching for the dawning
> Of eternal day.
>
> —WILLIAM PENNEFATHER

HYMN: "Jesus Shall Reign," or
"O Zion, Haste."

INVOCATION:

Have mercy upon me, O God, according to thy loving-kindness; according unto the multitude of thy tender mercies blot out my transgressions. Wash me thoroughly from mine iniquity, and cleanse me from my sin. . . . Create in me a clean heart, O God; and renew a right spirit within me. Amen.[1]

AFFIRMATION OF FAITH:

We believe in the one God, Maker and Ruler of all things, Father of all men; the source of all goodness and beauty, all truth and love.

We believe in Jesus Christ, God manifest in the flesh, our Teacher, Example, and Redeemer, the Saviour of the world.

We believe in the Holy Spirit, God present with us for guidance, for comfort and for strength.

We believe in the forgiveness of sins, in the life of love and prayer, and in grace equal to every need.

We believe in the Word of God contained in the Old and New Testaments as the sufficient rule both of faith and of practice.

We believe in the Church as the fellowship for worship and for service of all who are united to the living Lord.

We believe in the kingdom of God as the divine rule in human society; and in the brotherhood of man under the Fatherhood of God.

We believe in the final triumph of righteousness, and in the life everlasting. AMEN.[2]

SCRIPTURE:

Then shall the King say unto them on his right hand, Come, ye blessed of my Father, inherit the kingdom prepared for you from the foundation of the world: for I was ahungered, and ye gave me meat; I was thirsty, and ye gave me drink: I was a stranger, and ye took me in: naked, and ye clothed me: I was sick, and ye visited me: I was in prison, and ye came unto me. . . . Inasmuch as ye have done it unto one of the least of these my brethren, ye have done it unto me.[3]

POEM:

> In suffering thou hast made us one,
>   In mighty burdens one are we;
> Teach us that lowliest duty done
>   Is highest service unto thee.
>
> Teach us, great Teacher of mankind,
>   The sacrifice that brings thy balm;
> The love, the work that bless and bind;
>   Teach us thy majesty, thy calm.
>
> Teach thou, and we shall know, indeed,
>   The truth divine that maketh free;
> And knowing, we may sow the seed
>   That blossoms through eternity.[4]

—RICHARD WATSON GILDER

STORY:

GOD HAS NO ORPHANS

WHEN Samuel Munson and Henry Lyman, Congregationalist missionaries, in 1834 first took the word of Christ to the Bataks they were one of the most feared tribes of the South Pacific. Several days after landing on Sumatra the two men were pushing through the dense, tropical jungle approaching the small village of Sacca. Suddenly surrounded by armed warriors they were killed, with only several native guides in their party escaping. The Batak women, who had begged that the visitors lives be spared, refused to cook the cannibal feast. The warriors prepared the meal, consigning the bones of Munson and Lyman to a refuse hole marked with three sticks. One stick took root and today towers as a great tree over the stone marker on the martyrs' graves. Other villages heard that two white men who had come to do good had been murdered. They attacked the village of Sacca, killed whomever they could find, burned the houses and uprooted the gardens.

Ironically, it was another violent murder of missionaries more than twenty years later that next brought the word of Christ to the Bataks. That martyrdom was in Borneo, and the Dutch government of the island refused to let the mission continue there. Receiving permission instead to work in Sumatra, the German survivors of Borneo followed the steps of Munson and Lyman. The church they founded is one of the marvels of Christian missions in its vitality and effectiveness.

In 1939 violence struck again. When Hitler invaded Poland the Batak church overnight was cut off from its parent church in Germany. With the outbreak of war, German churches could send neither missionaries nor money overseas. The next May, when Germany attacked Holland, every German male missionary in Dutch territory was interned. Thus that young church without warning was stripped of its missionary leadership and the help of missionary funds. The thrilling story of the survival and continued growth of that church even during Japanese oppression is a part of the great story of "orphaned missions."

World War II severed one fifth of all Protestant missions from the support of their parent churches. One hundred twelve major mission fields were thus isolated from their home bases in France, Germany, Holland, Belgium, Denmark, Norway, and Finland. Those fields are scattered through Asia, Africa and the islands of the sea. Many were centers of intense fighting and destruction. Yet not one of those fields was abandoned. In the Church's finest hour Christians of many denominations and many lands sacrificed, shared, took new responsibilities, that the ways of war might not stop anywhere the work of the Prince of Peace.

The Church of Scotland sent resources to German missions in the Gold Coast. Swiss funds carried on German work in the Cameroons. The Dutch Reformed Church in South Africa and America supported the Rhenish work in Angola. Canadians sent funds to French work in Basutoland and Barotseland. The Church of Sweden underwrote support of the Leipzig mission in India. British funds went to French Madagascar. Mission boards contributed large sums to the International Missionary Council to distribute according to need. With efficiency and wisdom that council administered those funds and gave guidance to the whole cooperative movement.

Christians in the orphaned missions responded magnificently. Many, like the Bataks, reorganized their churches and took burdens of responsibility which no one—least of all themselves—thought they could carry. They gave, often lavishly, both to help themselves and each other. The Tamil church in Ceylon sent volunteers to help the Danish work in India, from which their own first growth had come. Native workers cut their own wages. Danish missionaries in India reduced their salaries by half. Danes in Syria cut their salaries to $16 a month for a man and $10 a month for a woman. Dutch missionaries in the Netherland Indies assessed themselves so much per month to help German missionaries who had been released to work again among the Bataks.

American GI's saw the need. From India, China, the Philippines, and the islands of the Pacific they sent their gifts to be used for orphaned missions. An American construction crew in Canada sent $60 to be used for missionaries without funds. GI's in New Caledonia gave $19,000 to support orphaned missions on that island. One of the agencies working there is the Paris Mission. It is the foreign missionary society of the major Protestant denominations in France. So effectively has it served in Africa, India, and the islands of the sea, that it numbers more Christians in its mission churches than the total number of Protestants in France.

The Bataks of Sumatra are no strangers to violence. Through tribal wars and world wars, through the depression and Japanese occupation, the Christian Church of these independent highlanders has steadily grown. Now it is stronger than ever before; stronger because it tested its strength under hardship and persecution; stronger because

231

in the midst of war it saw an unforgettable demonstration of Christians, whose nations were at war, banded together to serve the Prince of Peace.

God never has any orphans. During World War II His people had to arrange many temporary adoptions to care for one another and in doing so brought His Church to its finest hour. Across boundaries of denomination, nationality, and race they reached out in mutual help to gird the earth for Christ.[5]

POEM:

> What is He building, the carpenter's Son
>   Of Nazareth town?
> He is building His Church, to stand unshaken
>   When storms sweep down.
>
> What are the timbers with which He builds,
>   This Toiler divine?
> He builds with knotty and cross-grained lives,
>   Like yours and mine.[6]

—EFFIE SMITH ELY

PRAYER:

Our Father, we thank thee for the first missionaries sent forth to tell the good news of the gospel. We thank thee for others who throughout the ages have labored to bring people into thy kingdom that they might have fullness of life. And we thank thee for thy laborers of our own age who have gone to the far islands of the sea to bring the people under thy influence. We pray for the missionaries in all parts of the world. Grant unto them a sense of thy presence at all times, encourage them in times of loneliness, strengthen them for their tasks, and prosper them in their labors. May they serve thee with patience, courage, and humility. Help us to co-operate by praying for them, by studying the needs of the fields, and by increasing our givings to missions. In Christ's name we pray. AMEN.

HYMN: "Christ for the World We Sing," or
  "We've a Story to Tell to the Nations."

BENEDICTION:

May our God hasten the time when every knee shall bow and every tongue confess thee as Lord and Master of their lives. AMEN.

SERVICE 33

SERVING THE LEAST
(*Missions Sunday*)

PRELUDE: Adagio from "Moonlight Sonata" by Beethoven.

CALL TO WORSHIP:

> Since there are those who trust me,
> God, help me to endure;
> Since there are those who love me,
> God, keep me clean and pure;
> Since there are those who need me,
> Keep thou my faith secure.
> The enemy is crafty
> The strength of none is sure.
> Hold thou my hand, Almighty God,
> And help me to endure! [1]

—RALPH S. CUSHMAN

HYMN: "Draw Thou My Soul, O Christ," or
 "O Master Workman of the Race."

SCRIPTURE:

At the same time came the disciples unto Jesus, saying, Who is the greatest in the kingdom of heaven? And Jesus called a little child unto him, and set him in the midst of them, and said, Verily I say unto you, Except ye be converted, and become as little children, ye shall not enter in the kingdom of heaven. Whosoever therefore shall humble himself as this little child, the same is greatest in the kingdom of heaven. And whoso shall receive one such little child in my name receiveth me. But whoso shall offend one of these little ones which believe in me, it were better for him that a millstone were hanged about his neck, and that he were drowned in the depth of the sea.

Pure religion and undefiled before God and the Father is this, To visit the fatherless and widows in their affliction, and to keep himself unspotted from the world.[2]

INVOCATION:

O Master of our lives, forgive us that in our selfishness we have neglected to minister to thy little ones; that we have been absorbed in trivial things and have crowded out eternal things; that we have been concerned with accumulating material things and have forgotten spiritual values; that we crowd thee out of our lives and miss the blessing of thy presence. Help us to amend our lives that we may live completely within thy will. In Christ's name. AMEN.

STORY:

MIRACLE IN PORTICI

THE night of the allied landing at Salerno, Italy, a group of orphans, recently evacuated from their bombed-out home near Naples, found themselves suddenly surrounded by battle. As they huddled in their temporary shelter the guns roared, bombs exploded, and all about them there were soldiers in action.

One little girl said to another, "Which soldiers do you like best: German, French, American, English, or Indian?" The other girl replied, "I don't know. I like Jesus best of all." These orphans had known many soldiers, for they had seen much of war, but there was more appeal in Jesus, the Prince of Peace, than in the soldiers about them.

Riccardo Santi, a Methodist pastor in Naples, remarked, "God surely wanted an orphanage at Portici, a suburb of Naples, for without his help, the institution could neither have started under the handicaps it faced, nor survived the dangers it has met."

The orphange began during World War I when Pastor Santi, walked through the city, saw a little boy and girl selling matches. Inquiring of them, he found that they had lost their parents and their home had been destroyed. He recalled that when he was an orphan the people in Venice had cared for him. A voice seemed to say to him, "What other people have done for you as a boy, try to render a similar service to other orphans."

When Pastor Santi took the two little waifs home, his wife wondered how they would manage, for they had two children of their own,

234

besides an aged grandmother to care for. But the members of his church, hearing of the need, gave money, as well as clothing, furniture, and other articles. Within a few weeks a great improvement was seen in the children because of the balanced diet and the excellent care they received. When Pastor Santi discovered other orphans wandering about the streets, he continued to bring them home until eventually larger quarters had to be secured.

At the close of World War I, when the need of the orphanage was presented to the Methodists in the United States, they raised money to buy the beautiful residence of the Prince of Monaco on the Bay of Naples as a home for the orphans. In this attractive home, now called Casa Materna, were housed over one hundred orphans. Everything moved along smoothly until the pastor started a school for the children and enrolled an additional one hundred day students. Then the trouble began.

Many unsuccessful attempts were made to drive Pastor Santi and his orphanage out of the city. At the time the school was opened in Portici, there was only one poorly supported school in that suburb of Naples. However, Pastor Santi's school stimulated the establishment of other schools until finally there were twenty in that section. The Santi family is grateful that their work caused the government to render greater service by providing schools for more children than they could ever have reached by their own efforts.

In 1938 more serious trouble came from Mussolini's government. A decree was passed ordering the Santi school closed on the ground that it was Protestant and thus against the religion of the state. Fabio, the lawyer son of the pastor, fought the case to the supreme court. However, the school was closed temporarily, until Fabio secured a decision to postpone the final hearing on the case until the close of World War II. Without this intervention the orphanage would almost certainly have remained closed.

Fabio Santi saved the legal status of the orphanage, but the bombs almost destroyed the building. Located near an important railway, the buildings were hit by British, American, and German bombs. The children were finally evacuated to a village near Salerno, but the shock and exposure caused several of them to have nervous disorders. Finally the legal status of the school and orphanage was affirmed on the principle of infringement of religious liberty when a Lutheran chaplain carried the case to the Allied Council in London.

During World War II, Casa Materna became a retreat for soldiers of many denominations from the United States. Presbyterians, Lutherans, Methodists, Baptists, and others came to spend their leave at the orphanage, to teach in the school, and to help wherever needed. One morning when a sergeant from California discovered that the children had no shoes, he went in search of leather. That afternoon he returned with a truck load of footballs, boxing and baseball gloves, from which shoes were made for all the children.

A Lutheran chaplain from Wisconsin, finding that food was desperately low at the orphanage, returned later with a jeep and trailer loaded with bread and beefsteak. Another chaplain from New Jersey replaced the Communion set which had been taken by Hitler's soldiers searching for silver. A chaplain from England was responsible for repairing the bombed chapel. The World Council of Churches, the Church World Service Committee, and the people of Switzerland sent money which supplied other needs.

Visitors at Casa Materna are impressed with the homelike atmosphere of the orphanage and with the happiness of the children. Most of the children have not only regained health but have been restored to normalcy again.

Amazing as this orphanage is, it is no more so than the Santi family. Riccardo and his wife, now on in years, have turned over the heaviest work to their children, while he continues to serve as pastor to the orphanage and the attached congregation. The lawyer son, Fabio, now director of Casa Materna, is also vice-mayor of Portici. Another son, Theofilo, a well-trained doctor who studied in Italian and German schools, carries on the medical work at the orphanage in addition to his large private practice. A daughter, Louisa, trained in social work at Columbia University, gives her full time to the orphanage. The third son, Emanuele, a Ph.D. from Columbia, is a pastor in New York and serves as secretary of the Casa Materna Aid Society.

A further step in enlarging the orphanage is now under way. The Methodists in the United States are providing the necessary funds for additional buildings which are badly needed. Yes, God certainly must have wanted to have this orphanage in Naples, but it cannot be kept there without our loyal support.[3]

PRAYER:

We praise thee, O God, for the little children given into our keeping. For their purity of heart, their constant simplicity, their natural and trusting affection, . . . we praise and bless thy glorious name. Continue, we beseech thee, thy protection to them; and grant to us such a measure of thy Spirit that we may work together with thee for their good.

We remember before thee the many children who are now denied a fair chance in life, all who are hindered by a bad environment, all who are made to toil at an early age, all who are unwanted, neglected, and ill-treated. Make haste, O Lord, for the help of these thy little ones. Suffer us not to add to their burden, or to leave them without a champion for their cause. Fill us with thy holy wrath toward the things whereby they are bruised and afflicted, and by thy great compassion bring us swiftly to their aid. All which we ask in the name of him who took little children in his arms and laid his hands upon them in blessing, thy Son Jesus Christ our Lord. Amen.[4]

HYMN: "Lift Up Our Hearts," or
        "O Holy City, Seen of John."

BENEDICTION:

Unto God's gracious mercy and protection we commit ourselves. May the Lord bless us all. Amen.

Appendix

NOTES

SERVICE 1, PIONEERING IN MEDICINE

1. "The Celestial Surgeon."
2. Georgia Harkness, *The Glory of God*, p. 76. Used by permission of Abingdon-Cokesbury Press.
3. Heb. 11: 1, 6, 13-16.
4. By Elsie McCormick. *Independent Woman*, Nov. 1948, as condensed in the *Reader's Digest*. Used by permission.
5. Georgia Harkness, *Through Christ Our Lord*, pp. 80, 147 (adapted). Used by permission of Abingdon-Cokesbury Press.

SERVICE 2, HONORING A GREAT MUSICIAN

1. "The Singers."
2. Ps. 40:3; I Cor. 14:15; Ps. 150.
3. "Invocation." Used by permission.
4. Adapted from the story by Bernice Littlestone, *Classmate*, Aug. 26, 1951. Used by permission.
5. "The Master's Touch."

SERVICE 3, ANSWERING THE CALL TO SERVE

1. Matt. 20:25-28; 6:24.
2. Frederick C. Gill, *John Wesley's Prayers*, p. 35 (adapted). Used by permission of Abingdon-Cokesbury Press.
3. By Bennie Bengston. *Classmate*, Apr. 22, 1951. Used by permission.
4. "God of the Common Life." From *The Glory of God*. Used by permission of Abingdon-Cokesbury Press.

SERVICE 4, BEING A GOOD NEIGHBOR

1. "Lift Up Our Hearts, O King of Kings."
2. Frederick C. Gill, *John Wesley's Prayers*, p. 64. Used by permission of Abingdon-Cokesbury Press.
3. Luke 10:25-36.
4. By Katharine E. Wilkie, *Classmate*, July 18, 1948. Used by permission.
5. "Count That Day Lost."
6. Ernest Fremont Tittle, *A Book of Pastoral Prayers*, p. 30. Used by permission of Abingdon-Cokesbury Press.

SERVICE 5, SELECTING A VOCATION

1. "Your Place" from *Bees in Amber*. Used by permission of Erica Oxenham.
2. Pss. 62:11-12; 104:23; II Tim. 2:15; Ps. 90:12.
3. "Invocation." Used by permission.

WORSHIP SERVICES FOR LIFE PLANNING

4. Adapted from the story by Ben F. Sheetz. *Classmate*, Dec. 24, 1950. Used by permission.
5. "The Sacrament of Work," from *The Fiery Cross*. Used by permission of Erica Oxenham and Harper & Bros.
6. Walter Rauschenbusch, *Prayers of the Social Awakening*, p. 144. The Pilgrim Press. Used by permission.

SERVICE 6, OPENING A CONTINENT

1. "Seekers." Used by permission.
2. Thomas à Kempis.
3. Matt. 9:36-38; 28:16-20.
4. "The Weaver." Used by permission.
5. Adapted from the chapter by Norman E. Richardson in *Vocations and Professions*, "Creative Personalities," Vol. I, ed., Philip Henry Lotz. Used by permission of Association Press.
6. "Promotion," from *Tamate*. Used by permission of Erica Oxenham.

SERVICE 7, SEEKING PEACE

1. From "The Arsenal at Springfield."
2. Pss. 85:8; 29:11; Ezek. 37:26-27; Matt. 5:9.
3. By Edna A. Bruner. From the Adult Program Packets, Dec. 1944. Used by permission.
4. "Dies Irae—Dies Pacis," from *All's Well*. Used by permission of Erica Oxenham and Harper & Bros.

SERVICE 8, BRINGING IN THE KINGDOM

1. Ps. 24:3-5.
2. Matt. 6:9-10; Luke 13:19, 21; Matt. 13:45-46; 7:21; Luke 17:20-21.
3. "God's Call to Youth." Used by permission.
4. Adapted from the story by Ben F. Sheetz. *Classmate*, Jan. 22, 1950. Used by permission.
5. "To Win the World," from *The Vision Splendid*. Used by permission of Erica Oxenham.
6. Walter Rauschenbusch, *Prayers of the Social Awakening*, p. 119. The Pilgrim Press. Used by permission.

SERVICE 9, CHANGING THE WORLD

1. Mic. 4:1-4; Isa. 65:17.
2. By Gladys H. Barr. *Classmate*, Nov. 2, 1947. Used by permission.
3. "A New Earth," from *The Vision Splendid*. Used by permission of Erica Oxenham and Harper & Bros.
4. Walter Rauschenbusch, *Prayers of the Social Awakening*, p. 29. The Pilgrim Press. Used by permission.

SERVICE 10, RULING THROUGH LOVE AND PEACE

1. Mic. 4:2; Rom. 14:19 (RVS); Mic. 4:3; Rom. 12:17-18.
2. "Prayer for Peace." Used by permission.
3. By Edna A. Bruner. From the Adult Program Packets, Dec. 1944. Used by permission of the author and the missionary education department, the United Christian Missionary Society, Indianapolis, Ind.

NOTES

4. "Stranger at the Peace Table." Copyright 1945, The Curtis Publishing Co. Used by permission.

SERVICE 11, APPRECIATING OTHER RELIGIONS
1. "Thou Light of Ages." Used by permission.
2. John 1:1-9 8:12.
3. By Maeanna Cheserton-Mangle. *Christian Advocate*, Dec. 15, 1949. Used by permission.

SERVICE 12, SWINGING TOWARD THE LIGHT
1. Mal. 1:11; Ps. 98:2; Isa. 60:3; II Pet. 1:19; II or. 4:6; Isa. 60:1.
2. "Swinging Toward the Light," from *The Glory of God*. Used by permission of Abingdon-Cokesbury Press.
3. By W. J. Faulkner. Used by permission.
4. "Stanzas on Freedom."
5. Walter Rauschenbusch, *Prayers of the Social Awakening*, p. 28. The Pilgrim Press. Used by permission.

SERVICE 13, GIVING A CUP OF WATER
1. "We Bear the Strain of Earthly Care."
2. Luke 4:18-19.
3. Matt. 10:42.
4. "Where Cross the Crowded Ways of Life."
5. Eugene L. Smith, *They Gird the Earth for Christ*, p. 49. Used by permission.
6. William L. Stidger, *Human Adventures in Happy Christian Living*. Used by permission of Fleming H. Revell Co.
7. "God of Our Fathers." Used by permission.

SERVICE 14, LIVING AS BROTHER TO EVERY RACE
1. Matt. 23:9; Acts 17:26; Luke 13:29; Rom. 10:12; Acts 10:34-35; Mark 3:35.
2. Anonymous. From the Chinese.
3. By Maeanna Cheserton-Mangle. Copyright 1945 by Maeanna Cheserton-Mangle. Used by permission.
4. *The Pulpit*, Feb. 1945. Used by permission.
5. "Who Is So Low?" Used by permission.
6. Georgia Harkness, *The Glory of God*, p. 123. Used by permission of Abingdon-Cokesbury Press.

SERVICE 15, REALIZING OUR WORTH
1. "America's Gospel."
2. Thomas à Kempis.
3. Ps. 8.
4. "The Quest Eternal." Used by permission.
5. Roy L. Smith. *Christian Advocate*, May 6, 1948. Used by permission.
6. "What Is Man?" from *All's Clear*. Used by permission of Erica Oxenham.

SERVICE 16, STANDING FIRM AND BOLD
1. Heb. 11:8-10, 23-27, 32-34, 39-40; 12:1-2, 11-23. Edgar J. Goodspeed, *The New Testament, An American Translation*. Used by permission of the University of Chicago Press.
2. "In the Morning." Used by permission.
3. By Gladys H. Barr. *Classmate*, Oct. 19, 1947. Used by permission.
4. "Thanksgiving for Brave Men." Used by permission.
5. Walter Rauschenbusch, *Prayers of the Social Awakening*, p. 30. The Pilgrim Press. Used by permission.

WORSHIP SERVICES FOR LIFE PLANNING

SERVICE 17, HELPING EACH OTHER

1. "For the Beauty of the Earth."
2. Rom. 12:9-21. Edgar J. Goodspeed, *The New Testament, An American Translation*. Used by permission of the University of Chicago Press.
3. *The Book of Worship for Church and Home*, p. 67. Used by permission of The Methodist Publishing House.
4. "Mountain Pines." Used by permission.
5. Adapted from the story by Frederick H. Hall. *Classmate*, Mar. 13, 1949. Used by permission.
6. "Making Life Worth While."

SERVICE 18, TESTING OUR LIVES BY THINE

1. Luke 23:13-21, 24-25, 29-43, 46-47.
2. "That One Face." Used by permission.
3. Adapted from the story by Roy L. Smith. *The Christian Advocate*, Apr. 10, 1941. Used by permission.
4. "The Dream." Used by permission.
5. Ernest Fremont Tittle, *A Book of Pastoral Prayers*, pp. 63, 84. Used by permission of Abingdon-Cokesbury Press.

SERVICE 19, SEEKING COURAGE AND CALMNESS

1. John 4:23-24.
2. "Prayer for Strength."
3. Pss. 62:1-2, 5-8; 37:3-5, 23-24, 34-37.
4. By Gladys H. Barr. *Classmate*, Apr. 3, 1949. Used by permission.
5. "The Coming Day," from *All's Well*. Used by permission of Erica Oxenham.

SERVICE 20, LIVING ON HIGHER LEVELS

1. *Julius Caesar*, Act IV, Scene 3.
2. John Ruskin, "Creed of St. George's Guild."
3. Phil. 3:13-15.
4. *The Book of Worship for Church and Home*, p. 125. Used by permission of The Methodist Publishing House.
5. Adapted from the story by Willis Lindquist. *Classmate*, May 1, 1949. Used by permission.
6. "Three Lessons."

SERVICE 21, SHARING IN HIS NAME

1. From "The Vision of Sir Launfal."
2. "Life in Prayer." Used by permission.
3. Mal. 3:8, 10; I Cor. 16:2.
4. From "The Vision of Sir Launfal."
5. By Paul K. McAfee. *Classmate*, Apr. 17, 1949. Used by permission.

SERVICE 22, GIVING NOT SEEKING

1. From "Awareness."
2. Eccl. 12:1; Ps. 37:5; Prov. 3:5-6; Matt. 6:19-20; II Cor. 9:6-7.
3. Augustine of Hippo.
4. Adapted from the story by Noble J. Hamilton, *Classmate*, Jan. 8, 1950. Used by permission.

SERVICE 23, PRACTICING HIS PRESENCE

1. Ps. 139:7-12, 17-18, 23-24.
2. Matt. 7:7-11.

NOTES

3. "The Secret," from *Spiritual Hilltops*. Used by permission of Abingdon-Cokesbury Press.
4. By Mrs. E. C. Cronk. *Front Rank*. Used by permission.
5. From "Morte d' Arthur."
6. Georgia Harkness, *The Glory of God*, p. 78. Used by permission of Abingdon-Cokesbury Press.

SERVICE 24, LIVING ABUNDANTLY

1. John 10:7-10.
2. Frederick C. Gill, *John Wesley's Prayers*, p. 103. Used by permission of Abingdon-Cokesbury Press.
3. Used by permission.
4. Adapted from the story by Willis Lindquist. *Classmate*, Mar. 19, 1950. Used by permission.

SERVICE 25, CHOOSING WORTHY GOALS

1. From "For an Autograph."
2. Phil. 3:4-9, 13, 19.
3. "A Prayer."
4. Adapted from the story by Willis Lindquist, *Classmate*, Feb. 27, 1949. Used by permission.

SERVICE 26, GIVING CHRIST FIRST PLACE (Christmas)

1. "Today in Bethlehem Hear I."
2. Luke 2:8-20.
3. "A Christmas Litany." Used by permission.
4. By Roy L. Smith. *Christian Advocate*, Dec. 25, 1941. Used by permission.
5. Ralph S. Cushman, "Busy Inns," from *I Have a Stewardship*, p. 110. Used by permission of Abingdon-Cokesbury Press.
6. Woodrow Geier. *Church School*, Dec. 1951. Copyright 1951. Used by permission.

SERVICE 27, BRINGING OUR GIFTS

1. "O Little Town of Bethlehem."
2. Matt. 2:1-12.
3. "Christmas Eve Meditation," from *Be Slow to Falter*. Used by permission of the author and the Kaleidograph Press.
4. Abridged from *Ben Hur, A Tale of the Christ*, p. 65.

SERVICE 28, OBSERVING EASTER

1. Matt. 28:5-8.
2. "The Man Who Rose." Used by permission.
3. Toyohiko Kagawa, *Behold the Man*, p. 339. Used by permission of Harper & Bros.
4. "Seeds." Used by permission of Erica Oxenham.

SERVICE 29, HONORING OUR MOTHERS

1. "Miriam."
2. Prov. 31:10-13, 25-31.
3. "The Mother's Hymn."
4. Adapted from Archer Wallace, *The Mothers of Famous Men*, p. 95. Used by permission of Harper & Bros.
5. "For a True Mother." *Charlotte Observer*. Used by permission.
6. Georgia Harkness, *The Glory of God*, p. 106. Used by permission of Abingdon-Cokesbury Press.

SERVICE 30, DECIDING FOR CHRIST

1. Isa. 55:1-3, 6-9, Matt. 6:33.
2. Christina Rossetti.

3. "I Need a Song." Used by permission.
4. Adapted from Toyohiko Kagawa, *Behold the Man*, pp. 241-48. Used by permission of Harper & Bros.

SERVICE 31, FOLLOWING CHRIST

1. Thomas Aquinas.
2. Walter Rauschenbusch, *Prayers of the Social Awakening*, p. 148. The Pilgrim Press. Used by permission.
3. Luke 9:23-24.
4. Adapted from the story by Frederick Hall. *Christian Observer*, Nov. 12, 1947. Used by permission of Mrs. Grace H. Ohl.
5. "Follow Me," from *Hearts Courageous*. Used by permission of Erica Oxenham and Harper & Bros.
6. Frederick C. Gill, *John Wesley's Prayers*, p. 36 (adapted). Used by permission of Abingdon-Cokesbury Press.

SERVICE 32, MINISTERING TO OTHERS

1. Ps. 51:1-2, 10.
2. The Methodist Hymnal, p. 512. Used by permission.
3. Matt. 25:34-36, 40.
4. "God of the Strong, God of the Weak."
5. Eugene L. Smith. *They Gird the Earth for Christ*, p. 81. Used by permission.
6. "The Carpenter's Son." Used by permission.

SERVICE 33, SERVING THE LEAST

1. "For Endurance," from *More Hilltop Verses and Prayers*, p. 19. Used by permission of Abingdon-Cokesbury Press.
2. Matt. 18:1-6; Jas. 1:27.
3. Adapted from Eugene L. Smith, *They Gird the Earth for Christ*, p. 64. Used by permission.
4. Ernest Fremont Tittle, *A Book of Pastoral Prayers*, p. 69. Used by permission of Abingdon-Cokesbury Press.

SOURCES FOR HYMNS

A ... New Hymnal for American Youth
B ... Broadman Hymnal (Southern Baptist Convention)
C ... Common Service Book (Lutheran)
D ... Church School Hymnal for Youth (Presbyterian U.S.A.)
E ... American Student Hymnal
F ... Hymnal for Youth (Presbyterian U.S.A.)
G ... Abingdon Song Book (Methodist)
H ... Presbyterian Hymnal (U.S.)
I ... Worship and Praise

J ... Hymnal for Christian Worship (Presbyterian U.S.)
M ... Methodist Hymnal
N ... Pilgrim Hymnal (Congregational, now United Church of Christ)
P ... The Hymnal (Presbyterian U.S.A.)
R ... Devotional Hymns
S ... Great Songs of the Church (Disciples)
T ... New Baptist Hymnal (Southern Baptist Convention)
W ... Christian Worship (Northern Baptist Convention and Disciples)

A Charge to Keep I Have
B—157; C—376; E—379; G—186; H—289; I—196; J—161; M—287; N—500; R—240; T—203; W—373

All Things Are Thine
B—493; H—383; J—293

Angels, from the Realms of Glory
B—145; C—27; D—86; F—69; H—49; J—71; M—87

Are Ye Able
B—396; E—174; G—184; J—189; M—268

Arise, My Soul, Arise
C—138; G—79; M—211

As with Gladness Men of Old
A—95; C—38; D—96; F—77; G—259; J—79; M—90; N—84; P—135; W—196

At Length There Dawns the Glorious Day

E—256; F—288; H—335; J—251; M—469

Awake, My Soul, Stretch Every Nerve
A—195; C—380; E—165; H—278; J—197; M—359; S—347

Beneath the Cross of Jesus
A—120; B—234; D—186; E—105; F—173; G—39; H—95; I—176; J—91; M—144; N—125; P—162; R—242; S—351; T—110; W—235

Be Still, My Soul
B—479; C—181; G—121; J—215; M—73

Be Strong!
A—182; D—214; E—185; F—229; M—300; N—253; P—488

Breathe on Me, Breath of God
A—61; B—417; D—152; E—98; F—130; G—76; J—123; M—180; N—201; P—213; T—146

Christ for the World We Sing
B—267; C—218; D—319; E—355;
F—250; H—404; J—266; M—481

Come, Ye Faithful, Raise the Strain
C—108; F—108; J—101; M—151;
N—134; P—168; S—363; W—242

Dear Lord and Father of Mankind
A—152; B—401; D—236; E—80;
F—150; G—137; H—242; I—238;
J—202; M—342; N—224; P—302;
R—280; S—366; T—63; W—411

Dear Master, in Whose Life I See
M—376; N—265; P—507; W—318

Draw Thou My Soul, O Christ
A—149; D—234; E—370; F—164;
G—151; H—250; J—160; M—297;
N—232; W—299

Fairest Lord Jesus
A—137; B—211; D—136; E—58;
F—119; G—55; H—72; J—113;
M—111; S—369

Fight the Good Fight
A—207; B—270; D—212; E—158;
F—288; G—204; H—299; J—201;
M—286; N—255; P—270; R—261;
S—375; T—200; W—376

God of Grace and God of Glory
F—236; G—115; M—279; W—378

Go Forth to Life
M—296; N—474; W—319

Go, Labor on!
F—249; H—285; J—198; M—292;
N—330; P—376; S—381; T—206;
W—473

Happy the Home When God Is There
G—242; M—428

Hark, the Voice of Jesus Calling
B—407; D—162; G—185; H—283;
M—288; S—392

He Who Would Valiant Be
A—204; E—169; F—233; J—193;
M—265; N—250; P—276; W-364

I Heard the Voice of Jesus Say
A—147; B—163; D—172; E—83;
F—216; G—174; H—183; J—163;
M—210; S—403

In Christ There Is No East or West
A—299; D—314; E—273; F—243;
G—221; H—375; J—234; M—507

It Came Upon the Midnight Clear
A—78; B—141; C—29; D—76;
E—245; F—64; H—58; J—73;
M—92; N—73; P—127; R—56;
S—416; T—85; W—191

Jesus Calls Us
A—144; B—159; D—168; E—106;
F—198; G—187; H—284; J—144;
M—233; S—420

Jesus Christ Is Risen Today
A—129; B—32; C—111; D—129;
E—331; F—103; G—48; H—118;
I—212; J—102; M—155; P—163;
R—94; S—358; T—115

Jesus Shall Reign
A—305; B—150; C—219; D—31;
E—380; F—248; G—220; H—392;
J—267; M—479; S—425

Joyful, Joyful, We Adore Thee
A—43; D—48; E—49; F—6; G—3;
H—25; J—5; M—12

Just as I Am, Thine Own to Be
A—145; B—411; D—181; E—136;
F—171; G—143; H—280; J—310;
S—131

Let All the World in Every Corner Sing
C—287; F—16; M—8

Let Us with a Gladsome Mind
A—32; D—60; E—40; F—41; G—8; J—39; M—81; S—433

Lift Up Our Hearts
A—295; E—176; G—180; J—253; M—472; N—154; P—405; W—372

Light of the World
A—9; D—5; E—19; F—281; H—398; J—277; M—114; S—137

Lord, Speak to Me
A—251; C—212; D—293; E—216; F—196; G—175; H—279; I—222; J—248; M—460; N—339; P—399; S—438; T—211; W—470

Love Divine, All Loves Excelling
A—67; B—19; C—276; D—231; E—356; F—153; G—111; H—21; I—2; J—176; M—372; N—270; P—308; R—81; S—440; T—183; W—379

March On, O Soul with Strength
A—184; D—220; E—110; F—234; G—192; H—300; M—264; N—247; P—273; W—359

Master, No Offering,
A—252; D—277; E—229; H—277; J—246; M—464

'Mid All the Traffic of the Ways
A—159; F—165; G—165; H—237; J—204; M—341; P—322

More Love to Thee, O Christ
B—218; D—200; F—191; G—110; H—224; I—240; J—168; M—364; N—146; P—315; R—283; S—148; T—195; W—390

My Jesus, as Thou Wilt
B—178; C—395; F—172; H—247; J—214; M—330; N—494; P—280; S—446; T—222; W—408

My Soul, Be on Thy Guard
B—247; C—272; E—378; H—295; I—245; M—277; N—256; R—279; T—177; W—300

Now in the Days of Youth
A—146; F—169; G—207; J—308; N—477; W—300

Now Thank We All Our God
A—325; C—283; D—358; E—303; F—17; J—289; M—7; S—560

O Brother Man, Fold to Thy Heart
A—244 B—403; D—283; E—258; F—260; J—254; M—466

O Come, All Ye Faithful
A—83; B—143; D—89; E—298; F—74; G—30; H—56; J—69; M—96; N—105; P—116; S—452; T—90; W—205

O for a Heart to Praise My God
C—264; G—176; H—257; J—177; M—370; S—456

O Happy Home
A—313; D—263; E—382; F—262; H—320; M—427;

O Holy City, Seen of John
E—63; H—354; J—269; M—474

O Jesus, Master, When Today
E—212; H—278; M—470; N—307; W—517

O Jesus, Prince of Life and Truth
D—224; F—182; N—257

O Love Divine and Golden
G—170; H—212; I—65; M—430; N—292; P—485; R—129; W—353

O Master, Let Me Walk with Thee
A—197; B—202; D—182; E—214;
F—166; G—116; H—271; I—263;
J—245; M—259; N—291; P—364;
R—19; S—468; T—274; W—306

O Master Workman of the Race
A—98; D—106; E—74; F—85;
G—59; H—82; J—86; M—118;
N—328; P—140; R—62; W—210

Once to Every Man and Nation
D—184; E—240; F—221; J—249;
M—263

O Perfect Love
C—415; H—484; J—296; P—484;
M—431; N—430

O Son of Man, Thou Madest Known
A—188; D—207; E—175; F—197;
G—61; M—121

O Thou Who Camest from Above
M—344

O Young and Fearless Prophet
G—212; M—266; W—362

O Zion, Haste
A—306; B—151; C—224; D—308;
E—270; F—240; G—222; H—395;
J—257; M—475; N—372; P—382;
R—131; S—474; T—264; W—529

Peace, Perfect Peace
C—413; H—231; J—205; M—354;
S—478

Prince of Peace, Control My Will
M—216; S—480

Rejoice, Ye Pure in Heart
A—27; B—285; D—139; E—199;
F—124; G—9; J—209; M—358;
N—476; P—297; R—181; S—483;
T—47; W—418

Rise Up, O Men of God
A—254; B—186; D—288; E—224;
F—258; G—203; H—274; J—252;
M—267; N—313; P—401; W—374

Saviour, Thy Dying Love
B—149; D—198; F—195; G—88;
H—273; J—171; M—219; S—492

Silent Night, Holy Night
A—81; B—146; C—530; D—83;
E—302; F—73; G—33; H—60;
J—74; M—106; S—494

Sing, Men and Angels Sing
M—152

Spirit of Life in This New Dawn
A—63; E—22; G—74; M—178

Still, Still with Thee
A—6; E—20; F—53; H—454;
J—18; M—40

Take My Life, and Let It Be
A—198; B—174; C—382; D—221;
E—142; F—175; G—131; H—268;
I—83; J—166; M—225; N—195;
P—242; R—244; S—501; T—329;
W—296

The First Noel
A—79; B—140; D—82; E—328;
F—70; G—35; J—72; M—97;
S—231

The King of Love My Shepherd Is
A—50; C—345; D—59; E—35;
F—57; G—108; H—80; J—51;
M—353

The Kings of the East Are Riding
A—92; E—326; M—101

The Light of God Is Falling
D—279; F—254; G—213; H—376;
J—250; M—468

There's a Wideness in God's Mercy
A—55; B—182; C—256; D—63;
E—39; F—50; H—18; J—54;
M—76

The Voice of God Is Calling
  D—284; E—235; F—202; G—205;
  M—454; N—337; W—490

True-hearted, Whole-hearted, Faithful
  and Loyal
  F—177; M—255; I—28; R—226;
  S—278; T—383

We May Not Climb the Heavenly
  Steeps
  M—120

We Thank Thee, Lord, Thy Paths
  of Service Lead
  A—249; B—301; D—287; E—223;
  F—203; G—206; M—458; P—367;
  W—495

We've a Story to Tell to the Nations
  A—302; B—379; D—306; F—238;
  G—215; I—146; J—261; M—501;
  N—374; R—124; T—261; W—530

When I Survey the Wondrous Cross
  A—123; B—191; C—97; D—118;
  E—376; F—96; G—44; H—88;
  I—215; J—97; M—148; N—122;
  P—152; R—247; S—532; T—108;
  W—228

When Morning Gilds the Skies
  A—2; B—7; C—310; D—1;
  E—201; F—19; G—20; H—453;
  J—21; M—31; S—533

Where Cross the Crowded Ways of
  Life
  A—265; B—405; D—268; E—60;
  F—253; G—214; H—330; I—230;
  J—268; M—465; N—140; P—410;
  R—24; S—536; T—276; W—519

Selected Bibliography

WORSHIP FOR YOUTH

Applegarth, Margaret T. *Restoring Worship.* New York: Harper & Bros., 1949.

Bailey, Albert Edward. *The Gospel in Art.* Boston: Pilgrim Press, 1916.

_____. *The Arts and Religion.* New York: The Macmillan Co., 1944.

Blackwood, Andrew W. *The Fine Art of Public Worship.* New York and Nashville: Abingdon-Cokesbury Press, 1939.

Bowie, W. Russell. *The Story of the Bible.* New York and Nashville: Abingdon-Cokesbury Press, 1934.

_____. *The Story of Jesus.* New York: Charles Scribner's Sons, 1937.

_____. *The Bible Story for Boys and Girls: New Testament.* New York and Nashville: Abingdon-Cokesbury Press, 1951.

_____. *The Bible Story for Boys and Girls: Old Testament.* New York and Nashville: Abingdon-Cokesbury Press, 1952.

Cavert, Walter Dudley. *Remember Now.* New York and Nashville: Abingdon-Cokesbury Press, 1944.

Cushman, Ralph S. *Practicing the Presence.* New York and Nashville: Abingdon-Cokesbury Press, 1936.

Fisk, Margaret Palmer. *The Art of the Rhythmic Choir.* New York: Harper & Bros., 1950.

Garrett, Constance. *Think on These Things.* New York and Nashville: Abingdon-Cokesbury Press, 1948.

Gilbert, Clark. *Devotions for Youth.* New York: Association Press, 1943.

Harrell, Costen J. *Walking with God.* New York and Nashville: Abingdon-Cokesbury Press, 1928.

Jones, E. Stanley. *Abundant Living.* New York and Nashville: Abingdon-Cokesbury Press, 1942.

_____. *The Christ of the American Road.* New York and Nashville: Abingdon-Cokesbury Press, 1944.

_____. *How to Pray.* New York and Nashville: Abingdon-Cokesbury Press, 1951.

_____. *Victorious Living.* New York and Nashville: Abingdon-Cokesbury Press, 1936.

_____. *The Way.* New York and Nashville: Abingdon-Cokesbury Press, 1946.

_____. *The Way to Power and Poise.* New York and Nashville: Abingdon-Cokesbury Press, 1949.

Jones, Rufus M. *New Eyes for Invisibles.* New York: The Macmillan Co., 1943.

Lotz, Henry P. *The Quest for God Through Understanding.* St. Louis: Christian Board of Publication (Bethany Press), 1937.

_____. *The Quest for God Through Worship.* St. Louis: Christian Board of Publication (Bethany Press), 1934.

Luccock, Halford E. and Brentano, Frances. *The Questing Spirit.* New York: Coward-McCann, 1947.

Mattoon, Laura and Bragdon, Helen. *Services for the Open.* New York: Association Press, 1947.

McDormand, Thomas Bruce. *The Art of Building Worship Services.* Nashville: The Broadman Press, 1942.

McIlwain, Orene. *Worship God.* Richmond: John Knox Press, 1947.

Myers, A. J. William, ed. *Enriching Worship.* New York: Harper & Bros., 1949.

Page, Kirby. *Living Creatively.* New York: Farrar & Rinehart, 1932.

_____. *Living Triumphantly.* New York: Farrar and Rinehart, 1934.

Palmer, Albert W., ed. *Aids to Worship.* New York: The Macmillan Co., 1944.

Paulsen, Irwin G. *The Church School and Worship.* New York: The Macmillan Co., 1940.

Pease, Dorothy Wells, ed. *Altars Under the Sky*. New York and Nashville: Abingdon-Cokesbury Press, 1942.

Petty, Carl Wallace. *The Evening Altar*. New York and Nashville: Abingdon-Cokesbury Press, 1940.

Phillips, D. B., Nixon, L. M., Howes, E. B., eds. *The Choice Is Always Ours*. New York: Richard R. Smith, 1948.

Porter, David. *Worship Resources for Youth*. New York: Association Press, 1948.

Quimby, Chester W. *Jesus as They Remembered Him*. New York and Nashville: Abingdon-Cokesbury Press, 1941.

——————. *The Jubilant Year*. New York and Nashville: Abingdon-Cokesbury Press, 1946.

Reid, Albert C. *Invitation to Worship*. New York and Nashville: Abingdon-Cokesbury Press, 1942.

——————. *Resources for Worship*. New York and Nashville: Abingdon-Cokesbury Press, 1949.

Rice, Merton S. *My Father's World*. New York and Nashville: Abingdon-Cokesbury Press, 1943.

Sadler, Alfred J. *Out of Doors with God*. New York and Nashville: Abingdon-Cokesbury Press, 1940.

Seidenspinner, Clarence. *Our Dwelling Place*. New York and Nashville: Abingdon-Cokesbury Press, 1941.

Smart, W. Aiken. *The Contemporary Christ*. New York and Nashville: Abingdon-Cokesbury Press, 1942.

Smith, H. Augustine. *Lyric Religion*. New York: D. Appleton-Century Co., 1931.

Smith, Roy L. *Making a Go of Life*. New York and Nashville: Abingdon-Cokesbury Press, 1948.

Snowden, Rita F. *While the Candle Burns*. London: Epworth Press, 1942.

Stuber, Stanley, ed. *Treasury of the Christian Faith*. New York: Association Press, 1949.

Toner, Helen L. *When Lights Burn Low*. New York and Nashville: Abingdon-Cokesbury Press, 1942.

Watson, Lillian Eichler. *Light From Many Lamps*. New York: Simon & Schuster, 1951.

POEMS

Armstrong, O. V. and Helen, comps. *Prayer Poems*. New York and Nashville: Abingdon-Cokesbury Press, 1942.

Bever, Patricia. *Steppingstones of the Spirit*. New York: Association Press, 1951.

Bruner, Margaret E. *Be Slow to Falter*. Dallas: Kaleidograph Press, 1941.

——————. *In Thoughtful Mood*. Dallas: Kaleidograph Press, 1937.

——————. *Midstream*. Kaleidograph Press, 1940.

——————. *Mysteries of Earth*. Dallas: Kaleidograph Press, 1934.

——————. *The Constant Heart*. Dallas: Kaleidograph Press, 1952.

——————. *The Hill Road*. Dallas: Kaleidograph Press, 1932.

Clark, Thomas Curtis, comp. *Poems of Justice*. Chicago: Willett, Clark & Co., 1929.

——————. *The Golden Book of Religious Verse*. New York: Garden City Publishing Co., n.d. 1941.

Clark, Thomas and Hazel. *Christ in Poetry*. New York: Association Press, 1952.

Clark, Thomas Curtis and Robert Earle, comps. *Poems for the Great Days*. New York and Nashville: Abingdon-Cokesbury Press, 1948.

Clark, Thomas Curtis and Gillespie, Esther A., comps. *1000 Quotable Poems*. Chicago: Willett, Clark & Co., 1937.

Cushman, Ralph S. *Hilltop Verses and Prayers*. New York and Nashville: Abingdon-Cokesbury Press, 1945.

——————. *Practicing the Presence*. New York and Nashville: Abingdon-Cokesbury Press, 1936.

SELECTED BIBLIOGRAPHY

Cushman, Ralph S. and Robert E. *More Hilltop Verses and Prayers.* New York and Nashville: Abingdon-Cokesbury Press, 1949.

Gibran, Kahlil. *The Prophet.* New York: Alfred A. Knopf, 1923.

Harkness, Georgia. *The Glory of God.* New York and Nashville: Abingdon-Cokesbury Press, 1943.

Hill, Caroline. *The World's Great Religious Poetry.* New York: The Macmillan Co., 1923.

Kagawa, Toyohiko. *Songs from the Slums.* New York and Nashville: Abingdon-Cokesbury Press, 1935.

Kagawa, Toyohiko and Cole, Franklin. *The Willow and the Bridge.* New York: Association Press, 1947.

Lowell, James Russell. *Complete Poetical Works.* Boston: Houghton, Mifflin Co., 1917.

Markham, Edwin. *Selected Poems.* New York: Harper & Bros., 1950.

Marlatt, Earl. *Cathedral.* New York: Harper & Bros., 1937.

Morgan, Angela. *Selected Poems.* New York: Dodd, Mead & Co., 1926.

Morrison, James Dalton, comp. *Masterpieces of Religious Verse.* New York: Harper & Bros., 1948.

Mudge, James, comp. *Poems with Power to Strengthen the Soul.* New York: Abingdon Press, 1907, 1909.

Oxenham, John. *Gentlemen—The King!* Boston: Pilgrim Press, 1928.

_____. *Hearts Courageous.* New York: Methodist Book Concern, 1918.

_____. *Selected Poems.* New York: Harper & Bros., 1948.

Piety, Chauncey R. *General Sam Houston.* Emory University: Banner Press, 1943.

Tagore, Rabindranath. *Collected Poems and Plays.* New York: The Macmillan Co., 1946.

van Dyke, Henry. *Collected Poems.* New York: Charles Scribner's Sons, 1920-25.

STORIES

Bartlett, Robert M. *They Dared to Live.* New York: Association Press, 1937.

_____. *They Did Something About It.* New York: Association Press, 1939.

_____. *They Work for Tomorrow.* New York: Association Press, 1943.

Bolton, Sarah. *Famous Men of Science.* New York: Thomas Y. Crowell Co., 1941.

_____. *Lives of Girls Who Became Famous.* New York: Thomas Y. Crowell Co., 1930.

_____. *Lives of Poor Boys Who Became Famous.* New York: Thomas Y. Crowell Co., 1947.

Cather, K. Dunlap. *Boyhood Stories of Famous Men.* New York: D. Appleton-Century Co., 1916.

_____. *Girlhood Stories of Famous Women.* New York: D. Appleton-Century Co., 1924.

Cheley, Frank H. *Stories for Talks to Boys.* New York: Association Press, 1932.

Eastman, Fred. *Men of Power.* Vols. 1-V. New York and Nashville: Abingdon-Cokesbury Press, 1938-40.

Eddy, Sherwood. *Pathfinders of the World Missionary Crusade.* New York and Nashville: Abingdon-Cokesbury Press, 1945.

Erdman, Mabel, ed. *Answering District Calls.* New York: Association Press, 1942.

Erdman, Walter C. *Sources of Power in Famous Lives.* Nashville: Cokesbury Press, 1936.

_____. *More Sources of Power in Famous Lives.* Nashville: Cokesbury Press, 1937.

Gill, D. M. and Pullen, A. M. *Adventures in Service.* New York: Missionary Education Movement, 1938.

_____. *Victories of Peace.* London: Student Christian Movement Press.

Hume, Edward H. *Doctors Courageous.* New York: Harper & Bros., 1950.

Lantz, J. Edward, ed. *Best Religious Stories.* New York: Association Press, 1948.

_____. *Stories of Christian Living.* New York: Association Press, 1950.

Lotz, Philip Henry, ed. *The Altar Hour.* St. Louis: Christian Board of Education, 1941.

—————. "Creative Personalities," vols. I-III, V-VII: *Vocations and Professions, Women Leaders, Founders of Christian Movements, Rising Above Color, Distinguished American Jews, Unused Alibis.* New York: Association Press, 1940-45.

Matthews, Basil. *Book of Missionary Heroes.* New York: George H. Doran Co., 1922.

Oxenham, John. *The Hidden Years.* New York: Longmans, Green & Co., 1925.

Parkman, Mary R. *Heroines of Service.* New York: D. Appleton-Century Co., n.d.

Sawyers, Mott R. *Famous Friends of God.* New York: Fleming H. Revell Co., 1933.

Snowden, Rita F. *Safety Last!* London: Epworth Press, 1946.

—————. *The Lark in the Sky.* London: Epworth Press, 1946.

—————. *Never a Dull Moment.* London: Presbyterian Bookroom, n.d.

Stidger, William L. *The Human Side of Greatness.* New York: Harper & Bros., 1940.

—————. *There Are Sermons in Stories.* New York and Nashville: Abingdon-Cokesbury Press, 1942.

—————. *More Sermons in Stories.* New York and Nashville: Abingdon-Cokesbury Press, 1944.

Turnbull, Agnes S. *Far Above Rubies.* New York: Fleming H. Revell Co., 1926.

Wallace, Archer. *Overcoming Handicaps.* New York: Harper & Bros., 1927.

—————. *Stories of Grit.* New York: Harper & Bros., 1930.

—————. *In Spite of All.* New York and Nashville: Abingdon-Cokesbury Press, 1944.

—————. *The Field of Honor.* New York and Nashville: Abingdon-Cokesbury Press, 1949.

—————. *100 Stories for Boys.* New York and Nashville: Abingdon-Cokesbury Press, 1947.

Wallace, Lew. *Ben Hur.* New York: Harper & Bros., 1880.

PRAYER

Abernathy, Jean Beaven. *Meditations for Women.* New York and Nashville: Abingdon-Cokesbury Press, 1947.

Andrewes, Lancelot. *The Private Devotions of Lancelot Andrewes.* New York and Nashville: Abingdon-Cokesbury Press, 1950.

Bowie, W. Russell. *Lift Up Your Hearts.* New York: The Macmillan Co., 1939.

Buttrick, George A. *Prayer.* New York and Nashville: Abingdon-Cokesbury Press, 1942.

Campbell, Donald J. *The Adventure of Prayer.* New York and Nashville: Abingdon-Cokesbury Press, 1949.

Cavert, Walter Dudley. *Remember Now.* New York and Nashville: Abingdon-Cokesbury Press, 1944.

Clough, William A. *Father We Thank Thee.* New York and Nashville: Abingdon-Cokesbury Press, 1949.

Cushman, Ralph S. *Hilltop Verses and Prayers.* New York and Nashville: Abingdon-Cokesbury Press, 1945.

Cushman, Ralph S. and Robert Earl. *More Hilltop Verses and Prayers.* New York and Nashville: Abingdon-Cokesbury Press, 1949.

Edmonds, Henry M. *Beginning the Day.* New York and Nashville: Abingdon-Cokesbury Press, 1951.

Finegan, Jack, *Book of Student Prayers.* New York: Association Press, 1946.

Fox, Selina F. *A Chain of Prayers Across the Ages.* New York: E. P. Dutton & Co., 1943.

Gill, Frederick C. *John Wesley's Prayers.* New York and Nashville; Abingdon-Cokesbury Press, 1951.

Harkness, Georgia. *The Glory of God.* New York and Nashville: Abingdon-Cokesbury Press, 1943.

—————. *Prayer and the Common Life.* New York and Nashville: Abingdon-Cokesbury Press, 1948.

—————. *Through Christ Our Lord.* New York and Nashville: Abingdon-Cokesbury Press, 1950.

SELECTED BIBLIOGRAPHY

Harlow, S. Ralph. *Prayers for Times Like These.* New York: Association Press, 1942.

Hayward, Percy R. *Young People's Prayers.* New York: Association Press, 1945.

Hoyland, J. S. *A Book of Prayers for Youth.* New York: Association Press, 1939.

Lester, Muriel. *Ways of Praying.* London: Independent Press, 1931.

Luccock, Halford E. and Brentano, Frances. *The Questing Spirit.* New York: Coward-McCann, 1947.

Morton, Richard K. *A Book of Prayers for Young People.* New York and Nashville: Abingdon-Cokesbury Press, 1935.

Murrell, Gladys C. *Channels of Devotion.* New York and Nashville: Abingdon-Cokesbury Press, 1948.

_____. *Doorways to Devotion.* New York and Nashville: Abingdon-Cokesbury Press, 1938.

_____. *Glimpses of Grace,* New York and Nashville: Abingdon-Cokesbury Press, 1941.

_____. *Patterns for Devotion.* New York and Nashville: Abingdon-Cokesbury Press, 1950.

Newton, Joseph Fort, *Everyday Religious Living.* New York and Nashville: Abingdon-Cokesbury Press, 1951.

Philips, D. B., Nixon, L. M. Howes, E. B., *et al. The Choice Is Always Ours.* New York: Richard R. Smith, 1948.

Rauschenbusch, Walter. *Prayers of the Social Awakening.* Boston: Pilgrim Press, 1925.

Snowden, Rita F. *Today.* London: Epworth Press, 1949.

Tittle, Ernest Fremont. *A Book of Pastoral Prayers.* New York and Nashville: Abingdon-Cokesbury Press, 1951.

Wyon, Olive. *The School of Prayer.* Philadelphia: Westminster Press, 1944.

The Kingdom, the Power, and the Glory (Services of praise and prayer for occasional use in churches; an American edition of the English *Grey Book*). New York: Oxford University Press, 1933.

INDEX OF STORIES AND SUBJECTS

Answer to Her Prayer .... Consecration to full-time service 40
Awakening, The .... Courage 136

Consecrated Genius (Johann
    Sebastian Bach) .... Dedication of one's talents 20
Count Me in, Too .... Tithing 157
Cup, The .... Racial prejudice 150
Cup of Cold Water in the Jungle, A ..... Sharing 98
Cup of Water, A .... Racial prejudice 97

David Livingstone .... Missions 46

Empty Tomb, The .... Victory over death 201

God Has No Orphans .... God's love and care for all people 230
God in Your Home, The .... Presence of God 165
Greatest Gift, The .... Self-sacrifice 169
Greatest of Them All, The .... Seeking peace 51

Heart of Hull House, The (Jane Addams) Social service 34

I Saw a Man Die Today! .... Sacrifice for others 130

Lady With a Lamp (Florence
    Nightingale) .... Pioneer in nursing profession 26
Land of the Enemy .... Living on higher levels 144
Light from the Past .... Appreciating other religions 81

Man from Shushan, The .... Helping one another 123
Miracle in Portici .... Missions—helping orphans 234
Mother of Booker T. Washington, The ... Appreciation of mothers 208
Mustard-Seed People (Samuel Meharry) ... Sharing educational advantages 90

Old Man and the Ram, The .... Worth of human personality 109
One More Song (Martin Luther) .... Religious freedom—changing the world 67

Renewal (John Wycliffe) .... Making the Bible known to common
    people 115

Shepherd Boy's Tale, The .... Giving Christ first place in one's life .. 185
Striving After the Wind .... of values 176

Tenth Jew, The .... Brotherhood 103
Thy Kingdom Come .... Building the Kingdom 59
Trail Blazer in Medicine (Elizabeth Black-
    well) .... Pioneering in medical profession 13

Understudy, The .... Following Christ 222
Upper Room, The .... Loyalty to Christ 213

Visit of the Wise Men, The .... Gifts for Christ 193

Yet They Seek Him, And .... Working for world peace 76